Washington Itself

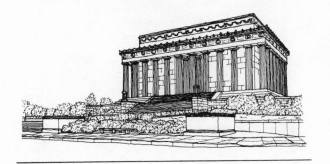

Washington Itself

AN INFORMAL GUIDE
TO THE CAPITAL
OF THE UNITED STATES

E. J. Applewhite

ILLUSTRATIONS BY FRED H. GREENBERG

Published by Madison Books
4720 Boston Way
Lanham, Maryland 20706

Washington Itself *was originally published by Knopf in
1981 and has been updated for this Second Edition.*

Distributed by National Book Network

The paper used in this publication meets the minimum
requirements of American National Standard for
Information Sciences—Permanence of Paper for
Printed Library Materials, ANSI Z39.48–1984. ∞™
Manufactured in the United States of America.

Library of Congress Cataloging-in-Publication Data

Applewhite, E. J.
Washington itself : an informal guide to the Capital of
the United States / by E.J. Applewhite ; illustrations
by Fred H. Greenberg. — 2nd ed.
  p.   cm.
Includes bibliographical references and index.
1. Washington (D.C.)—Guidebooks.   I. Title.
F192.3.A7   1993
917.5304'4—dc20   93–17776 CIP

ISBN 1–56833–008–1 (pbk. : alk. paper)

Contents

Contents

The Mall 168

Downtown 211

Southwest 230

Capitol Hill 237

Foggy Bottom 271

Georgetown 285

Wisconsin Avenue 294

Northeast 307

CONTENTS

Preface to Second Edition

In the years since this guide first came out, Washington, D.C. has become virtually a completed city. In the early 1980s half of the office blocks downtown consisted of parking lots. Now the infill of shiny new hotels and lawyers' offices complete the urban grid—softened by new trees and old vestiges of L'Enfant's diagonal vistas. The trees in Constitution Gardens along the Mall from 17th Street, N.W. to Bacon Drive have almost reached maturity, justifying the scale of the original design.

Construction is well underway at the last big urban tracts—the Portal complex at 14th Street and Maryland Avenue, S.W. and the International Center at the last prominent corner of the Federal Triangle at Pennsylvania Avenue and 14th Street, N.W. While the city of New York seems permanently doomed to be called "the unfinished city", Washington, in contrast, is now just about finished, with all the parking lots gone underground and not a vacant lot in sight!

Virtually all of the houses, museums and monuments described when this guide first came out remain intact—thanks in part to a flourishing program of historic preservation—enhanced now by a more mature urban character and context. My method in describing the city's chief ornaments has been to say something of the architecture and then a little of what goes on inside; What do the people who work or live inside these buildings actually do? I was afraid that this propensity would hurt people's feelings. After all not everything in the capital is great and good, and I have a few uncharitable observations about some of the ancient institutions like the DAR, the Society of the Cincinnati, and Brookings Institution. I have friends who work in those places and I thought I would have to cross the street when I saw them coming. But to my surprise they seemed to relish the criticism and didn't mind being called snobs of one sort or another, as long as we took notice. It is now a great pleasure to see these observations weather the test of time as they appear in this second edition.

E. J. Applewhite
June 1993

Scope of the Guide:
A Note to the Reader

This is a personal guide whose aim is to inform the visitor, entertain the resident, and—at times—admonish some of the guardians of the sacred places. It is my goal to provide fresh descriptions of the buildings, museums, and monuments of the nation's capital in terms of the social and esthetic values of the 1980s. Each architectural description is presented in the context of what goes on inside the building itself: lobbying, policing, giving grants, displaying objects—a setting for work or prayer or homage or escape.

The book originates in part out of frustration with official guides, stressing as they do the size and cost of buildings and accepting uncritically the purity of the institutions that occupy them; such guides tend to have too much history, too many pictures, and an excess of zeal. While I have no desire to give offense to authority, I want to write about the White House and the Capitol without any official obligation to assure the reader of the worthiness of their incumbents.

Since I first came to Washington in 1947, I have been beguiled by the rich range of the city's monuments and memorials, sometimes moving in their symbolism and associations, sometimes embarrassing in striving for effects beyond their means, but always abounding in enough paradoxes and ambiguities to sustain the most jaded of observers. I write of these matters as a layman—a conscientious amateur—with no pretensions to scholarship. I am addressing the average citizen—the government's proper client—and I will succeed if I can provide information not easily available elsewhere, if I can sharpen his eye by causing him to look freshly at what has become too familiar as well as what has escaped notice, and if I can help him decide what he may like or not like and why.

Geographically the guide is limited to places within the District of Columbia proper, but not out of disrespect for the many marvels across the Potomac and within the Beltway; to cover them in detail would require a separate book. Nor is this a history of Washington; places are discussed in the form—for better or worse—in which they survive today.

There is nothing in these pages about where to eat, shop, or take children on a rainy day, but hints of this kind of ephemeral information are contained in the sources listed in the bibliography.

The buildings discussed are presented in convenient groupings along the city's main avenues; although no specific walking or driving itineraries are suggested, articles appear in a general geographical sequence.

E. J. Applewhite
3 July 1981

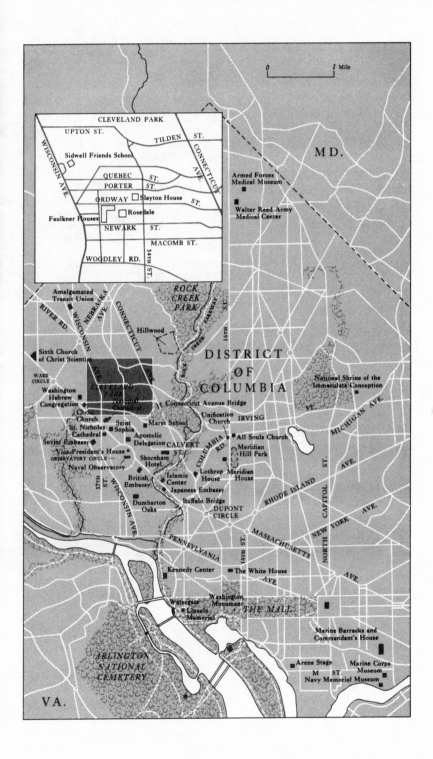

0   1 Mile

MD.

CLEVELAND PARK

UPTON ST.

TILDEN ST.

CONNECTICUT AVE.

WISCONSIN AVE.

Sidwell Friends School

Armed Forces Medical Museum

QUEBEC ST.

PORTER ST.

ORDWAY ST.

Slayton House

Walter Reed Army Medical Center

Faulkner Houses

Rosedale

NEWARK ST.

MACOMB ST.

34TH ST.

WOODLEY RD.

ROCK CREEK PARK

Amalgamated Transit Union

RIVER RD.

NEBRASKA AVE.

WISCONSIN AVE.

CONNECTICUT AVE.

Hillwood

ROCK CREEK PARKWAY

16TH ST.

DISTRICT OF COLUMBIA

Sixth Church of Christ Scientist

WARD CIRCLE

Washington Hebrew Congregation

GLOVER PARK

National Shrine of the Immaculate Conception

MICHIGAN AVE.

Connecticut Avenue Bridge

Christ Church

Saint Sophia

St. Nicholas Cathedral

Maret School

Unification Church

IRVING

All Souls Church

Soviet Embassy

Apostolic Delegation

CALVERT ST.

COLUMBIA RD.

Meridian Hill Park

Vice-President's House

OBSERVATORY CIRCLE

Naval Observatory

Shoreham Hotel

Meridian House

Lothrop House

17TH ST.

WISCONSIN AVE.

British Embassy

Islamic Center

Japanese Embassy

Buffalo Bridge

RHODE ISLAND AVE.

NORTH CAPITOL ST.

NEW YORK AVE.

Dumbarton Oaks

DUPONT CIRCLE

MASSACHUSETTS AVE.

PENNSYLVANIA AVE.

14TH ST.

Kennedy Center

The White House

AVE.

Watergate

Lincoln Memorial

Washington Monument

THE MALL

Marine Barracks and Commandant's House

ARLINGTON NATIONAL CEMETERY

Arena Stage

M ST.

Navy Memorial Museum

Marine Corps Museum

VA.

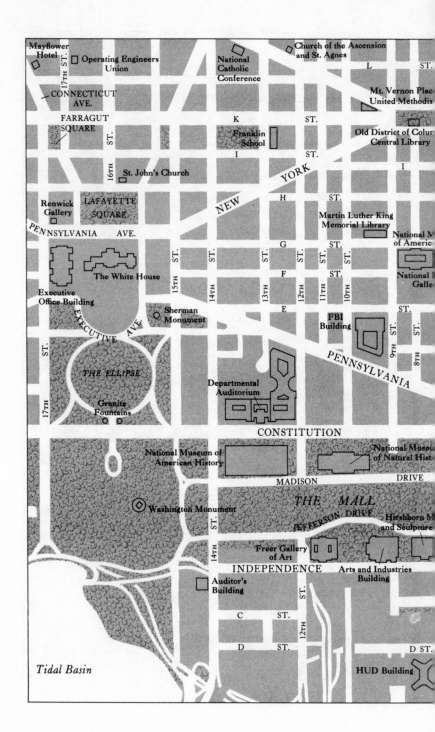

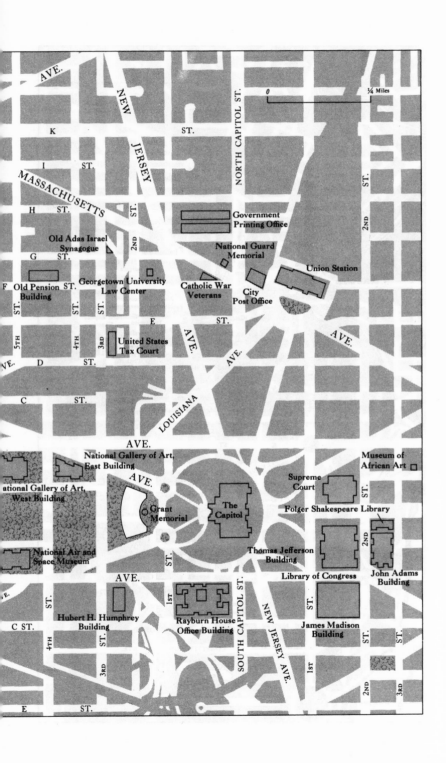

D.C.:
Name of the Place

The name almost succeeds: District of Columbia. The last word soars. Hail Columbia, happy land, the gem of the ocean discovered by the admiral from Genoa, Cristoforo Columbo, the Admiral of the Ocean Seas. But the word *district* has all the wrong connotations, as in water and sewer district or garment district or district jail; the term is inherently local and provincial, devoid of the dignity accorded to a *state*.

These disparate terms—abbreviated as D.C.—capture the intent of the founding fathers to describe a neutral isolated seat of government as well as the capital of a great future nation in which sovereignty would be retained by the separate states. The title conferred by the early federal bureaucrats, District of Columbia, enshrines a paradox like Browning's—it comforts while it mocks. The whole idea was to celebrate the ideal of the republic without creating a rival to the ultimate dominion of the states.

The capital belongs to all the people, to all the states and not to any one of them; and this is a notion which to this day—despite all demographic logic to the contrary—impedes the acceptance of the residents of the District as worthy of full representation in Congress.

America

Christopher Columbus and Amerigo Vespucci have provided America with the most splendid eponyms since Rome was named for Romulus. The name *America* was invented by and for Europeans to describe an unpredicted geographical obstacle to traffic between Europe and Asia. The word first appeared in a map drawn by Martin Waldseemüller in 1507. The attribution went to Amerigo Vespucci by default as Columbus had died the year before, insisting to the end that what he had discovered was Asia.

3

New City
on the Potomac

History gave Congress many reasons to be jealous of its identity and vigilant in its sense of place. Before being established in its own buildings in the Capitol—where to this day it maintains its own independent police force*—Congress led a nomadic existence. During its first 15 years it had convened in eight different cities: Philadelphia, Baltimore, Lancaster, York, Princeton, Annapolis, Trenton, and New York. When it authorized a statue to George Washington in 1783, Francis Hopkinson, a signer of the Declaration of Independence from Philadelphia, suggested the base be placed on wheels so it could follow Congress wherever it met. (Hopkinson's son with a similar crazy zeal was later to compose the patriotic anthem "Hail Columbia.") Congress convened most frequently in Philadelphia and might have continued to do so had not the session in 1783 been stormed by mutinous Continental soldiers demanding their hard-earned back pay. The members felt it prudent to hold their next sessions in Princeton, whose Nassau Hall was the largest building in the colonies, though the rest of the town was too small to accommodate them easily.

The members from the South were reluctant to meet in the cities of the North where they feared the government might be dominated by the wealthy residents of the large cities. The members from the North were loath to move south as every additional 30 miles' distance meant an added day in travel time. The separate loyalties of the North and the South were so divisive, the confederation of the colonies so loose, the debts to its impatient army so pressing, and the potential for revenue so innocently unrealized, that Congress lacked authority with its constituents and recognition from its adversaries.

* Not to mention its own Sergeant at Arms and its own Doorkeeper of the House, the latter thoughtfully provided with a limousine and chauffeur—how else could one keep a door?

6

Inspired by reckless boosterism many small towns offered land and other inducements for Congress to settle permanently in their midst. It was assumed, mistakenly, that the new federal capital—wherever established—would become a thriving center of commerce and industry; for this prize the competing colonies were prepared to surrender some control of their territory. Among the chief contenders were Kingston, New York; Williamsburg, Virginia; Nottingham, New Jersey; Carlisle, Reading, and Germantown, Pennsylvania. Vice-President John Adams, perhaps smarting over the fact that the South had won the presidency, voted for Germantown, a city whose name would have proved particularly awkward for a nation destined to fight two major wars against Germany.

The southern states had paid their troops in the Continental Army throughout the revolutionary campaign, but the northern states had not. Thus the southern delegates, already fearful of the growing commercial independence of the North, were wary of Alexander Hamilton's efforts to bail out the North by having Congress assume state debts. The history books tell us that Thomas Jefferson as secretary of state in Washington's first administration negotiated a compromise: this issue was decided in Hamilton's favor, while the South was placated by a federal city sited on the banks of the Potomac. Thus the federal capital was born of expedience, one might say of logrolling—an exchange of political favors.

The first Congress under the Constitution, sitting in 1790, authorized President Washington to select a site "not exceeding 10 miles square" (not 10 square miles) anywhere along an 80-mile-stretch of the Potomac north of the junction of the Anacostia River. Never before had a nation established its permanent capital by legislative action. Never before had the metes and bounds of any city been so precisely described.

When Congress settled the question of establishing the nation's capital on the banks of the Potomac, the country was still 97 percent rural. There were only six cities with a population of 8,000 or more, five of them in the North—Boston, Salem, New York, Philadelphia, Baltimore; the sixth, Charleston, was in the South.

Landowners and speculators had a great stake in the site the president would select, as did the legislatures of Maryland and Virginia, which had each promised funds for the purchase of land. Washington was besieged by petitioners whose arguments were as vociferous as their interests were narrow. He chose a 10-mile-square diamond with the junction of the two rivers at the center and the four corners at the cardinal points of the compass; the scheme embraced the town of Alexandria on the Virginia side and Georgetown in Maryland. The Potomac would link up with the projected Chesapeake and Ohio Canal as a route for commerce with the frontier to the west, and the Anacostia would provide a deep-water ocean port—considered essential—and a favorable location for a navy yard.

The choice was objective and magnanimous. It vindicated the dictum of one of Washington's many English admirers, Samuel Taylor Coleridge: "Among a people eminently querulous and already impregnated with the germs of discordant parties, he directed the executive power firmly . . . and did those things only which only he could do." There we have in all its double-onlyness the essential character of the man who was first in war and first in peace, but second—after Lincoln—in the hearts of his countrymen.

Capitals at the Fall Line

Thus the new federal city was *located* (then a new American expression, later to be adopted in England) at the head of navigation where the Potomac River makes its last plunge over the rocks below Great Falls and sprawls out beyond Alexandria to the drowned river valley that feeds the estuary of Chesapeake Bay. The city itself is bisected by the Piedmont Plateau, conspicuously along the line of old Boundary Street (now Florida Avenue) between Meridian Hill Park and the Washington Hilton Hotel. The tide reaching Washington is almost two days later than the crests and troughs entering Chesapeake Bay between Cape Henry and Cape Charles 200 miles to the south.

All 50 states of the union have as their capitals cities situated on a river. Most of the state capitals of the former original colonies along the eastern seaboard are not only riparian but situated at the head of navigation of a river—at the *fall line*, where the fresh water of the "falls" and rapids meets the tidewater of the river estuaries. This fall line roughly parallels the Appalachian system, with an average rise of 200 feet at the point where the Atlantic coastal plain abuts the Piedmont plateau.* Thus the rivers are navigable up to the site of many of the capitals; this is true not only of Washington on the Potomac, but of Augusta on the Kennebec, Hartford on the Connecticut, Albany on the Hudson, Trenton on the Delaware, and Richmond on the James. The neighboring states of Maryland and Virginia have made the name *Tidewater* their own.

Piedmont is a geographical analogy from the Piedmont region of Italy, which in turn is from the Latin for "at the foot of the mountains." At the fall line, rivers pass from the more resistant rocks of the Piedmont, the geologically older formations, to the easily eroded, unconsolidated sands, gravels, and sediments of

---

* This joining of the two geological systems is most conspicuous in Washington where 16th Street rises at the edge of Meridian Hill Park.

the coastal plain. These places as far as boats can go also afford the easiest river crossings by ferry or bridge. In fact the oldest highway in the east, the old U.S. Route 1, traces the northeast-to-southwest path of these river crossings.

It is also partly a matter of geological determinism that the more desirable residential areas of the capitals and cities which grew at the fall line are located on the higher, solid terrain of the cities' northwest sections, while the slums tend to lie to the southeast.

Since the capital was first established it has aroused in the rest of the country feelings of profound ambivalence that are peculiarly American, feelings of allegiance and distrust, devotion and suspicion, contradictions of dependence and rejection that remain unresolved. At bottom it is American patriotism itself that is paradoxical, attempting in the federalistic phrase *e pluribus unum* to resolve the contradictions of the pluralistic culture, to make the many into one.

The Metro System: Swing Low, Sweet Chariot

The Russians did it with marble; we did it with shadows.
—Harry Weese, architect of the Metro system

For any city in the world that has one, a subway system becomes an emblem of civic identity with feelings ranging from shame to tolerance to fierce pride. If New Yorkers cared what tourists think—which they don't—they would probably forget their subway's efficiency and be ashamed of its shabbiness. Washingtonians, as the custodians of a system built under federal auspices as a model for the nation if not the world, are more sensitive to the opinion of strangers, and they are generally proud and defensive of their costly new subway; citizens of Moscow are said to feel much the same about their palatial old one.

Metro: the name has now become generic for a subway system, as in Paris's *Métropolitain,* Moscow's *Metropoliten,* and Rome's *Metropolitana.* But strictly speaking, Washington's Metro is not a subway but a *rapid rail* system, since as much of its track is on the surface and on aerial pylons as is under the ground.

The subway itself is essentially a 19th-century invention; in the revival of this long-established idea, Washington joins such newcomers to the world of mass transit as Seoul, Tbilisi, Rome, and Buffalo.

Metro has its critics, of course, among both natives and strangers: the natives deplore the complex fare system and the frequent breakdowns of the high-technology equipment; visitors complain mostly that the entrances are hard to find and that the stations, once entered, seem dimly lit with unfamiliar light. (As the clients of remote bureaucratic forces, subway riders are difficult to please. According to transportation planner Lee H. Rogers, what riders want most are reliability of service and frequency of trains; all other requirements are way down the list—comfort, cleanliness, good lighting, low decibels, and even low fares. It is the arrival and not the journey that matters.)

The entrances to Metro stations are hard to find because they are announced only by a single bronze pylon capped with a backlit letter M and because the open, street-level escalators are concealed behind plain granite balustrades. The effect is deliberately unobtrusive and rigidly functional. (The Commission of Fine Arts even decreed that there should be no maps of the system on display at street level. Their initial ban on advertising, however—adopted in an excess of design purity—was rescinded, so that now a limited number of cards and posters are permitted to bring some welcome light and movement to the platform areas and the subway cars themselves.)

There are no Art Nouveau trellises, no noodle filigree tulip gates like those Hector Guimard designed for the Paris Metro. Some of the Washington escalators are woven discreetly into the corners and lobbies of the existing fabric of commercial and retail buildings. Where such discretion is not practicable, the escalators descend baldly from an opening in the pavement into gaping holes; the station mezzanine is never in view from above. There are no stairs in the system, only escalators. And there are few graphic indicators to orient an unfamiliar traveler or prepare him for the starkness of the descent.

Typical escalators are grouped in two to four parallel grooves, many of them very long indeed. The longest in the system are at the Rosslyn Station, where it takes almost a minute and a half to descend or ascend the 210 feet, 8 inches. (In

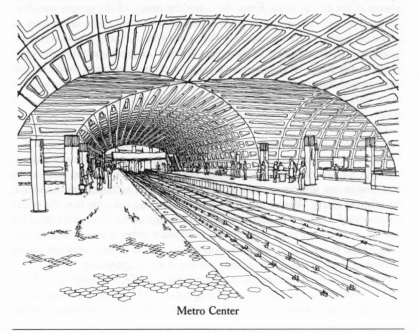

Metro Center

The air in the underground Metro stations is conditioned through filters and cooled by refrigerating coils, so it is often purer and pleasanter than what we have to breathe outside. On a muggy August day the stations are not only echoless gray chambers, but they are cool. The architect thought it would add drama and excitement to this neutral scene if the trains rushing into the long platforms were painted a bright red. Red trains is what the architect prescribed, but the engineers balked, preferring cars of brushed aluminum with bronze bands between the windows and thin red, white, and blue stripes around the canted owlish face of the cars, front and rear.

The trains glide quietly over the welded rails set a quarter of an inch closer than standard to reduce sway. In many areas the rails float on elastomer or fiberglas pads, cushioned to absorb noise and vibration. When the trains come in, what you hear is more of a whoosh of air than a clatter of steel wheels and rails; their approach is signaled by blinking floor lights set into the pinkish granite edges of the tiled subway platforms. When Metro car doors are ready to close, warning chimes sound the first two notes of "Swing Low, Sweet Chariot"—that is, the "Swing Low," sometimes a little off-key.

The 75-foot-long cars are clean and roomy, with big windows and industrial carpeting in earth tones. The squeamish may note that the doors of the cars have no handles—in Paris you have to open the door manually to get out—and there are no emergency break-out panels like those commonly found on buses and airplanes. The reliance on electronic automation is total. Claustrophiles might delight in such hermetic womb-tomb confinement; others may have more disturbing dread of incarceration. The situation invites what the Germans call *torschlusspanik,* the fear of being locked in. Passengers are not permitted to walk from car to car. Only the guards have keys to the outer doors, due to the danger of allowing passengers access to the tracks—loaded as they are with 750 volts of electricity.

The projected final budget for Metro is running to $8 billion and still counting. *Fortune* magazine has described it as "The Solid Gold Cadillac of Mass Transit." The capital cost of the system has been estimated as sufficient to provide every family in the region with a secondhand car. The costing of Metro is very conspicuous, and the 80 percent federal subsidy for construction invites outrage because it comes from appropriated funds. (We are not so painfully aware of the 90 percent federal subsidy of the Interstate highway system because it comes from dedicated revenues earmarked to the highway trust fund.) The most certain long-term beneficiaries of the government subsidies to Metro are the commercial and real estate developers whose projects flourish near the Metro stations. Some of these benefits are partially recaptured by local governments in the form of increased revenue from property taxes; and in a few of the commercial developments Metro itself retains a direct investment in the property.

After its first five years of operation the transit system has generated more than $1 billion of private real estate development, and much further intensive construction—clustered around Metro stations—is still under way.

There are always cynics who say that Metro not only costs too much, but that it has come too late. New York's subway was launched before the advent of the automobile, and fortunately before electronic gadgetry could have coped with anything but a single flat fare for the whole system. As a result New York was integrated in a profound way, and the meadows of Brooklyn and Queens were converted to row housing without the benefit of freeways. In Washington the subway has come only after the 67-mile Capital Beltway had determined the pattern of suburban growth; at the same time Metro introduced a possibly too sophisticated technology, vulnerable to slight overloads and dependent on a highly trained labor force. Also Washington's downtown building height maximum of 160 feet—130 feet in most areas—restricts the kind of intensive land use compatible with high-speed mass transit.

Perhaps Metro illustrates the latest example of the Clipper Ship Effect, in which the fastest sailing ships were introduced into world commerce only decades after the advent of the steamship. Could an earlier Metro have forestalled construction of the aging expressways—Interstate 295 and Interstate 395—designed to let every man drive his own car through the city at high speeds? Mass transit patterns change from one mode to the next with an unpredictable fickleness. Trolley cars reached their peak in 1906; they have now been rechristened *interurbans* and may be staging a comeback. New York's subway reached its greatest saturation in the 1930s, two decades after the motor car. Will airplanes some day go the way of the passenger train?

In an age of oil shortages it is possible that the Capital Beltway may become obsolete before the Metro. Operating and maintenance costs, not capital costs, are the darkness at the end of the economic tunnel.

Massachusetts Avenue (East)

Massachusetts Avenue is the longest avenue in the District and it displays the greatest variety of residential and institutional buildings, the heart of Embassy Row, churches, synagogues, and a mosque. Most of the avenue just east and west of Union Station is in the process of recovering from decades of neglect and disuse.

City Post Office   *Massachusetts Avenue at North Capitol Street, NE*

This commanding structure of white Italian marble on a granite base was designed by Daniel H. Burnham to harmonize with but in no way rival his neighboring Union Station. (Burnham's only other work in the city is a commercial office building, the Southern Building at 1425 H Street, NW.)

The City Post Office was completed in 1914 as a major increment of the McMillan Plan, which was to line the city's avenues with uniform classic facades as a Beaux Arts legacy of the Chicago Exposition of 1893. President Charles W. Eliot of Harvard was commissioned to compose the inscriptions chiseled in marble over the east and west entrance pavilions; he is said to have completed them in the course of a single afternoon's sailing in Maine . . . but not without a little help from his friends. President Woodrow Wilson, who had also been a university president, condensed and refined the inscription on the west portal. The texts are given here not only because they are inconvenient to read from street level but because they are the incarnation of romance, zeal made manifest, mementoes of a day when the postal service enjoyed a broader base of popular affection.

   West portal

> MESSENGER OF SYMPATHY AND LOVE
> SERVANT OF PARTED FRIENDS
> CONSOLER OF THE LONELY

City Post Office

BOND OF THE SCATTERED FAMILY
ENLARGER OF THE COMMON LIFE

East portal

CARRIER OF NEWS AND KNOWLEDGE
INSTRUMENT OF TRADE AND INDUSTRY
PROMOTER OF MUTUAL ACQUAINTANCE
OF PEACE AND GOOD WILL
AMONG MEN AND NATIONS

Government Printing Office

*North Capitol Street between G and H Streets, NW   Not open to the public
Main retail bookstore, 710 North Capitol Street, NW, open weekdays 8–4.*

Avoid contractions such as *don't,* . . . use *do they not.* The abbreviation
etc., must be made to read *and so forth.* Profanity, obscene wordings,
and extreme vulgarisms are to be deleted and a 3-em dash substituted
therefor.
—*GPO Style Manual*

In a capital city noted for a paucity of manufacturing activities it is appropriate
that the largest single industrial employer should be the Government Printing
Office (GPO), providing the legislative branch with transcripts of sessions (the
Congressional Record), hearings, bills, acts, and laws; the judicial branch with
decisions, briefs, and decrees; and the executive branch with regulations (the
Federal Register), budgets, rulings, and proclamations—the very end product of
government. This largest printing complex in the world has 35 acres of floor
space paved in wood blocks. It processes 10 freight car loads of paper every
working day. (Freight car loads are unfamiliar magnitudes to most of us; it may
lend perspective, if not comfort, to reflect that the Brown and Williamson Tobacco Company ships two freight car loads of snuff every day out of Louisville.)

It is curious that Congress has retained control of the GPO as part of the legislative branch. Thus the *Congressional Record* is not so much a verbatim record
of what was said on the floor of the House or Senate, but a record of what the
honorable members want to say they said: they are free to refine a metaphor
or tone down a reckless sally up till the midnight press deadline of the day of
debate.

The head of the GPO has the honorific title of Mr. Public Printer, and he is
required by statute to be "a practical printer versed in the art of bookbinding."
The Public Printers are appointed by the president, and they have all been journeymen printers who rose through the union ranks.

In the summer of 1906, after Congress had adjourned, President Theodore

Roosevelt sent a letter to the Public Printer directing him to adopt the revised orthography of the Spelling Reform Committee, which prescribed simplifications for some 300 words. *Though* was made *tho* and *through* was made *thru* and *fixed* was made *fixt*. When Congress reconvened in December it was outraged, and the members had their own means of dealing with the situation: they simply attached a rider to the GPO appropriation stating that no compensation shall be paid to the Public Printer unless he conforms to the spelling recognized by accepted dictionaries of the English language. If President Roosevelt was still carrying his big stick, he wisely refrained from further joining the issue.

Until the 1960s the GPO admitted public visitors; the practice has been abandoned for safety reasons. There are electric forklifts running the corridors with pallets of heavy paper and six-foot-long pneumatic paper knives, not to mention hot lead and high-speed presses. As befits a free economy, the GPO functions as a printer of last resort; it contracts out to commercial printers about two-thirds of all the printing produced for the government. What it ends up printing itself is mostly orders on short deadlines, of short runs in quantity or with a large number of pages—marginal work for private printers who are not about to bring charges of creeping socialism. There are also security considerations, and the GPO prints civil service examinations, passports, and postcards in areas behind wire grilles. (The Treasury's Bureau of Engraving and Printing prints stamps and currency; the GPO prints postcards.)

These enormous buildings are full of many small job shops like boutiques in a department store. They have some of the most advanced high-speed presses (many of them from Germany) as well as virtual antiques held together as makeshifts. They have no four-color presses and no gravure or silk-screen capability. Jet-scan printers and microfiche and tape processors come in on one floor while on another floor a half acre of Mergenthaler linotypes become candidates for the Smithsonian—artifacts embracing the entire printing technology of a century. The GPO plans to complete the transition from hot metal to photocomposition by 1984 in a program that involves retraining hundreds of journeymen printers at the new electronic terminals.

Some of the ancient crafts survive amid all the high technology. Highly skilled artisans marbleize by hand the peacock-feathered edges of pages for decoration and protection; others stamp gold leaf on book covers or hand etch Morocco bindings with silk linings.

The two huge GPO buildings, however grand in their prime, are now obsolete and grossly inefficient. They are both of finely detailed red brick and are the design products of government architectural bureaucracies. The older is GPO Building No. 2 at the corner of G Street completed in 1901 under the direction of Captain John S. Sewall of the U.S. Army Corps of Engineers. Building No. 3

at the corner of H Street was completed in 1938 as a symmetrical echo of the earlier one but in a more modern idiom; it was constructed under the supervision of Louis A. Simon, the last supervising architect of the Treasury before that office was superseded by the Public Buildings Service of the General Services Administration. Simon was a conservative designer, even insisting that his project architects and draftsmen wear coats and ties at the drawing board.

Directly across North Capitol Street from the two behemoths is a minor gem of late Art Deco architecture, a GPO warehouse by architect Victor D. Abel. The fine ornamental low reliefs on the third story overlook some of the bleakest parking lots in the city.

The main entrance lobby of Building No. 3 is graced with a bronze plaque on which the following text is inscribed:

THIS IS A PRINTING OFFICE

CROSSROADS OF CIVILIZATION

REFUGE OF ALL THE ARTS AGAINST THE RAVAGES OF TIME

ARMORY OF FEARLESS TRUTH AGAINST WHISPERING RUMOR

INCESSANT TRUMPET OF TRADE

FROM THIS PLACE WORDS MAY FLY ABROAD

NOT TO PERISH ON WAVES OF SOUND

NOT TO VARY WITH THE WRITER'S HAND

BUT FIXED IN TIME

HAVING BEEN VERIFIED BY PROOF

FRIEND, YOU STAND ON SACRED GROUND

THIS IS A PRINTING OFFICE

—Beatrice L. Warde

National Guard Memorial   1 *Massachusetts Avenue, NW*
Open weekdays 9–4.
This rather splendid exhibition hall, which calls itself the National Guard Heritage Gallery, presents to visitors of every age dramatic episodes and artifacts from the history of the citizen soldiers who make up the militia. There are animated displays of sound and light in which you hear Paul Revere galloping through the night and see how the advancing British Redcoats must have looked to the untested American amateurs. There are miniature figures of the National Guardsmen of every state in their various uniforms, as well as models of military aircraft from 1909 to the present.

The front of the building on Massachusetts Avenue is dominated by a 20-foot-high statue of the Minute Man, a stylized version by Felix de Weldon of the mythic figure first created by Daniel Chester French for the town of Concord and subsequently appearing on millions of postage stamps and war bonds.

The Minute Man was called that because he promised to take arms at a *minute*'s notice; he still symbolizes the tradition of the citizen soldier for whom the profession of arms is an avocation, a secondary calling.

The 100-year-old National Guard Association, which has its headquarters here, exists to support and improve a system in which (in peacetime) the federal government organizes and arms the militia units while the states man and control them until mobilized—a unique resolution of the conflict between the needs of the military and the values of a liberal democracy. Much of the landmark legislation creating and regulating this system resulted from the initiative and sponsorship of the National Guard Association. (And many of the quirky pay and retirement benefits of army and air force reservists result from the association's effective lobbying on Capitol Hill.)

The building was designed by Louis Justement and was dedicated in 1959. Visitors should not be discouraged by the unfortunately forbidding effect of the monolithic solid chrome front doors; they look like a bank after closing hours, with no suggestion of the friendly welcome awaiting within.

"The reserves," says Gen. DeWitt C. Smith, commandant of the Army War College, "are, in a sense, the alternative to nuclear war."

Catholic War Veterans *2 Massachusetts Avenue, NW*
At the apex of Massachusetts Avenue at its junction with North Capitol Street is the relic of the old Childs Restaurant chain, a 1930s sandstone palace with high arched windows, now sheltering the Catholic War Veterans. The Catholic War Veterans was founded in 1935 by a former Army chaplain to promote the values of God and Country and Home and to combat the forces of paganism.

Georgetown University Law Center *600 New Jersey Avenue, NW*
This Law Center building (1971) is one of Edward Durell Stone's last variations on the theme of verticality capped by a Mexican hat cornice—conceivably sired by the National Geographic Building (1964) with the Kennedy Center (1969) as dam.

A law school brochure states that the center is "literally" within the shadow of the U.S. Capitol," so either this "literally" means "figuratively" or we're dealing with a seven-block-long shadow. Anyway, it handsomely accommodates Georgetown's 1,800 law students in convenient proximity to the U.S. Supreme Court, the Library of Congress, the lower District courts, and the Tax Court, in a graduate center three miles east of the main campus in Georgetown.

In this building Stone's vertical spandrels are composed economically but elegantly of face brick rather than the customary marble. The ample podium beneath the superstructure houses a large moot court as well as a chapel.

When the Law Center was dedicated the *Washington Post* heralded the occasion by describing its style as "Late Mussolini" or "Early WPA," and including the following stern admonition:

> The Law Center's aloof monumentality—particularly its imposing and forbidding temple stairs along New Jersey Avenue, leading to an enormous terraced forecourt—isolates it from the surrounding community almost as much as though it were located way out in some rusticated academe. We realize, of course, that what with that awful freeway trench cutting off the center from downtown and all those parking lots, desultory and dilapidated buildings and vacant sites surrounding the rest of it, there is not much of an immediate community in evidence. One great hope for the Law Center is surely, however, that it becomes a catalyst for a healthier, more vibrant, more democratically active community life, that it becomes part of the capital city and "civitas." To that hope, we are afraid, the architecture is a hindrance. It is just not very inviting.

Old Adas Israel Synagogue   *G Street at 3rd Street, NW*

This was the first building in the city constructed specifically for use as a synagogue, and despite more than its share of vicissitudes its red brick walls and narrow double-hung windows have the same appearance today as when first erected in 1876 in the Federal Revival style. The consecration of this synagogue, originally built at 6th and G Streets, NW, was the first in the history of American Judaism to be attended by a president of the United States, Ulysses S. Grant.

The building was in continual use until 1907, when the congregation moved to larger quarters at 6th and I Streets, NW. After it moved out, the building was sold to the Gatti family and used as the Greek Orthodox Church of Saint Sophia; later it was used by the evangelical Church of God. Since 1946 it has served as a carry-out food shop and even as a barber shop. In 1950 the Adas Israel established a new congregation at Connecticut Avenue and Porter Street, NW.

The 6th and G Street site was preempted by the Washington Metropolitan Area Transit Authority for its Metro headquarters, and the building was skidded down the street to a triangle of land at 3rd and G. The separate gallery for women (Adas Israel was, and is, a Conservative congregation) and the original ark survive intact. The one-time synagogue also serves as the site of the Lillian and Albert Small Jewish Museum.

Old District of Columbia Central Library
Mt. Vernon Place, Massachusetts Avenue at 8th and K Streets, NW

President Theodore Roosevelt and Andrew Carnegie were both present for the ceremony in 1903 dedicating the city's first public library and the most recent

Carnegie benefaction at a time when he was dotting America's urban landscape with hundreds of monumental public libraries.

The architectural firm of Ackerman and Ross of New York won the design competition for this exuberant Beaux Arts style building, perhaps with less effort than might be expected since it is closely modeled on a similar Carnegie library that it had designed four years earlier for the city of Atlanta, Georgia. In a sense this library was obsolete at the time it was built as it was designed for closed stacks just when open stacks were first coming into fashion. Today it stands not only more obsolete than ever but vacant and unclaimed, its fate hanging on the future development of the University of the District of Columbia campus in the Mt. Vernon Place area.

Mt. Vernon Place United Methodist Church
Massachusetts Avenue at 9th Street, NW

The Southern branch of the Methodist Episcopal Church resulted from a schism over the slavery question before the Civil War. Because the Southern Methodists wanted a permanent symbol of their denomination in the nation's capital, members from 15 southern states raised most of the money to build this large Doric porticoed church in 1917. The architects were Sauginet and Staats of Fort Worth, and the Neoclassic temple that resulted was constructed exclusively of material from the South: marble from Georgia and wood from Louisiana and the Carolinas.

Mt. Vernon Place Methodist has traditionally had the largest congregation of any Protestant denomination in the city.

Church of the Ascension and St. Agnes
Massachusetts Avenue at 12th Street, NW

I, sweetly tolling men do call to taste the meat that feeds the soul.
—Inscription on east tower sacring bell

The Anglican communion—organized in the United States as the Episcopal Church—admits a broad latitude in the celebration of ritual within its various parishes, ranging, as a piece of 19th-century doggerel has it, from low and lazy to broad and hazy to high and crazy. Within that spectrum the combined parish of Ascension and St. Agnes has traditionally been of the last persuasion, with the habitual employment of votive candles and incense, violins and trumpets, matins and confession—"bells and smells"—and an emphasis on the role of the clergy. In its own words it is "a church for all who enjoy the fine art of Old Prayer Book Worship, Magnificent Liturgical Music, Sound Gospel Preaching." (St. Paul's

Episcopal Church at 2430 K Street, NW, in Foggy Bottom, would have to be ranked as equally high church.)

The Church of the Ascension and St. Agnes is a well-preserved example of the High Victorian Gothic style, built in 1875 on a piece of land donated by

Church of the Ascension and St. Agnes

W. W. Corcoran. It was designed by two prominent Baltimore architects of the day, Thomas Dixon and Charles Carson, and is executed in the oddly discordant combination of Maryland white marble and light pink and orange Ohio sandstone. The roof ridge is graced with an ornamental iron railing.

Though the congregation—like Mr. Corcoran—sympathized with the Confederacy, Ascension and St. Agnes was among the first churches in Washington to be integrated. At a time when Washington had an Episcopal bishop but no cathedral, it served as a procathedral until the Washington Cathedral completed its Bethlehem Chapel in 1912. Since 1961 the church has been responsible for community housing and social service programs that have done much to alleviate the blight and decay of its run-down neighborhood.

Ascension and St. Agnes has a rich tradition of ambitious musical programs enhanced by the superb acoustical properties of the interior and nurtured by a dedicated organist and choirmaster who have recently rebuilt the baroque pipe organ. The balcony accommodates a full orchestra and the altar area is unusually ample for a parish church, providing uncluttered space for the full liturgy. Every spring the church sponsors an impressive Bach festival during Ascension week.

The wide nave in the interior is suspended by slender cast iron columns ornamented with scroll work and rising above the surviving original pews made of dark walnut. The highly stylized altar mural was painted by John de Rosen in 1956 and portrays the Ascension of Our Lord; clouds of silver leaf punctuate the blue sky and a gold leaf nimbus frames the Virgin clothed in salmon and pale blue. The very modern nave windows by Henry Lee Willett are semi-abstract and made of faceted glass set in epoxy. A chief ornament on the altar is a papally authenticated relic of St. Agnes—a particle of bone; Father Frederic Howard Meisel, the rector, says that no other Anglican church of St. Agnes has such a relic of its patron.

**National Conference of Catholic Bishops and
United States Catholic Conference** *1312 Massachusetts Avenue, NW*
The entire facade of this headquarters building for the organization of the Catholic bishops in the United States serves as a limestone niche framing a gigantic bronze statue of Christ rising over a plinth with the arresting legend from the scriptures: I AM THE LIGHT OF THE WORLD. The great scale of the work permits it to prevail over its disadvantageous setting at a point where Massachusetts Avenue divides for an underpass.

Most Washington statues—and there are over 200 of them—honor military figures, especially generals and a few admirals; next most common are statesmen, or at least politicians, and then inventors, scientists, and poets. But as of 1936 the capital had no statue of the founder of the Christian religion, when

Bishop John F. Noll of Fort Wayne, Indiana, initiated a national drive for funds to repair the omission. Finally, in 1949, the 22-foot statue was completed and dedicated. The sculptor was Eugene Kormendi of Notre Dame University in South Bend, and the architect was Frederick V. Murphy of Catholic University in Washington.

The National Conference of Catholic Bishops and the United States Catholic Conference are the two principal national organizations sponsored by the nation's Catholic bishops. A forerunner of these two groups was founded in 1919 in a wartime service program; it was later named the National Catholic Welfare Conference, a title intended to indicate that it had no ecclesiastical jurisdiction. In its early years the assembly of bishops raised some doubts in the Vatican since church law decrees that no body shall stand between the local bishop and the Holy See. Not until Vatican Council II in 1966 legitimized—indeed mandated—regional meetings of bishops, was the National Catholic Welfare Conference reorganized into its present Conference of Bishops, a religious organization, and the Catholic Conference, a secular social welfare and action organization. Their programs are funded in part by diocesan assessments estimated to average seven cents annually per Catholic in the United States.

Metropolitan AME Church   *1518 M Street, NW*

The Metropolitan African Methodist Episcopal Church is the National Cathedral of African Methodism; it is also known as the "connectional" church for all the African Methodist Episcopal (AME) congregations throughout the country. Member AME churches from California to Florida are represented in the nation's capital in the 18 stained glass windows they have donated in recognition of this place as their metropolitan temple.

The AME church movement grew out of black dissatisfaction with the discrimination practiced in Methodist parishes in Philadelphia, Baltimore, and Washington. It had no doctrinal disputes with the mother church; the considerations promoting disaffection were strictly sociological. Some of the AME's first ministers were ordained and later its own bishops were consecrated by Bishop Francis Asbury of the Methodist Episcopal Church. After the Civil War the church spread rapidly from the northern states into the South; it now has over a million active members and it initiated one of the earliest black missionary programs to Africa and the West Indies.

The land for this church was acquired in 1838 and construction stretched over the period from 1854 to 1881. Some of the funds for construction were raised from an assessment of five cents from every member of AME churches all over the world. The thick bearing walls of used brick, two feet thick, support a large sanctuary on the second floor with a wide clear span free of supporting columns. The church recapitulates many episodes of black religious life since the days of slavery: the catacombs of its subbasement harbored fugitives traveling the underground railroad; church members helped many slaves purchase their freedom for sums in the neighborhood of $1,000; it was a social service center for poorer parishes in the depression of the 1890s; in 1913 it was the scene of an overflow mass meeting protesting segregation in the federal government; and during the Vietnam War in the 1960s it was a refuge and mass shelter for the many young demonstrators—black and white—who camped in the church with their bedrolls and backpacks and are reported to have left the place as clean as they found it.

For years city high schools and Howard University used Metropolitan AME Church for their graduation ceremonies. Its pulpit has served as a rostrum for President William Howard Taft, Mary McLeod Bethune, Eleanor Roosevelt, and President Jimmy Carter. The pews of two of its most distinguished parishioners, Paul Laurence Dunbar and Frederick Douglass, are marked with a brass plate.

The church was designed by Samuel T. Morsell in an eclectic Victorian Gothic style and has been designated a Category II Landmark by the Joint Commission on Landmarks. It represents a unique architectural relic, a living artifact, in an area saturated with commercial buildings. Though it is now far removed from the homes of most of its members, more than 500 loyal adherents flock downtown from distant suburbs to attend regular Sunday services, at a time when few downtown congregations have survived the onslaught of commercial development.

National City Christian Church
Thomas Circle, 14th Street at Massachusetts Avenue, NW
In 1926 the International Convention of the Disciples of Christ meeting in Memphis, Tennessee, approved a project to erect "a National Church in Washington"—perhaps as a symbolic escape from any lingering regional identity. As a result, the present building, designed by John Russell Pope, was dedicated in 1930 at the Disciples' First World Convention.

This is the church attended by President Lyndon B. Johnson; prior to that the most distinguished member of its congregation (then meeting in a smaller church, since destroyed) had been President James A. Garfield. Charles Guiteau, who assassinated Garfield just four months after his inauguration, had stalked him at services in the old church for the three preceding Sundays.

National City Christian Church is a monumental rendition of the simple New England frame churches with columned porticoes and a steeple; it copies the finer English Georgian stone models. Here it rises larger than life over Thomas

Circle, with a tower and lantern cupola so well proportioned that you don't realize they exceed Washington's normal building height limit—the tip of the spire is 200 feet above the pavement, or as high as a 20-story building.

Metropolitan AME Church

National Paint and Coatings Association   *1500 Rhode Island Avenue, NW*

> This former millionaire's mansion is now the new headquarters of the
> National Paint, Varnish and Lacquer Association . . . located on U.S.
> Route No. 1, the main artery of travel from Maine to Florida.
> —*National Painter's Magazine*, 1940

In its succession of prominent owners and tenants, this fashionable town house occupying the entire trapezoidal block at 1500 Rhode Island Avenue near Scott Circle recapitulates the last 100 years of Washington's social history. The house was built in 1879 by Lt. John Brodhead, who must have enjoyed rather easy circumstances for a junior officer in the Marine Corps. (When he was asked to take a three-year assignment in China, he declined.) Brodhead commissioned the architect John Fraser to build a 40-room red brick mansion in the Victorian Gothic style complete with turrets and gable roofs and bay windows. (Fraser designed the surviving James G. Blaine House at Dupont Circle in the same red-brick castle style.) Of Fraser's original flamboyance at 1500 Rhode Island Avenue nothing now remains; in 1912 John Russell Pope completely remodeled the house into the classic symmetry of a Beaux Arts version of an Italian Renaissance palace. So we see it today.

In 1882 Brodhead sold the house to Gardiner Greene Hubbard, the founder of the National Geographic Society, who gave it as a wedding present to his daughter upon her marriage to Alexander Graham Bell, the inventor of the telephone and the father of what was to become the Bell System. The couple lived there for the first five years of their marriage, then decided to move to Georgetown to be closer to the Volta Laboratory, which Bell had built with his telephone earnings.

Levi P. Morton, the New York financier, bought the house when he arrived in Washington three days before his inauguration as vice-president under Benjamin Harrison. After serving one four-year term he failed to be renominated and returned to New York and his other house on Fifth Avenue. He decided to retain possession of 1500, however, and rented it to Congressman Charles Sprague of Massachusetts, the first of a series of distinguished Morton tenants.

When Sprague died in 1903 Morton leased the house to Count Arturo Cassini for use as the Imperial Russian Embassy.* He was the last diplomat to represent the Romanovs in Washington and launched the house at 1500 on its

---

* In the twilight of Empire the Russians apparently had a short supply of persons trained in the profession of diplomacy and had to impress many non-Russians—Italians, Monegasques, and others—into their service.

career as a celebrated setting for lavish entertainment, featuring masquerade balls and great Sunday dinners.

Count Cassini arrived in town with a legend of untidiness in marital affairs, a social hurdle that he survived with personal panache and the indulgent acquiescence of Washington society. For fear of offending Czar Nicholas II, he kept his second marriage to a Mme. Stein a secret, although by the time he arrived in Washington he was already estranged from her and accompanied instead by Stephanie Scheele, a member of a theatrical troupe, whom he had met in Hamburg. Cassini introduced Stephanie as his housekeeper and as the governess of his "niece"—their natural child Marguerite, whom he later adopted. The transparency of this improvisation did not deter Presidents McKinley and Theodore Roosevelt from frequent attendance at the embassy dinners.

On reaching the age of 18 the spirited Marguerite shared the duties of embassy hostess. She kept 20 wolfhounds at the embassy and was one of the first women in Washington to play golf, drive her own car, and smoke cigarettes in public. (Her friendship with Alice Roosevelt cooled when she confided that Nicholas Longworth, Alice's husband-to-be, had proposed to her.) Not until Count Cassini retired to Paris was he able to marry Stephanie; there he learned that Mme. Stein had, in fact, been married to a German doctor for 15 years. Years later, Marguerite was also to marry in Paris, assuming the name of Loiewski-Cassini; her two sons Oleg and Igor were to adopt their maternal grandfather's name and title on their road to fashion-mongering and professional celebrity.

Levi P. Morton next rented 1500 to Elihu Root, who lived there while secretary of war and secretary of state. Morton's last tenant was John Hays Hammond, who had made his fortune in South African diamond mines; he installed the first elevator ever to grace a private house in the city. In 1912 Hammond moved to the English Tudor style house at 2221 Kalorama Road that was later to become the French Embassy.

At this point Morton commissioned John Russell Pope to renovate the basic Victorian house completely in a more fashionable formal style, after the model of a 16th-century Italian palace. Pope added a new porte cochere at the main entrance and a spectacular oval spiral staircase with the monogram *M* woven into the gilded grillwork. Presumably pleased, Morton moved back to Washington and resided in the refurbished 1500 until his death in 1920 at the age of 97.

Morton's daughter subsequently rented the house to Ogden Mills when he was undersecretary of the treasury in the Hoover administration and notable for having commissioned a custom-designed limousine with a higher than usual roof to accommodate the silk hat that he habitually wore driving to the office. After Mills moved out, the mansion was leased to the National Democratic Club for use as a clubhouse. In 1939 it was purchased by one of the new trade associations which were beginning to flock to Washington to represent the interests of their industry; this was the paint lobby now known as the National Paint and Coatings Association.* The association has carefully preserved the character of the house inside and out in an imaginative example of what the preservation professionals call *adoptive reuse* (or worse, *commercial recycling*). While the building is not generally open to the public, the association is hospitable to casual visitors who want a peek at the ceremonial entrance hall and its oval staircase painted with great sensitivity in shades of gold, black, chamois, putty, white, and vermilion.

General Scott Apartments   *1 Scott Circle, NW*
The General Scott was Washington's premier luxury residential apartment house of its era, the first in the city to be centrally air conditioned and the last of the Art Moderne style to be completed in 1942 before all construction was halted by World War II. The architect was Robert O. Scholz, who is also responsible for several nearby surviving buildings of the same genre: the World Center Building at 16th and K Streets, the Bay State Apartments at 1701 Massachusetts Avenue, and the Boston House at 1711 Massachusetts Avenue.

Now on the brink of condominiumization, the building has enjoyed a remarkable continuity of management by Mrs. Lillian E. Bowen of Herbert Harvey, Incorporated, since it opened 40 years ago; she was the first woman in the industry to manage commercial property. Under her custodianship the original walnut veneer paneling of the lobby has been preserved without any disturbing anachronisms. To walk into this sleek hermetic lobby in the ocean-liner style of the 1930s is like plunging into the smoking room of the old R.M.S. *Queen Mary.*

Australian Embassy Chancery
1601 Massachusetts Avenue, NW, at Scott Circle
This chancery building was completed in 1965 to the rather unimaginative architectural design of Bates, Smart, and McCutcheon of Melbourne. The cobblestone forecourt is distinguished by stone bollards to keep cars on the right path. A large bronze sculpture emblematic of the Commonwealth of Australia features a composite seal of the country's six states supported by a kangaroo and an

---

* Such large houses had become white elephants, costly to maintain. The trade association was able to purchase the house for the same price—$95,000—Levi P. Morton had paid the Hubbards for it in 1889.

emu rampant. A permanent exhibit of Australian crafts—ceramics, glass, and especially fine leatherwork—is open weekdays from 9 A.M. to 5 P.M.

This building provides the eastern anchor to Embassy Row as it proliferates along Massachusetts Avenue between Scott Circle and Observatory Circle.

National Rifle Association   *1600 Rhode Island Avenue, NW, at Scott Circle*
Museum open daily 10-4, free.
Except for abortion, no abiding issue in our national life arouses more mindless passion than gun control. The attitude toward guns polarizes two divergent strains in the American character—as described by a neutral observer quoted by the NRA itself in *The Public Interest*, fall 1976: On the one hand is the rational model of people "for whom hunting is atavistic, personal violence is shameful, and uncontrolled ownership is a blot on civilization." The other model is the conservative for whom " 'sociological' is an epithet. Life is tough and competitive. Manhood means responsibility and caring for your own."

The National Rifle Association and its membership of over a million—possibly the largest consumer lobby in town—attest to the lively support for the latter persuasion. For them, freedom is symbolized by the right to bear arms. Their executive vice-president, Harlon B. Carter says, "Ours is not the lighthearted pursuit of a sport, though there's nothing wrong with that. Ours is the deep and serious voice of a people determined to be free." Equally serious arguments to the contrary may be found two blocks away at the National Council to Control Handguns, 810 18th Street, NW. (In 1979 a federal judge ruled unconstitutional a United States law that required a person to be a member of the NRA in order to buy surplus army rifles—usually at a fraction of their cost.)

The bland and institutional NRA headquarters building was designed by Antonio C. Ramos of Clas, Riggs, Owens & Ramos of Silver Spring, Maryland.

Chilean Embassy Chancery   *1732 Massachusetts Avenue, NW*
This severely unadorned 1890 mansion of dark brick and sandstone has recently been described by architectural historian Sibley Jennings as "austere Art Nouveau (rather than whimsical, sinuous or organic) though many interior elements are related to the Arts and Crafts movement."

It is one of three surviving Massachusetts Avenue residences by the influential Washington architect Glenn Brown, who is also responsible for the equally somber Beale House at 2012 and the more fanciful Egyptian Embassy residence at 2301, as well as the Buffalo Bridge that takes Q Street across Rock Creek Park. Brown was a guiding spirit of the 1901 McMillan Plan for Washington and an instigator of the Commission of Fine Arts; his books include a two-

Mrs. Moore remarried and lived on at 1746 (at least several months a year) until 1927, when she sold it to accommodate the new Canadian Legation, that country's first diplomatic mission in Washington. The deed recorded the transfer of the property as "from Mabelle Swift Wichfeld (formerly Moore) to His Majesty King George V, in Right of Canada, represented herein by the Minister of Public Works of Canada."

Diplomatic relations between Ottawa and Washington were inhibited for years by Canada's understandable regard for the priority of its Imperial ties with Great Britain. But once the post was established, her appointments to Washington were awarded to men of singular distinction: the first minister who presented his credentials to President Coolidge in 1927 was Vincent Massey (a relative of the actor Raymond) who was later to become the first Canadian to serve as governor-general. Lester Pearson, who served as ambassador here during World War II, subsequently became prime minister. (The State Department's *Diplomatic Lists* for 1946–53 record the fact that the Canadian ambassador H. Hume Wrong had as one of his aides a first secretary named H. Hume Wright.)

All Canadian chancery offices and consulates are relentlessly bilingual: they even answer the telephone in both French and English before the caller has had a chance to identify himself.

Brookings Institution   *1775 Massachusetts Avenue, NW*
Open by arrangement (797-6000).

Bad politics cause poverty more often than bad business.
—Hugh Thomas, *A History of the World*

Washington is a city preoccupied with the practice, rather than the theory, of government. Into this inhospitable milieu the Brookings Institution seeks to bring the blessings of objective nonpartisan analysis of government policy and practice: the social sciences, practically applied. The emphasis at Brookings is on economics and political science. The injunction of W. H. Auden—"Thou shall not commit a social science"—is at least partially honored in Brookings's disdain for social anthropology and social psychology.

Brookings is a sanctuary, but an antiseptic one with the atmosphere of a laboratory, where scholars recognize two types of research: that which is "of Brookings quality" and that which is not. (In an in-house joke they refer to each other as members of the PBI—with the *P* standing for prestigious.) In these gray precincts the staff is composed of accredited academics free of the constraints of academe, obliged neither to meet a payroll nor to defend their budgets to any outside body; they are insulated by endowment from the competitive pressures of the flamboyant think tanks that decorate the Capital Beltway.

A forerunner of the Brookings Institution was the privately financed Institute for Government Research organized in 1917 to provide government policy makers with some of the insights available from the inexact sciences. In her *Washington: A History of the Capital,* Constance McLaughlin Green writes:

> Research in the social sciences, intensified by the troubles of wartime agencies in assembling precise information . . . [demonstrated] the need of a clearer understanding within the federal government of the principles of political and business economy. Robert S. Brookings, a wealthy St. Louis manufacturer [of rope and cordage] who had served on the War Industries Board, took the lead. In 1919, a slim, handsome, white-haired, trimly bearded man of 69 whose formal education had ended when he was 16 but whose intellectual interests deepened as his fortunes grew, Brookings virtually singlehanded raised the money to prevent the threatened demise of the privately supported Institute for Government Research. From the institute's dispassionate factual studies came the recommendations that Congress wrote into a law of 1921 creating an executive accounting system and the Bureau of the Budget.

With his own funds and with aid from the Carnegie and other foundations, Brookings's initiatives evolved in 1927 to the present institution, which can since be credited with further government reforms such as the establishment of the Congressional Budget Office and the (increasingly controversial) program of federal revenue sharing with the states.

In less tangible ways the Brookings staff members spend as much as a fifth of their time testifying on Capitol Hill on government policy and proposed legislation. And they issue any number of weighty published studies. The bottom line of a Brookings study is to answer the question: What should U.S. government policy be? (This is in contrast to the adversary posture of the more overtly business-oriented American Enterprise Institute—around the corner at 1150 17th Street—whose purpose is to counter existing policies with preferred alternatives.)

The titles of Brookings studies are broadly polemic, *Red Tape: Its Origins, Uses, and Abuses;* and relentlessly interrogatory, *Must Corporate Income Tax Be Taxed Twice?* and *Must We Bus?;* and on a more desperate note, verging on the nihilistic, *Can Organizations Change?*

When Robert Brookings was lobbying businessmen to support his transition of the temporary Institute for Government Research into the permanent Brookings Institution, he would ask them such questions as, "Do you want logrolling or a scientific tariff? Do you want pork barrel bills or a budget?" Brookings survives as a convenient object of regard for observers who believe in the conspiracy theory of history and for writers who believe in "The Establishment" school of journalism, for those who hold the conviction that somehow, somewhere, there are people—if only we could find them—who really are running the place.

Brookings Institution practices explicit partisan neutrality from one presidential administration to the next, affording the same hospitality to a loyal opposition as to incumbents. At a time when federal law provided no official abode for presidents-elect and their staffs, Brookings supplied office space for President-elect John F. Kennedy and his not yet confirmed cabinet. Different presidents respond in different ways. Nixon's Watergate operatives regarded Brookings as subversive of their mode of governance and laid plans to detonate its files. Presidents who were trained as engineers, such as Herbert Hoover and Jimmy Carter, seem to share Robert Brookings's faith in a social science approach to political problems.

The sanitary Brookings office building at 1775 Massachusetts Avenue, NW, by the architectural firm of Faulkner, Kingsbury, and Stenhouse (1960) looks like neither a government agency nor commercial law offices but like something in between, which is what it is: a nonprofit corporation employing largely private funds to study public problems of politics and the economy. The joyless pastel facade achieves severity without any redeeming grace of self-confidence or originality.

Both sides of this 1700 block of Massachusetts Avenue are zoned Special Purpose, an innovative category designed to serve as a buffer between the business district and residential areas. This zoning remedy was adopted by the District in 1958 on the advice of a New York planning consultant, Harold M. Lewis. It permitted the conversion of existing structures to chanceries or institutional purposes as a matter of absolute right; but, more recklessly, it also permitted the construction of new hotels, apartments, or office buildings, for institutional or nonprofit use, to a height of 90 feet subject to zoning board approval—seldom denied. The result was a wholesale destruction of former row house elegance, including in the case of Brookings the demolition of the handsome residence of Senator Henry Cabot Lodge and the conversion of other houses of equal merit into Brookings parking lots. The damage of this perfectly legal devastation was atoned for in part by the generosity with which Brookings salvaged the neighboring apartments at 1785 until they could be permanently restored by the National Trust for Historic Preservation.

Dupont Circle

Dupont Circle has as its focal point a fountain dedicated to Samuel Francis Dupont, a rear admiral in the Union Navy. (It was commissioned as a memorial by his family of Wilmington, Delaware, where the name is spelled du Pont.) Many of the surviving Victorian mansions of this formerly residential area have been converted to embassy or institutional functions. The surrounding neighborhood of tree-lined streets is the most cosmopolitan—or at least most heterogeneous—area of the city. In addition to diplomatic missions, there are many specialty shops, hotels, pubs, bookstores, cafés, and combined bookstore-cafés. The Dupont Circle branch of Riggs National Bank does more retail business in the exchange of foreign currencies than any other bank in the city.

National Trust for Historic Preservation *1785 Massachusetts Avenue, NW* *Open for public business weekdays 9–5.*

> The National Trust has chosen . . . to show other institutions how a historic downtown property can be rejuvenated and preserved.
> —*Washington Post,* 19 January 1977

This large apartment house at 1785 Massachusetts Avenue accommodates only six apartments, and they are the most opulent luxury apartments ever to be built in the city. They were designed by Jules H. de Sibour in his customarily palatial Beaux Arts style, but in this example an air of restrained grandeur prevails. Designing street facades that "turn a corner" with grace and assurance is said to be a test of an architect's skills; here that test is passed with high marks as the designer effectively features the corner entrance axis of a difficult trapezoidal site plan. The construction is of brick on steel, well concealed by a veneer of limestone fabric with Louis XVI motifs. (De Sibour also designed the neighboring Canadian Chancery at 1746 Massachusetts Avenue and the severely stark Yater

Clinic—originally the M. E. Ingalls residence—directly across the street to the south.)

1785 Massachusetts Avenue has sheltered a long roster of socially and politically prominent tenants. Most of them were birds of brief passage; they rented their apartments for just a few years of career tenure in Washington, and even then they actually lived in them only part of the year—sometimes staying as briefly as six weeks—between winter sojourns on Jekyll Island or summers in Newport or Bar Harbor.

A typical apartment was entered through an oval entrance foyer giving access to a living room 45 feet long; there were six bedrooms, six fireplaces, and 14½-foot ceilings. Each apartment had 11,000 square feet, or about seven times the size of an average house today. The floors were of herringbone wood parquet and the doorknobs were plated with silver or gold. There were silver vaults, wine closets, and trunk rooms, and the servants' rooms were set in eight mezzanine levels with lower ceilings. Among the innovations were a central vacuuming system, centrally refrigerated tap water, and separate laundry chutes to individual electric washing machines in the basement.

Before this marvel of luxury was built, the site had been occupied by the Belden Noble House, a massive red brick mansion in the 13th-century Romanesque Revival style. In 1906 the Noble House was bought by Stanley McCormick, a son of the inventor of the reaper and founder of the International Harvester Company. He remodeled the place but never moved into it, and in 1915 demolished it to build his new apartments in an action that might have had considerable opposition if the preservation movement—it was then virtually nonexistent—had been as strong as it is now. In 1917 the new de Sibour apartments were completed and the first tenants moved in.

But Stanley McCormick's role as the entrepreneur is an obscure one, as he was a tragic victim of a mental illness diagnosed as dementia praecox and malignant compulsion neurosis. He spent most of his adult life behind protective bars on an isolated estate near Santa Barbara, California, until he died in 1947 at the age of 72. He had been first declared legally incompetent by a California court in 1906. Why and how these apartments were built in his name is a minor mystery of McCormick family history, especially since no McCormicks ever lived there.

Among the earliest tenants (from 1920 to 1922) was Thomas Fortune Ryan, one of the great tycoons of railroads and minerals, whose personal property included one of the largest diamond fields in the Belgian Congo.

In 1921 Andrew W. Mellon came to town from Pittsburgh and moved into 1785 to become its richest and—eventually—most famous and most long-tenured tenant; he lived there for ten years as secretary of the treasury under three presidents and intermittently thereafter until his death in 1937. In fact it was Mellon's top floor apartment with the skylight over the oval foyer that was to become the birthplace of the National Gallery of Art with a little help from his fellow tenant (from 1936 to 1937), Baron Duveen of Millbank. The role of these two men in that achievement is dramatically documented in S. N. Behrman's engaging biography *Duveen*.

Mellon was the son of a Pittsburgh banker who had taken over control of his father's enterprises while he was still in his 20s. He went on to found the Aluminum Company of America and helped establish and eventually dominated the Gulf Oil Corporation. By the time he came to the capital he was one of the richest men in the country and a director or officer in more than 60 corporations. As secretary of the treasury he was opposed to taxation as an instrument of social policy; he advocated repeal of the excess profits tax and proposed an individual income tax rate ceiling of 10 percent. He was the apostle of the "trickle down" theory of economic growth, what would now be called "supply side" economics, and during his tenure the national debt was actually *reduced* by more than a

National Trust for Historic Preservation

third. But these policies did not forestall the social devastation of the Depression years, and in 1932 growing popular criticism made timely his appointment as ambassador to the Court of St. James's.

Just before he left for London, the Soviet government began to sell the art treasures of the Hermitage to pay for tractors and industrial development, and Mellon began to buy them. With Knoedler and Company as agents Mellon purchased $6 million of Old Masters including Raphael's *Alba Madonna* at over $1 million, then the highest price ever paid for a single picture. Mellon's individual purchases amounted to one-third of all Soviet exports to America in 1931.

Lord Duveen, perhaps the most flamboyant art dealer of all time, was determined to outdo Knoedler; he had built his career on "the simple notion that Europe had plenty of art and America had plenty of money." In 1936, after Mellon had returned to 1785 Massachusetts Avenue, Duveen prevailed upon the family living in the apartment directly below Mellon to transfer the lease to him. Behrman offers a firsthand account:

> Duveen said to Mellon one day, "You and I are getting on. We don't want to run around. I have some beautiful things for you. You don't want to keep running to New York to see them; I haven't the energy to keep running to Washington. I shall arrange matters so that you can see these things at your convenience and at your leisure."
> ... He then moved in all the wonderful things and the result was very beautiful and very expensive. He installed a caretaker, engaged several guards to keep an eye on the apartment, gave Mellon the key, and went back to New York.
> The caretaker confided charming vignettes of the tenant on the upper floor, in dressing gown and carpet slippers, leaving his own apartment to bask in Duveen's more opulent environment. ... There came a moment when he felt he couldn't go on living a double life. He sent for Duveen and bought the contents of his apartment, lock, stock, and barrel. This was the largest transaction ever consummated in the world of art.

Andrew Mellon paid $21 million for 24 paintings and 18 sculptures; for once he was short of cash and had to pay Duveen in securities. Thus was assembled the nucleus of the collection that launched and justified the National Gallery of Art.

After all that, the remaining catalog of tenants of the apartment house has to be a little anticlimactic; they were (with their terms of residence) Sumner Welles (1921–27), diplomat and undersecretary of state; Robert Woods Bliss (1920–23), art collector, diplomat, and founder of Dumbarton Oaks; Alanson B. Houghton (1930–34), former president of the Corning Glass Works and later ambassador to Germany and to Great Britain; and Mrs. Perle Mesta, ambassador to Luxembourg and inspiration of Ethel Merman's role in the musical *Call Me Madam*.

World War II ended all that. The millionaires were politely evicted and the entire building was turned over to the British government for the British Purchasing Commission and the British Commonwealth Scientific Office. The once great rooms were partitioned and the bureaucrats moved in their drab furnishings. When the British moved out, the place was taken over for 20 years by the American Council on Education. Fortunately, the neighboring Brookings Institution bought 1785 and rented the office space to a string of learned societies and eleemosynary organizations. As a responsible landlord Brookings kept commercial real estate speculators at bay until the National Trust for Historic Preservation could raise the funds to buy the building in 1977 and restore it as a model of sensitive and pragmatic historic preservation which enhances its urban environment. To this end it has planted sturdy wisteria vines and a ground cover of vinca minor to relieve the starkness of the iron railings along the basement light wells. That these plantings are continuously being vandalized is a sad comment on civic decency in the Dupont Circle community. Must wisteria vines, like bicycles, be padlocked when left unattended at night?

Sulgrave Club *1801 Massachusetts Avenue, NW   Private club.*
The rounded apex of this triangular building is gracefully oriented toward the center of Dupont Circle. It was built in 1901 by Herbert and Martha Wadsworth; he was a large landowner from the Genesee Valley of New York State and they were both amateur designers and decorators. The identity of the architect, if any, is unknown, and Mr. Wadsworth graciously allowed that the only thing the house lacked was a sign over the arched carriage entrance in Gothic letters saying "Marfy done it!"

That carriage entrance originally went straight through the ground floor of the house as a fully sheltered porte cochere; this area under a Palladian window has since been closed in as a wood-framed vestibule. During World War I the Wadsworths turned the entire house over to the use of the Red Cross. In 1932, at the depth of the Depression, it was sold for $125,000 to a small group of Washington matrons who wanted to convert the residence into a women's social club. In that bicentennial year of Washington's birth they decided to name the club for his ancestral home in England, Sulgrave Manor.

The club survives as a refuge of the city's cave dwellers, relatively impervious to the transience of Washington's political life. Members of the diplomatic corps are welcome as guests, but not as members; and press photographers are strictly barred at all times. It was a place where President Eisenhower could have a cozy breakfast with Republican women, where Frances Parkinson Keyes could give dinners to launch her novels, and where Arthur Rubinstein could play informally for a coming-out party.

The main floor of the club—the second floor—features an oval drawing room overlooking Dupont Circle, a circular morning room in the southeast corner, and a squarish ballroom with gilded mirrors. In a 1955 article in the *Washington Post,* society columnist Mary Van Rensselaer Thayer wrote that "dancing groups, which night-club-less Washington favors, meet there regularly. . . . The Dancing Class . . . The Waltz Group . . . the Friday Cotillion . . . have all twirled on the Sulgrave parquet."

Washington Club   *15 Dupont Circle, NW   Private club.*

Washington was the one city in the East where any woman with money and talent could set up housekeeping and become an important hostess.
—A. A. Hoge, *Cissy Patterson*

For a generation of older Americans one of the most familiar newspaper pictures of their lives was that of Charles A. Lindbergh flanked by President and Mrs. Coolidge waving from a Washington balcony on his triumphal return to the United States from Paris in June of 1927. In any other year he would have been given a White House welcome, but the president's home was undergoing one of its periodic renovations. The Coolidges were required to accept the hospitality of Mrs. Patterson at 15 Dupont Circle. For three days after his return the circle was filled with cheering crowds wanting a glimpse of their new hero. It was from the balcony of this house that he appeared to them—and on the front pages of every newspaper in the land.

The house was built for Robert W. Patterson in 1903 by McKim, Mead and White, with Stanford White as the partner-in-charge. (White was also responsible for another residence that still stands nearby: the Thomas Nelson Page House of 1897, 1759 R Street, NW.) The Patterson House survives today as a women's social club.

Euram Building   *21 Dupont Circle, NW*

A piece in the *New Yorker* once described Washington's downtown office buildings as looking like ice cubes poured out of a tray. Certainly most of them fill out their zoning envelopes with a bland uniformity that does little to add to the variety or gaiety of the urban scene. A rare exception to the conventional formula for speculative office buildings is the Euram Building at 21 Dupont Circle. It is such an exception, in fact, that a lot of people find it hard to get used to; they say they don't like it because "it looks funny." Well, they should count their blessings. The Euram Building is original and beautiful; unique in its site plan, original in its clear-span structural armature, and striking in the refinement of its brick and glass fabric.

The success of Euram is as much a tribute to the taste and boldness of the client as it is to the ingenuity of its architects. The Institutio Mobilare Italiano (IMI), a financial group based in Rome, had the princely attitude of a patron; it wanted a work of quality that would make an esthetic contribution to the Dupont Circle area, and to that end provided the architects with a budget of $2 million in 1971 to come up with 43,000 feet of net rentable floor space out of a total building area of 75,000 square feet. When the Washington architectural firm of Hartman-Cox got the commission, it responded with a resourceful inter-

Euram Building

Normandy was much prized by the builders of Canterbury Cathedral, Westminster Abbey, and Buckingham Palace, who imported it from France for carving and decorative work. Mr. Sanson decreed that this stone should be granulated, pulverized, and reconstituted so it could be cast *in situ* as tawny sculptured reliefs or simulated blocks with white-painted mortar lines.

All this sumptuous detail and lavish scale was designed for a kind of social life that was to disappear from the scene less than two decades after it was completed. By the time the Depression arrived, Mr. Belmont was hard pressed to find a new owner who could preserve such a vast domestic monument at even a custodial level of care. If he had sold the house to an embassy, the public room would almost certainly have been divided up into smaller offices. Records indicate that in 1933 he applied for a zoning change to permit the building to be converted into six luxury apartments. Nothing came of that plan; we are told only that he was determined that the place should not "stand as a monument to the Depression."

Mr. Belmont was a master Mason, and he finally turned to an affiliated organization, the Order of the Eastern Star, to which he agreed to sell the house in 1937 for $100,000—virtually a gift, for the sum would not even touch the worth of the ornaments and furnishings included.

The fate of Belmont House is like that of Anderson House as bequeathed to the Society of the Cincinnati; they remain intact because their owners left them in the hands of established fraternal organizations, more or less exclusive clubs with vaguely patriotic purposes. Anderson House is tax exempt and nonprofit; the society maintains a library and museum open to the public. Belmont House is nonprofit but not tax exempt (it pays real estate taxes to the District of over $1,000 a month), and open only to members and their guests.

The Order of the Eastern Star is not just a women's auxiliary of Freemasonry, as men who are Masons may also join. Women must be female relatives of master Masons to qualify for membership. In the words of its own statement of purpose, "The Eastern Star strives to take good people and through uplifting and elevating associations of love and service, through precept and example, build an Order which is truly dedicated to Charity, Truth, and Loving-kindness." The order makes substantial financial contributions to cancer research and a variety of Masonic charities. Since it is international in scope, it flies no flag over its temple. Though it professes the deep spiritual conviction of its members, "it is not a religion . . . it is open to all faiths, except no faith."

The temple is maintained through an endowment fund created by an almost unanimous record of each member making a once-in-a-lifetime contribution of one dollar. Members regard the building as a hallowed shrine to their high ideals and purposes, and they describe it as "This Temple Beautiful." The Right Worthy Grand Secretary of the General Grand Chapter has a small administrative office in the basement where financial and membership records are kept, and bound records of the Triennial Sessions of the order are kept in the upstairs library, but neither local nor General Grand Chapter meetings are held at the headquarters, and its institutional functions are largely symbolic.

For a residence with 54 rooms, it is rather curious that there are only three bedrooms for family and guests. (Like Hillwood under the regime of Mrs. Post, there was minimal provision for houseguests.) Mr. Belmont first married at the age of 49—to a Miss Vanderbilt—and they occupied separate bedroom suites on the first floor. On the far northwest corner is a third bedroom suite with sitting room and bath, but quite small in view of the general scale of the house. It is this third bedroom that was occupied for ten days in November 1919 by the Prince of Wales—later King Edward VIII and duke of Windsor. Blair House had not been established as a presidential guest house, and the illness of President Wilson prevented the prince from being entertained at the White House. Perry Belmont and his wife were happy to oblige as quasi-official hosts; it is the kind of thing that must have been one of their motives for choosing to live in Washington, though they did so for only one or two months a year. In previous years they had entertained at 1618 New Hampshire the prime minister of Italy, the president of Brazil, and various naval missions from Japan. Mr. Belmont must have had particular satisfaction in entertaining the Japanese as he could use the silver dinner service he inherited from his godfather and grandfather, Commodore Matthew C. Perry, who opened the ports of Japan to United States trade.

Nowadays Mr. Belmont's bedroom is reserved for the use of the General Grand Chapter's Most Worthy Grand Matron on her occasional visits to the capital; the guest bedroom is similarly reserved for the Most Worthy Grand Patron; while Mrs. Belmont's suite of sitting room, bedroom, and bath with a large sunken marble tub, is allotted to the Right Worthy Grand Secretary (and her husband) in accordance with "the law of the lodge" as her ex officio year-round residence, a rather splendid perquisite of high fraternal (or sororal) office.

The third or attic floor of the house was for servants only. This floor is set back under a mansard slate roof with green copper-trimmed gable windows behind a marble balustrade deck with urns. Thirty-four servants were accommodated in a total of 17 bedrooms, but for a staff of that size there were only two servants' bathrooms—a rather mean, not to say imprudent, allocation of resources. The main house has an opulent oval elevator richly paneled in golden oak. But for the servants there are only dumbwaiters and a backstairs rising seven flights from the kitchen level to the attic bedrooms.

Most of the Belmont family furniture and works of art were auctioned off or

In 1979 the property was on the verge of being redeveloped into 30 condominiums when it was boldly rescued by a neighbor, Mrs. Stellita Stapleton Renchard, in an impulse of notable benefaction to the city. Since her purchase, Codman House has been designated a Category II District of Columbia Landmark and listed on the National Register of Historic Places. Plans are underway to install in the principal public rooms of the mansion a museum of Latin American art. It will be the first such museum in the United States devoted exclusively to works of art of Central and South America that flourished under the dominance of Spanish, Portuguese, and French rule during the colonial period 1500–1830.

Decatur Terrace Steps and Fountain
22nd Street between Decatur Place and S Street, NW

These steps and fountain are an unusually happy example of city planning gone absolutely right—a blend of private benefaction and bureaucratic designs. In 1911 the District's Office of Buildings and Grounds determined that the rise of 22nd Street toward S Street above Decatur Place—though less than 20

Decatur Terrace Steps

feet—was too steep to be broken through as a connecting street and that the public throughway should be completed on a pedestrian scale. The adjoining property at 1743 22nd Street was owned by Mrs. Mary Vaux Walcott who deeded a strip of her land to the city for this purpose. The result is a delightful stone and concrete staircase, framed by inviting ornamental lampposts and graced with a quietly plashing lion's head fountain. This is a rare amenity, the kind of urban streetscape design for which we seem to have lost the knack.

People in the neighborhood often refer to it as the "Spanish Steps," not because there is anything Spanish about it, but because they have sufficient imagination (or presumption) to compare it with the grand stair complex rising from the Piazza di Spagna in Rome.

Massachusetts Avenue (West)

James Bryce, who was the British Ambassador to the United States between 1906 and 1913 and the author of *The American Commonwealth*, declared that the intersection of Massachusetts and Wisconsin Avenues afforded the most beautiful view in the city. In an article he wrote for the *National Geographic* of June 1913 he said: "You all know the spot . . . just opposite where the Episcopal Cathedral is to stand. At that point you look down upon the city, you see its most striking buildings . . . and beyond them the great silvery flood of the Potomac." He urged that new building be limited in height so as not to obstruct the view. A triangular park at this site opposite the cathedral has been landscaped in recent years and named Bryce Park in his memory.

Phillips Collection   *1600 21st Street, NW   Open Tuesday–Saturday 10–5, Sunday 2–7, suggested contribution   Concerts September–June Sunday at 5.*

> Visitors to the gallery should be . . . welcomed to feel at home with the pictures in an unpretentious domestic setting.
> —Duncan Phillips

The Phillips Collection opened in 1921 as the first permanent museum of modern art in this country. In the words of its founder it was to be "a public gallery with its main stress on living painters," both American and European, and "those works of previous period which . . . would be forever modern." Thus the collection has a subtitle: A Museum of Modern Art and Its Sources. To Duncan Phillips, the term *modern* embraced the work of both contemporary living painters and those of the past who were innovative in spirit, and visitors should thus be prepared to encounter the paintings of Giorgione, El Greco, Goya, and Daumier. Phillips refrained from describing these earlier artists as *pre-modern*, thus happily obviating the equally vexing notion of *post-modern*. (That the terms *modern* and *contemporary* are ambiguous is an accident of 20th-century life. In any event, Phillips's striking phrase "forever modern" seems to have anticipated intuitively a trend by which the word will eventually become capitalized as *Modern*, even as in *Baroque* and *Classic*).

The Phillips is "one of the world's great one-person museums," in a phrase proposed by the art critic John Russell to describe "an institution founded, formed, and funded by an individual human being in the likeness of his own personal tastes." Other examples of the genre in this country are the Isabella Stewart Gardner Museum in Boston and Paul Mellon's Center for British Art at Yale. Such collections are mirrors of the personalities who created them; it is quite a different strategy from that of the grand acquisitors like Morgan, Frick, Widener, and Andrew Mellon, who simply sent out agents to buy up whatever was best and available in any particular field. There could be as many different kinds of one-man museums as there are collectors with the means and energy and originality to conceive of them.

Duncan Phillips was one of the originals; he declared, "I have no advisors, and I have no agents at all among the dealers. The capacity to decide for oneself is one's only safeguard against the contagions of fashion in art. . . . My special function is to find the independent artist and to stand sponsor for him against the herd mind." The impulse is aristocratic and self-confident; the approach is that of a connoisseur. When he admired an artist, he wanted to buy those paintings which would enhance the total effect of his collection and evoke in the viewer the enthusiasm of the collector; he particularly liked pictures that would communicate joy, as the joy of the viewer was for him the chief object of a museum.

When the family of Major Duncan Clinch Phillips moved to Washington from Pittsburgh, they were, unlike many other millionaires from the heartland, not motivated by social or political ambition; they came in all innocence to seek a milder climate for reasons of health. During the winter of 1896, which turned out to be a balmy one, they decided to make their permanent residence in Washington, and they commissioned the fashionable architectural firm of Hornblower and Marshall to build them a town house on the corner of 21st and Q Streets, NW. The result is the red brick building with brownstone and terra-cotta trim in a restrained Georgian Revival style.

The outside of the house is staid and a little cheerless, a nondescript relic of the turn of the century. Though the architects could have had no inkling that the house was destined one day to accommodate an art gallery, they fortuitously introduced large plate glass windows admitting floods of light as an eclectic departure from the Georgian tradition. Inside, the house is furnished in unobtrusive comfort. The pictures are now shown at eye level in mostly small rooms with overstuffed sofas and easy chairs; books are left out on tables; people do not talk in hushed tones; and there is an ample supply of ashtrays and an absence of uniformed guards. The guards, in fact, are apt to be artists or art students.

Duncan Phillips was a boy of 11 when his family moved into 1600 21st Street. His maternal grandfather was the Laughlin of the Jones and Laughlin Steel Company; this heritage assured him the means to indulge his talents as a collector and museologue. Though he was quite thin and ascetic looking (he was found to be 40 pounds underweight when rejected for military service in 1917), he was a keen athlete and full of energy and curiosity. As an undergraduate at Yale he majored in literature, but his interests turned more and more to art and esthetics. Even as a very young man he was a cosmopolite, equally at home in Pittsburgh, New York, and Paris. While he was still in his 20s he pinch-hit for Frank Crowninshield as managing editor of *Vanity Fair* and went on to become the youngest member of New York's Century Club. Although he never met Bernard Berenson, he had the temerity to sustain a lengthy correspondence with him arguing the attributions of works of certain early Italian Masters. He was also something of a painter, working with oils on still lifes and landscapes, with sufficient ability to address the artists he collected on the level of a colleague. His wife Marjorie was more accomplished and many of her works are in the collection; their son Laughlin Phillips, who now heads the collection, has also been a painter, not a bad discipline for someone who has to manage a gallery.

Like most museum people Duncan Phillips was leery of an architectural setting that would compete with the picture for the attention of the client; he wanted the setting and the picture to be complementary. The first wing had been added to the house in 1907. In 1917 McKim, Mead and White added a second-floor skylight gallery, quite ample but not out of scale with the rest of the family home. Then in 1924 Phillips took an option on a tract of land that has since become the site of the Washington Hilton hotel, and commissioned McKim, Mead and White to design a new museum building for the collection. The architects presented renderings of an elaborate Italianate villa, but for various subtle reasons the project never materialized. The collection put its money into acquisitions instead of real estate, and 1600 21st Street became the permanent home of the gallery by virtual default. In 1960 an awkward and incompatible wing* was added, and plans for further expansion are now under way—perhaps a "post-modern" caprice echoing the earlier Hornblower and Marshall facade.

If the architectural setting was a secondary consideration, the arrangement of the pictures in their various rooms was not. Phillips's instinct as a collector was

---

* The sculptured bird design over the door to the annex was copied from Georges Braque with permission.

manifested and enhanced by a concern for how the pictures acquired would look together, how one work of art would interplay with another in an intimate setting.

His way of hanging pictures was unorthodox; he liked the intuitive juxtaposition of the work of art of one artist against that of another without regard to academic periods or schools or the conventional labeling of curators. He wanted to avoid the clutter of unnecessary labels. And he had a particular eye for the display of little masterpieces in small furnished rooms.

His collection started with purchases from American Impressionists and the Ashcan School. He was an enthusiastic and early collector of the abstractions and visionary landscapes of Augustus V. Tack and Clyfford Still. Other American artists to whom he made early commitments were Arthur Dove, John Marin, and Georgia O'Keeffe. Throughout his career he was predisposed to recognizable and natural subjects, fine painterly brushwork, and above all color and colorists. His conversion to modernism was slow to ripen, and even then he never collected at the cutting edge of the avant-garde. He was wary of falling into the traps of cults and movements. He bought few of the Fauves, among Cubists he preferred Braque to Picasso, among the Abstract Expressionists his favorite was Mark Rothko. He preferred the contemplative to the raucous, and structured assurance to the technically experimental. He was, for instance, appalled by what he called the stupefying vulgarity of the New York Armory Show of 1913, and he bought none of the excessive and abrasive examples of the Paris avant-garde that he found there.

We can get some notion of the audacity required to open a new kind of museum in 1921 when we reflect that almost a decade would pass before the Museum of Modern Art would open its doors in New York, and when it did so it would concentrate almost exclusively on the celebration of European artists. The idea of a museum as a guardian of only past treasures was so firmly rooted that even Gertrude Stein said of the prospective Museum of Modern Art that it couldn't be done: her exact words were, "You can be modern or you can be a museum, but you can't be both." Maybe she was just anti-museum. Some years later when she appeared at the Phillips Gallery in 1934 and gave a public lecture at the invitation of its director, her opening remark was, "When I am at a picture gallery my one idea is to look out a window."

The Phillips Collection is epitomized by two works of European artists: the oldest picture in the gallery, a lyric landscape panel attributed to Giorgione called *The Hour Glass,* and the gallery's most familiar picture, Renoir's *Luncheon of the Boating Party,* surely one of the happiest pictures ever painted. The same woman posed for at least three of the figures in the boating party, and it is not surprising that she later became Mme. Renoir. In Duncan Phillips's own description "every inch of the canvas is alive and worth framing for itself, yet an integral part also of the complex pattern ... of inverted perspective." He bought it shrewdly in 1923 for $125,000 (then something of a record), and he was later to decline the offer of a blank check for it from Lord Duveen. It has been occasionally and generously lent to exhibitions around the world: Duncan and Marjorie Phillips always seemed to get a thrill of satisfaction, the ultimate confirmation of their taste and judgment, in the flood of requests from other institutions to borrow items from the collection.

The gallery refers to groups of paintings by artists on whom it has chosen to concentrate as *units*. The Bonnard unit, for instance, is among the most splendid, as the Phillips started to collect his paintings at a time when almost nobody else did. The gallery prefers to deal directly with artists—as it did with Bonnard—avoiding dealers whenever possible.

Phillips also made a point of buying the works of local artists and even art students in what he referred to as his "encouragement collection," a generous but undiscriminating policy that made much less of a contribution to the Washington art scene than did the availability of pictures by non-Washington artists when his gallery was haunted by Morris Louis, Kenneth Noland, Howard Mehring, Thomas Downing, Paul Reed, and Gene Davis—for whom there was no other place in town to see such an array of first-rate modern paintings. In this sense Duncan Phillips was the real progenitor of the Washington Color School.

After Duncan Phillips died in 1966, James R. Mellow of the *New York Times* wrote, "His whole approach to museum practice is very different from the brisk traffic in attendance figures. . . . Phillips was still promoting the taste of angels in a profession that was running to the devil of hard-sell."

The Phillips Collection sponsors a distinguished program of recitals and concerts on Sunday at 5 P.M. from mid-September through May. Admission is free and no reservations are taken for the 120 seats in the living room, so there is always an overflow crowd in the adjoining rooms.

Society of the Cincinnati/Anderson House   *2118 Massachusetts Avenue, NW House open Tuesday–Saturday 1–4, free   Research library and occasional concerts open to the public   Closed Saturdays in summer.*

> These treasured documents are gifts from a member of the Society . . .
> who is a four times great grandnephew of George Washington.
> —Society of Cincinnati monograph of 1967

When Mr. and Mrs. Larz Anderson built this palatial town house between 1902 and 1905, it was their express intention that it should become the headquarters—the last refuge—of the Society of the Cincinnati, and much of its interior and exterior iconography was designed with that particular destiny in mind. For this project the Andersons commissioned the Boston architectural firm of Little and Browne—who specialized in building stately homes for the wealthy throughout New England—and this residence at 2118 Massachusetts Avenue, NW, is considered their masterpiece.

Anderson House today represents not only the national headquarters of a patriotic society but serves as a home for other activities contributing to the cultural life of the city. It has a substantial research library covering the military history of the Revolutionary period; it sponsors a program of musical concerts; it affords a dignified setting available for the ceremonial entertainment of foreign officials visiting the capital; and it is also a well-preserved architectural period piece with eclectic interior furnishings serving as a permanent documentation of the opulent life style of wealthy Americans during the early 20th century. Like the Perry Belmont House, it is an artifact of social archeology.

The lavish scale of the house is signaled at the outset by the entrance courtyard partially obscured from the mob by a high formal stone wall terminating in two archways, and with the carriage court itself paved with gravel. There is not even the narrowest sidewalk provided for a possible pedestrian visitor; this is a house designed for the carriage trade. The two-story semicircular portico, spanning three bays, has a curved cornice and balustrade supported by only four composite columns spaced almost 12 feet apart; the three curved cornice-arc-segments of the architrave connecting the capitals are each carved from a single block of granite. The result is both a considerable technical accomplishment and

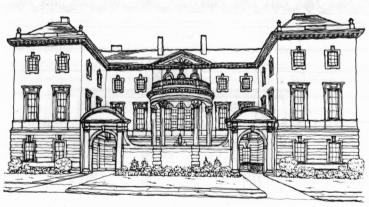

Society of the Cincinnati/Anderson House

which he surrendered his martial role to return to the plough. The legend of this civilian general captured the imagination of the veterans of the War of Independence as they themselves had been mostly part-time soldiers. The city of Cincinnati, Ohio, was named in honor of the society by the territorial governor who was then president of the Pennsylvania Society.*

In choosing the very name of Cincinnati (as a symbol of the soldier returned to civilian life) the society has in fact secured its own redemption. The fears of Thomas Jefferson and the other founding fathers are now seen as unwarranted; the values of our national life have evolved in a way that has made institutions based on ancestral lineage irrelevant as founts of honor for individuals. Certainly there is a limit to the number of generations in which a child can wear his father's medals. The Society of the Cincinnati has none of the impulses of Junkerism and it has not perpetuated a military caste. Most of the descendant members fought—as officers and as enlisted men—in the country's later wars, but in the spirit of Cincinnatus, their service was regarded as the interruption of normally civilian careers. And yet the society remains a sentimental anachronism, discriminating against women, against descendants of nonofficers, and against younger brothers. In one of the club's few new wrinkles, sons may now be taken into membership without waiting for the demise of their father—but some of the old-timers are uncomfortable with this indulgence.

The society has no dues. Each founding member paid in one month's salary, at whatever his rank was, to endow the membership for posterity. The Cincinnati is a confederation of 14 independent constituent societies (that is the 13 original colonies, plus one for the cadre of French officers) that have never ratified George Washington's proposal to abolish hereditary membership, made as a condition of his accepting its leadership. State societies have discretion to waive primogeniture in order to bar membership to those "unsuitable." The state societies contribute to the annual support of Anderson House and its museum, library, and concerts.

Larz Anderson was a great-grandson of a founder of the Cincinnati. He was the third in his family to be named Larz—which sounds vaguely Scandinavian—but there is no record of how it was adopted in a family of Scotch-Irish descent. He spent most of his career in the United States diplomatic service at a time when it was administered separately from the consular service. In 1893, while he was serving as first secretary to the embassy in Rome, he married Isabel Weld Perkins, a Boston heiress. They had no children, but they both liked to travel and they loved to entertain. After completing their new house at 2118 Massachusetts Avenue, he served as minister to Belgium and ambassador to

---

* I had a great-uncle named Cincinnatus Batte—known in the family as Uncle Cince.

Japan. And he was the last diplomat in the American service to wear a diplomatic uniform of gold lace tailcoat and trousers with a fore-and-aft hat like an admiral's; this complete outfit is now displayed in a glass case in the second-floor gallery.

After Ambassador Anderson retired from the service he made his house available at the request of the president or the secretary of state for the entertainment of foreign officials and dignitaries visiting the capital—Belgian royalty, Italian nobility, French generals of World War I, and princes from Japan. This was done from a sense of duty as well as pleasure. In the spring of 1929 Larz Anderson wrote: "Our dinners proved successful. The house was full of flowers—azaleas, orchids, lilies, and tulips. We remained, I believe, the only house in Washington, except the Embassies, which turned out the servants in full-dress livery, shorts and stockings, buckled shoes and braided coats. These dinners were the swan songs to the old order." In 1931 the Andersons vacated the house entirely to turn it over for the state visit of the king and queen of Siam.

When World War II was declared the society suspended its normal activities and turned Anderson House over to the use of the U.S. Navy for the duration. The navy installed its office of public relations there, and when the officers moved in they immediately covered all the parquet and marble floors with wall-to-wall carpeting—presumably to help them better relate to the public. And when the war was over and they moved out, they took all the wall-to-wall carpet with them.

Anderson House is now available for official entertaining at the request of the president, vice-president, members of the cabinet, the mayor of the District of Columbia, and ambassadors of foreign embassies. It has been the scene of receptions or dinners for Nikita S. Khrushchev, Chancellor Adenauer of Germany, French Premiers Mendes-France and Giscard d'Estaing, Ali Bhutto, Anwar Sadat, and the shah of Iran. Countries with small embassies in Washington find it an appropriate place to return White House hospitality. When the king of Jordan visits, he stays at Blair House but he may entertain at Anderson House. Outsiders using the house customarily offer an honorarium to compensate for the wear and tear.

The 10,000-volume library of the society specializes in the military history of the Revolution and the period 1750–1800. It is an open-shelf facility in the west basement of the mansion. Scholars and high school students are welcome. As a museum, the 50-room house is of interest in part for its collection of relics and regalia of the Revolutionary War period, but more importantly to most visitors as a social artifact, a cultural capsule of a vanished life style of the rich. In winter months when the Andersons were in residence wood fires were kept burning all

the patronage of King Farouk. The Egyptian Ministry of Works engaged an Italian professor of architecture, Mario Rossi, to design the project. Rossi had been a longtime student of the ancient mosques of Cairo and designed a number of modern mosques in Cairo and Alexandria. He became a convert to Islam late in his life and completed the pilgrimage to Mecca shortly before his death in 1961.

The Washington architectural firm of Irwin Porter and Sons collaborated with Rossi in the building's construction. The net result of their efforts is an eclectic mixture of Syrian and Moorish elements, recognizably Islamic but described by one Arab scholar as "Mid-Atlantic Mameluke." The north wing along the avenue frontage accommodates a library, and a director's office and bookstore are to the south. At the heart of the complex is the mosque itself, placed on a skewed axis from the street grid so that the *mihrab*—the semicircular niche used by the prayer leader, or *imam*—can point in the true great-circle direction of Mecca. Prayer services are held regularly five times a day: at dawn, noon, in the afternoon, after sunset, and at night. On many occasions people come from great distances to celebrate weddings and funerals in the mosque.

The United States now has a Muslim population of over two million, constituting, after Christians and Jews, the third largest religious community in the

Islamic Center

country. There are other mosques in North America, notably those in Montreal, Boston, Chicago, and Los Angeles. But the Islamic Center assumes a unique national function in the service of Islam: it publishes an annual calendar for the guidance of worshipers, including a comparative table of religious days and festivals and schedules of the daily prayers required of all adult Muslims. The center sponsors lectures, conducts religious training classes, provides guidance on questions of religion, and serves as an anti-defamation organization to defend the faith against misunderstandings and false charges.

Visitors to the mosque must be properly dressed—that is, they must have no bare arms or legs and they must remove their shoes before entering the sanctuary. To wear shoes in a mosque is a grave offense, and they certainly are not needed here, as the floors are covered with deep-piled Persian rugs—a gift from the former shah of Iran. The interior of the mosque is richly ornate with a two-ton chandelier from Egypt, blue wall tiles from Turkey, and red and yellow stained glass from Iraq. The graceful minaret tower is 160 feet high, exempt (as all towers are) from the normal height restrictions of the city. A modern loudspeaker system carries the voice of the *muezzin* calling the faithful to prayer.

British Embassy *3100 Massachusetts Avenue, NW*

> Lutyens "could be depended upon to design something dignified, austere and sterile, buildings for an empire at its apogee which could conceive of no alteration to its prestige and power."
> —*Times Literary Supplement,* 12 November 1976

This imposing—almost pompous—British Embassy residence and chancery complex houses the second largest diplomatic mission in Washington. (In the 1960s the Russians overtook the British as the largest.) Like the White House itself, this embassy is an adaptation of an English country house plunked down in the middle of a city—although it was on the edge of town at the time it was built.

Here is a stately home in the Queen Anne style,* converted to official diplomatic purposes by the greatest British architect of his generation, Sir Edwin Landseer Lutyens. This embassy is his only work in the Western Hemisphere, and his sheer panache has produced one of the capital's few buildings of genuine and unquestionable architectural distinction.

Lutyens was born the same year—1869—as Frank Lloyd Wright, but while

---

* The reign of Queen Anne was 1702-14. Her name does not easily lend itself to the adjectival mode; for some reason the literature of her reign is termed Augustan, while the architecture and furniture are called Queen Anne.

the greatest American architect of his day made a clean break with historic forms, Lutyens was the last of the British architects to work within the traditionalist mold. With particular regard to his emphasis on the delights of verticality, he is regarded as a modern successor to Christopher Wren. The early years of his career were devoted to the domesticity of English country houses. As in all of his work, he achieved in these private commissions a sophisticated combination of conventional eclectic detail and originality of space and arrangement. His career culminated in the 15-year-long design and construction of the Viceroy's House in New Delhi. Completed in 1931, it was a tour de force on a Roman scale of magnificence combining Mogul and Palladian elements; and it was the commission that earned him his knighthood. (That imperial Viceroy's House—No. 1 Bungalow—is now the home of an ascetic president of India.) Lutyens designed the monumental Cenotaph in London's Whitehall as a memorial to Britain's unknown soldier of World War I, prompting *The Times* to herald it in an editorial as "grave, severe, and beautiful."

The embassy was Lutyens's last great commission and in a way it recapitulates his career, combining the amenities of a country house with the official pomp of a building to serve as a symbol. Everybody feels that this is exactly the way an embassy should look. Though the design was imported, all the craftsmanship and materials that went into its construction are strictly American— from the handmade bricks from Pennsylvania to the pillars and capitals carved of Indiana limestone. The floor plan links the U of the chancery on the avenue front with the T of the residence facing a private garden in the rear, these two elements being joined by a broad porte cochere entrance on the ground level and by the ambassador's study on the main floor above. (The convenience of the arrangement must be the envy of every other ambassador in town.) The avenue frontage is punctuated by four driveways framed by eight tall vertical limestone

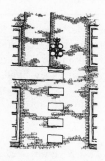

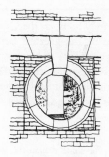

Trompe l'Oeil Pilaster

Oriel Stone Window

pylons, those In and Out to the chancery capped by urns, those In and Out to the residence capped by lions and unicorns. This is a design for Rolls Royces, not pedestrians.

Above the roof of the chancery portico facing the courtyard on the avenue— atop two buttresses linked to the higher structure of the residence—are two statues of crouching lions. The lions are hard to see from the street level, but they are remarkable beasts for they are *streamlined* with manes and haunches in stylized curves like the cowling of 1930s locomotives. They are a bold display of Lutyens's ardor for paradox, of his having brought Queen Anne to terms with Art Moderne. The building is replete with many traditional icons reclothed in modern dress.

The chancery court is furnished with Art Deco lanterns capped by a royal crown and accenting a trompe l'oeil pilaster that really isn't there: only its suggestion. The rectangular stone quoins are abstracted and generalized, set in a flat brick wall and not at a corner as our eye expects them to be; the pilaster has only the one edge of an overlapping wall. An oriel stone window is set in a brick wall with a stylized keystone intersecting the stone circle in a severely modern manner never before seen on land or sea. Such caprices and anachronisms—such a juggling of motifs—would be mere pastiche in less-skilled hands, but one

British Embassy

can see what led the architectural historian Nikolaus Pevsner to characterize Lutyens's work as "naughty." Lutyens himself described his architecture as "the High Game." (Lutyens's extravagant playfulness was not confined to his professional life. Once in New Delhi when he committed a minor faux pas—he was a few minutes late to tea—he tendered to the viceroy's wife, Lady Hardinge, the sylleptic apology: "I will wash your feet with my tears and dry them with my hair. True, I have very little hair, but then you have very little feet.")

One of the high points of Washington's spring social season is the annual celebration of the Queen's Birthday in May with a large and showy garden party on the lawn to the south of the residence. On these occasions the rare horticultural specimens (Japanese spider maples and wisteria trees) and the Henry Moore sculpture and the long pastel skirts of the ladies offset each other to great advantage. In 1949, when Great Britain was just weathering the crisis of devaluing the pound and pressing the United States for extensions of loans, Ambassador Sir Oliver Franks displayed the tact and prudence to celebrate the Queen's Birthday with tea and cookies instead of the customary strawberries with Devonshire cream and champagne—a practice since resumed.

Chancery Annex. In the 1960s the embassy added a large chancery annex ranging from three to seven stories along Massachusetts Avenue as it rises toward Observatory Hill. The design is generally timid, but with enough character to appear vaguely British; it was perhaps a wise choice not to attempt to compete in complexity or subtlety with Lutyens's original, which it blandly adjoins. The architect was Eric Bedford, sharing honors—or culpability—with the British Ministry of Works. The chief ornament of the avenue facade is a three-story-high wall of sheer red brick into which has been chiseled a heroic scale coat of arms of the sovereign complete with lion and unicorn supporters. To dispel any remaining doubt about the ownership of the place, there are large backlit letters over the chancery door reading HBM Chancery—Her Britannic Majesty's, of course.

The annex contains a large library visible on the ground floor (but not open to the public), a cafeteria on the roof which is said to have a fine view of downtown Washington, and a circular glass-walled conference room, 57 feet in diameter, like a copper-sheathed tent pitched on the front lawn. The cornerstone for the annex was set by Queen Elizabeth during her visit to the United States in 1957; for this ceremony she was provided with the trowel used by George Washington to set the cornerstone of the Capitol.

Churchill Statue. Few modern outdoor sculptures have solved the problem of putting a contemporary figure in a business suit in bronze or marble without making him look ridiculous. The capital's worst example of the genre is probably that of Senator Robert A. Taft standing miserably at the base of his carillon on Capitol Hill. The sculptor of Franklin D. Roosevelt's statue in London's Grosvenor Square made good use of the president's famous cape. Here on Massachusetts Avenue William McVey has cast Winston Churchill forthrightly in coat, vest, and trousers. Churchill's right hand is giving the "V for Victory" salute, while his left clutches a walking stick and a cigar. There was a lot of talk at the time the statue was unveiled—1966—about the propriety of showing the prime minister with a cigar. (Duke University quadrangle has a sedentary statue of James D. Duke with a firm grip on a stogie, but tobacco was the source of Duke's wealth and he was not a prime minister.)

Churchill is reported to have been pleased with the notion that this statue would be situated so that his right foot is over the boundary in United States territory along the Massachusetts Avenue right of way while his left is firmly planted in the extraterritoriality of the embassy's Crown property. Beneath the plinth on which the statue stands has been placed soil from Churchill's mother's home in Brooklyn, from his birthplace at Blenheim Palace, and from the rose garden of his home at Chartwell.

This statue specifically commemorates Churchill's honorary citizenship of the United States, conferred on him in 1963 by President John F. Kennedy. The time capsule in the base of the figure is scheduled to be opened on the centenary of that event in 2063.

Observatory Circle *Massachusetts Avenue at 34th Street, NW*

The first Naval Observatory was built on a knoll north of where the Lincoln Memorial now stands, near the corner of 23rd and D Streets, NW, and Lieutenant Matthew Fontaine Maury was its first superintendent. By 1880 it was recognized that the marshy ambience of Foggy Bottom and the increasing traffic of the area made it inappropriate as a site for astronomical observation. As a result, President Rutherford B. Hayes named a commission to select a site for a new observatory "upon an even degree of longitude west of Greenwich, and to possess . . . clearness of atmosphere, freedom from obstruction from the horizon, and freedom from objectionable vibrations from traffic." This resulted in the selection and purchase of 72 acres of Mrs. M. C. Barber's place on Georgetown Heights known (in the Maryland tradition of naming manorial properties) as Pretty Prospect.

It was not until 10 years later that funds were appropriated to construct the observatory, by which time the D.C. Department of Highways had started to survey the extension of Massachusetts Avenue cutting straight through the Barber tract. An alert superintendent of the Naval Observatory began immediately to excavate for the basement of his future house. He also surveyed a perimeter of a 1,000-foot radius from the hilltop site of the observatory upon which no encroachment would be permitted. The carts and heavy wagons of the day would be kept at a safe distance to avoid disturbing the navy's sensitive clocks and instruments. As a result—and to the dismay of the highway engineers—Massachusetts Avenue still curves today in that great arc from Whitehaven to Calvert Streets as Observatory Circle.

And the 26-inch telescope itself was erected on the exact even 77 degrees 4 minutes longitude west of Greenwich.

Naval Observatory

Observatory Circle, Massachusetts Avenue at 34th Street, NW   90 min. tours, Monday nights at 8:30, free;   Recorded information 653-1507.

When President John Quincy Adams went before Congress in 1825 to plead for an astronomical observatory there was no such facility in the Western hemisphere. For almost two decades Congress reacted with doubts that it had the authority to charter such a novel venture. Finally it assigned the function to the navy—to the Depot of Charts and Instruments—because it was necessary to know the precise time in order to determine longitude at sea.

The U.S. Naval Observatory is the source for all standard time in the country, and it is the sole authority in the United States for astronomic data required for navigation, civil affairs, and legal purposes. It is one of the few institutions on earth where the coordinate positions of the sun, moon, planets, and stars are continually determined. The largest telescope on the Naval Observatory grounds is a 26-inch refractor more than 100 years old but still in service; it was first used at the old site in Foggy Bottom, and was modernized in 1960. In 1877 Dr. Asaph Hall used this telescope to discover the two moons of Mars on which he bestowed the melancholy names of Deimos and Phobos—Anxiety and Fear. On nighttime tours visitors are allowed to peer through this same instrument to see Mars and double stars and galaxies whole light years away.

By the the turn of the century, the best marine chronometers had achieved an error factor of no more than one second every five days. By 1950 the average error of the time signals broadcast from the Naval Radio Station at Annapolis was less than a hundredth of a second. The tolerances achieved with atomic clocks is now far in excess of that required for marine navigation; the launching of artificial satellites and the operations of advanced space research generate an appetite for the most exquisite kinds of time. And that is just what the cesium beam atomic clock delivers at its steady pace of nine billion cycles a second—constant to within one 10-millionth of a second per day.

The observatory provides signals and data on three kinds of time. The first is now called Universal Time (UT, also known as Greenwich Mean Time), based on the period of earth's rotation about its axis; for this purpose clock readings are corrected by star positions recorded at their zenith. Second is Ephemeris Time, defined by the orbit of the earth about the sun and determined in practice by observing the position of the moon relative to the stars. Third is Atomic Time (called A.1), which has been kept, since 1958, by the cesium beam atomic clock. Since the rotation of the earth about its axis slowly decreases, it is necessary to adjust Universal Time by occasionally adding or dropping exactly one second at the end of a month.

For reservations for nighttime tours or for an excellent free booklet on observatory operations, write to the observatory at the above address and zip code 20390. If you are tired of your local telephone time signal and would like to hear a navy signal that is precise to a millisecond, call (202) 254-4950, but bear in mind that the response is subject to slight degrading by telephone circuit delays.

Vice-President's House/Admiral's House
Observatory Circle, Massachusetts Avenue at 34th Street, NW
By the time the new house for the superintendent of the Naval Observatory was completed in 1893, Washington's enthusiasm for the Victorian style was on the wane. What the Washington architect Leon E. Dessez produced was a modified late Victorian house with one turret, several dormers, and some vaguely Queen Anne and French Provincial elements, surrounded on three sides by one of those ample turn-of-the-century porches.* The original red brick has been painted white, robbing it of some of its period identity. As a Category II Historic Landmark, it qualifies more by the prescribed "cultural heritage" than by any attributes of "visual beauty."

The superintendent lived in the house for its first three decades, until 1928, when it was taken over as the official home of the chief of naval operations—a splendid perquisite of military office of a kind not provided for his civilian boss, the secretary of the navy. For 40 years it was used as Admiral's House, home port for the CNO, officially designated as Quarters A. When Admiral Radford became the first member of his service to be chairman of the Joint Chiefs of Staff, there were for the first time two naval top dogs in town and there was something of an unseemly struggle over who was to live in Admiral's House. They did not draw straws; the chairman was about to pull rank on the CNO when he was persuaded that the precedent might tempt future chairmen from other services to claim a right to live on Observatory Circle. So Admiral Rad-

* Admiral's House was not considered worthy of inclusion in Henry H. Glassie's *Victorian Homes in Washington* (Washington, D.C.: Columbia Historical Society, 1965).

ford moved into a house in the Navy Yard, and the question became moot as the CNO was soon to be evicted from Admiral's House for other reasons.

In the mid-1960s there was increasing public discussion of the need for establishing a suitable official residence for the vice-president, with specific speculation about the appropriateness of the Naval Observatory as a secure and convenient location. The navy was beginning to feel under siege,* and in 1969 the Office of Naval History issued a document entitled "The Chief of Naval Operations and Admiral's House," a heart-wrenching rationale for its claim on this particular piece of real estate. Some historian or public relations officer put the question in the context of the nation's defense:

> The senior naval officer of today's mighty forces for freedom, in the brief times he can be home, appropriately lives like the commander afloat admidst unresting machines and men ever probing out into the seas of earth and space, on watch for America. . . . It is fitting indeed that the Chief of Naval Operations of America's complex scientific navy, steaming with wide-open throttle into the space age, should dwell in Admiral's House admidst the Navy's oldest and first famous venture into the mysteries of the heavens.

But it was all to no avail—all that lovely prose. What the Congress giveth it can also taketh away, and in 1974 the old superintendent's house was officially designated as the vice-president's first official residence. Characteristically, the move was in fact presented as an economy measure; it had simply cost too much for the Secret Service to provide adequate physical security for the relatively modest houses where vice-presidents had lived in recent years. And ironically, the first vice-president eligible to move into the security of the new residence chose not to do so; Nelson Rockefeller preferred his even more spacious home on Foxhall Road. Congress intended this house to be only a temporary solution to the problem of housing the vice-president, to be occupied only until a permanent home can be built—perhaps on some site at the Naval Observatory.

Meanwhile, with Vice-President Mondale as its first official resident, it proved to be a spacious and comfortable home for family living, but—unlike the White House—with no rooms set aside for official entertaining. Mrs. Joan Mondale made the house a modest showplace of American art, inaugurating a program of borrowing paintings and sculptures from museums throughout the country in successive displays representative of artists from various regions.

Some day they may build the vice-president a proper house, and then the navy may even get Admiral's House back. But don't count on it.

---

* Admiral Zumwalt testified in 1973 that the roof leaked and the dining room seated only 18.

Apostolic Delegation *3339 Massachusetts Avenue, NW*

As its facade suggests, this building houses an institution that is half American and half Italian and enshrines many religious and cultural traditions of Roman Catholicism. Here in buff Indiana limestone is a stylized Art Moderne version of a Roman Renaissance palace. Over the central front door is the only indication of the identity of this official residence: a conventionalized sculpture of the papal crest with tiara and crossed keys, the same symbol appearing on the yellow and white Vatican flag flown above the entrance on holidays.

This is the home of the apostolic delegate, a tailor-made title for the papal representative in the United States. In most countries papal envoys are known as nuncios or (less importantly) pro-nuncios: they are accredited to the host government as well as representing the church organization; in many countries they are ex officio deans of the diplomatic corps. Here in Washington the apostolic delegate is relieved of such ceremonial diplomatic duties. The United States has a constitution that is particularly delicate on questions of religion, and thus it maintains no formal relations with the Holy See.* The apostolic delegate functions exclusively within the hierarchy of the Catholic Church. In the words of the delegate's secretary: "The ordinary function . . . is twofold. He keeps the Pope and his collaborators informed about the needs and thinking of the bishops, the clergy, religious and laity throughout the country. On the other hand, he conveys the mind of the Universal Shepherd of the Church, the Bishop of Rome."

Since the post was established in 1893 there have been ten apostolic delegates to the United States—all but one of them Italian. The small staff, which does its own typing and filing for reasons of discretion as well as convenience, consists half of American clerics and half of Italians trained at the Vatican's Diplomatic Academy. During the terms of their tenure the delegates have an invisible but significant role in the selection of new bishops for the American church. On the completion of their tour delegates are invariably elevated to the College of Cardinals.

The residence is richly furnished with Flemish tapestries, portraits of princes of the church, a portrait of Pope Pius IX by G. P. A. Healy, and contemporary works by the Jewish artist Abraham Ratner. On the ground floor is a chapel redecorated in modern liturgical style in 1961. There is an outside entrance on the west side of the building, and outsiders are welcomed to services by prior arrangement and on a restricted basis (the American church has a policy of encouraging Catholics to worship in their assigned parishes, and the delegation does not want to invite exceptions from that pattern). In a curious excess of dis-

* Only a personal representative of the president.

cretion, the mailing envelopes of the delegation provide only a street address and zip code; the telephone number is unlisted.

The residence, constructed in 1938, was designed by Frederick Vernon Murphy, who was associated with the Department of Architecture at Catholic University. The noble front of this building is being increasingly obscured by overgrown spruce trees and other casual shrubs long overdue for removal. A formal paved courtyard would become the facade better than the present narrow driveway and concrete path.

The large, red brick, Georgian style house just south of the delegation belongs to Mr. and Mrs. Clark Thompson. He is a former congressman from Texas, and like many such veterans, once he got used to the capital he decided to stay on. In a neighborly gesture the Thompsons turned their house and pool over to the use of the apostolic delegation during the visit of Pope John Paul II in October 1979.

St. Nicholas Cathedral   *3500 Massachusetts Avenue, NW*

Just around the curve above Observatory Circle looms as exotic a structure as any in the city, the small but towering St. Nicholas Cathedral completed in 1963 to serve the local Russian Orthodox congregation as well as to be a National War Memorial Shrine of the Orthodox Church in America. It was subscribed to by parishes across the country to commemorate victims of their faith who lost their lives in the Bolshevik Revolution and in all world wars since.

The architect of the church was a Russian, Alexander Neratov, who chose as his prototype the Church of St. Dimitri built in the city of Vladimir in 1195— typical of northwest Russian ecclesiastical architecture of the period. The helmet-shaped dome was a precursor of the familiar onion-shaped dome to proliferate in Russian churches several centuries later; it is employed here as appropriate for a war memorial. This helmet dome is surely the first ever constructed of an alloy of titanium.

The architect's widow, Rima Neratov, is an iconographer who in recent years has completed a new *iconostasis*, the conventional screen in Orthodox churches that separates the *bema*, or sanctuary, from the nave and the congregation. Mrs. Neratov's screen is of predominantly pale pink and pale green hues, giving an effect of permanent Easter morning to the otherwise stark white interior illuminated by daylight filtered through long, attenuated slit windows.

The congregation habitually stands* for services in the nave under the dome, and the deep vigor of the singing recalls all the Old Russia of the Don Cossack Chorus. Services are conducted alternate Sundays in English and Slavonic.

* The early church forbade kneeling, a Western custom of late medieval origin.

Saint Sophia: Greek Orthodox Cathedral
Massachusetts Avenue at 36th Street, NW

The chief distinction of this Greek Orthodox cathedral is its exquisite interior mosaic work. Since its altar must face east, its outside west front is relentlessly oriented on a half-block spur of 36th Street canting off the axis of Massachusetts Avenue. Some of the present factory-type windows will eventually be replaced by stained glass. An education and recreation center is planned for the sloping hill to the south.

Every dome and gable is surmounted by a Greek cross. The two towers

St. Nicholas Cathedral

framing the dome from the west are an eclectic concession, not particularly Byzantine but integrated into the basic scheme by their domed capitals. Atop the arched entrance portico looms the two-headed eagle representing the church and emperor sharing a common body, united in purpose, the emblem of allegiance to the patriarch of Constantinople as the heir to Byzantium.

The cornerstone of the cathedral was laid in 1956 in the presence of President and Mrs. Eisenhower. The architect was Archie Protopapas of New York, who had designed many other Greek Orthodox churches throughout the country.

The name Saint Sophia—*Hagia Sophia*—means "Holy Wisdom," referring to Christ as the embodiment of God's wisdom and not to any historic personage. (There is no canonization in Orthodoxy.) Saint Sophia is a seat in Washington of the archbishop of the Greek Orthodox Archdiocese of North and South America, whose principal base is in New York City. The cathedral here is the largest Greek Orthodox church in the United States.

Byzantine art is inseparable from religion; it is an integral part of worship, the translation of church theology into artistic terms. The edifice of the church is a replica of the glorified cosmos from the paved floor of the Earth to the blue dome of Heaven. The mosaic decorations incorporate the liturgy of worship; in fact, Greek Orthodox worship is inconceivable without the accompaniment of Byzantine art and music. It is said that the Eastern Church has two gospels: one written, the other visual. The icons throughout the church are holy art, visual sermons whose two-dimensionality reflects their abstract spiritual quality. (Three-dimensional sculptural representations of the saints are not employed. In Orthodox theology the icon is a key to the understanding of the dogma of God's appearance in physical human form.)

By convention, the plan of the church is symmetrically cruciform, with a dome over the center and the interior spaces divided into three main parts: the narthex, or vestibule; the nave, or main church; and the sanctuary containing the altar. The nave is now furnished with pews, but in ages past the congregation assumed the priestly standing posture during the entire worship service. The altar is separated from the rest of the church by an iconostasis, a screen of three doors of which the central, or holy gate, is used for the celebration of the Eucharist. Male communicants may enter the sanctuary through the side gates. Ideally, the church is not too large to enhance the sense of community in worship.

The narthex is the area to which the penitents and unbaptized used to retire during certain parts of the liturgy. It is now an area where the worshipers customarily make an offering, receive a candle, and light it in prayer before an icon; then they may join the congregation in worship by passing through the doors to the nave.

In the nave the gospel is proclaimed and the sermon is preached. (The word *nave* is cognate with the Latin for *ship;* the shape of the conventional nave as an inverted ship suggests the church as a vessel for salvation.) The dome rises over the nave above a circular ambulatory balcony from which the choir sings—a capella—during services. The mosaics of the dome depict the celestial hierarchy in which an enthroned Christ (said to be the largest in the Orthodox world) is surrounded by a host of seraphim standing in a zone of tongues of fire according to the vision of Isaiah. Here in Saint Sophia the effect of the dome is starkly electric, a graphic exhortation.

In the apse over the sanctuary is a mosaic mural of the Virgin Mary with Jesus; she is in blue against a background of gold. This is an icon of the complexity of the relations between Heaven and Earth; it is called the *Platytera,* an elaborate metaphor designed to instruct us that Mary was "like a ladder that God used to come down to Earth."

On the iconostasis and elsewhere throughout the interior of the church are more than 50 Old and New Testament figures in mosaic, all of intricate iconographic significance, representing a sophisticated interplay of art, dogma, and history. Demetrios Dukas is the iconographer and mosaicist of this scheme, which is now nearing completion. In executing the mosaic program the church has benefited greatly from the invaluable and generous counsel of leading scholars at the Dumbarton Oaks Center for Byzantine Studies of Harvard University. Mosaicists and scholars working together have drawn their liturgical motifs chiefly from surviving examples of that sustained period of Byzantine culture under the Macedonian dynasty, from the 9th to the 11th centuries—at the end of the Iconoclastic Controversy and before the schism with Rome.

The parish of Saint Sophia was founded in 1904 by a group of 35 newly arrived Greek immigrant families. In its early years the congregation met in the former Adas Israel synagogue, which was then located at 6th and G Streets, NW.

The best time to visit the cathedral is during regular Sunday services: matins at 9 A.M. and liturgy at 10 A.M. Weekday services vary according to the church calendar, but they begin at 9:30 A.M. Arrangements for special tour groups may be made through the church office (333-4730).

Christ Church of Washington *Massachusetts Avenue at Idaho Avenue, NW*
For many years the intersection of Massachusetts and Idaho Avenues was identified on D.C. Highway Department maps as Hamilton Circle. After the plans for Christ Church were completed, the highway people decided that this was one circle the District could do without, but the modernistic facade of the church survives well back of what would have been the circle's perimeter. The angular

prismatic front of the church looms over its setting like the ungainly prow of a stranded ship.

The church was designed by its pastor, the Reverend McArthur Jollay, whose chief interest was architecture before he was called to the ministry and who had designed and built two other churches in Michigan and Kentucky. Milton Prassas, the architect of record, was responsible mainly for the structural and mechanical engineering. Pastor Jollay's unorthodox design accommodates a sawtooth ceiling for indirect lighting and results in acoustics of excellent quality. Together with adjoining chapels the sanctuary seats over 1,800 people. It was completed in 1967.

Christ Church is an independently chartered denomination, loosely cooperative with the Assembly of God churches. The congregation is evangelical in its emphasis on the Gospels and broadly ecumenical in its hospitality to charismatic worshipers ranging from Catholics to Pentecostalists. It celebrates the sacrament of full immersion baptism, for which a large glass-walled pool is provided to the left side of the central pulpit.

On the Massachusetts Avenue frontage there is a standard glass-covered notice board of white plastic letters set into black felt strips. In addition to announcing the names of the clergy, the times of services, and the subject of the next Sunday's sermon, it proclaims the church's self-characterization as "Delightfully Different," a rebuke to any who might not think that a church has at least as much right as a restaurant to call itself different—or, for that matter, delightful.

Washington Hebrew Congregation
Massachusetts Avenue at Macomb Street, NW

The Washington Hebrew Congregation is Washington's oldest, largest, and richest Reform synagogue. It is also one of the city's most progressive and innovative temples, and its 2,300 families constitute one of the five largest congregations in the United States. (Other Reform congregations in the District are Temple Sinai—700 families—on Military Road, NW, and the avant-garde Temple Micah in Southwest. The leading Conservative congregation is Adas Israel on Connecticut Avenue, NW, and the chief Orthodox temple is Beth Sholem in Silver Spring.)

The modern temple building, of white Indiana limestone with black marble trim at the entrance, rises abruptly over the junction of Glover-Archbold Parkway and Macomb Street, presenting a sheer and unrelieved semicircular wall containing the main sanctuary in a striking example of almost vernacular architecture. The dramatic effect could be enhanced by improved landscaping, as the few scattered trees and shrubs are the result of amateur and voluntary efforts.

The architect of record was F. Wallace Dixon, but the resulting edifice is largely the product of an enthusiastic layman and member of the congregation, Gustave Ring, a real estate developer and amateur designer of his own office building, the Ring Building off Connecticut Avenue at 1200 18th Street, NW.

The temple of the Washington Hebrew Congregation is, like most of Washington's other synagogues, boldly functional and devoid of identification with any particular architectural tradition. This void may be due in part to the anti-iconic principles of Judaism.

The cornerstone of the temple was laid by President Harry S Truman in 1952, and President Dwight D. Eisenhower presided over the dedication in 1954. The semicircular sanctuary seats 2,300, with every seat individually reserved months in advance of the High Holy Day services. Two gigantic stone tablets at the rear of the sanctuary, behind the rostrum, slide apart during services to reveal the ark containing the scrolls of the Torah. Above the rostrum is a large choir area and an Aeolian-Skinner organ. Inside the lobby is a group of three bronze sculptures of the prophets by Albert Weinberg. Although the main doors are usually locked on weekdays, access may be had to the lobby and the library through the temple offices at the parking lot to the east. As in the case of nearby Washington Cathedral, the sanctuary is frequently borrowed for interfaith and ecumenical gatherings; the American University at Ward Circle has no large auditorium and regularly uses the temple for its annual commencement celebrations. Throughout the year the congregation sponsors a Sunday Scholar Series of free lectures (at 10:30 A.M., open to the public, phone 362–7100) by distinguished scholars on Judaism and related religious, philosophical, and cultural subjects.

The congregation has the unique distinction of possessing its own congressional charter by an act of Congress of 1855. From 1898 to 1952 the Washington Hebrew Congregation met in the old temple building at 816 8th Street, NW, with its two tall onion-domed towers, now the home of the Greater New Hope Baptist Church. In 1876 a conservative group of its members split off to form the Adas Israel Congregation, partially in protest against the plan to install an organ. Adas Israel's new temple on Connecticut Avenue now has an organ.

Ward Circle   *Massachusetts and Nebraska Avenues, NW*
Ward Circle was not named for Artemus Ward, the pseudonym of the first in a long line of American humorists indulging in dialect and misspellings. (His description of a census: "Did you ever have the measels, and if so, how many?") Even less well known to posterity is the Maj. Gen. Artemas Ward, whom the circle does memorialize. This Ward was a colorless commander of troops in the Revolutionary War who did not get along well with George Washington and

eventually resigned. The general's great-grandson felt that this ancestor's memory had been slighted, and he left more than a million dollars to Harvard University on the rather extraneous condition that Harvard erect and maintain in Washington, D.C., a statue of Ward. Harvard offered $50,000 for the statue in 1927 and awaited congressional approval; that amount was insufficient to provide the general with a horse, a consequence of the rising price of bronze in the pre-war year of 1938 when the project was completed.

The surrounding grass lawn and bed of pink roses are regularly maintained, but whether by Harvard or the Park Service, I cannot say. There is no pedestrian access to the circle. The inscription reads:

ARTEMAS WARD, 1727–1800, SON OF MASSACHUSETTS, GRADUATE OF HARVARD COLLEGE, JUDGE AND LEGISLATOR, DELEGATE 1780–1781 TO THE CONTINENTAL CONGRESS, SOLDIER OF THREE WARS, FIRST COMMANDER OF THE PATRIOT FORCES

Sixth Church of Christ, Scientist   *4601 Massachusetts Avenue, NW*

Christian Science is a denomination with neither clergy nor institutional hierarchy, so the architect's clients in this case were the entire congregation acting as a Committee of the Whole. The local firm of Chatelain and Gauger were architects for the first stage of the building, which was completed in 1962 and now serves as a Sunday school wing. For the second stage, which was completed in 1978, the congregation-committee selected Faulkner-Faulkner, a Chicago architectural firm making a specialty of Christian Science churches, but the clients reserved many of the design decisions to themselves. Their express ideal was that of distant Williamsburg, but the final result is closer esthetically and geographically to the middle-class respectability of the nearby Spring Valley shopping center. The steeple as well as the Corinthian style columns of the main porch are fabricated of hollow metal.

The neighboring Arabic Baptist Church, with its vernacular front porch, serves a Protestant congregation of Christian Arab descent. As the last Massachusetts Avenue church within the District, it is a testament to the avenue's ecumenical range.

Lafayette Square

Lafayette Square
Pennsylvania Avenue between Jackson and Madison Places, NW

> There is in Washington, in Lafayette Square . . . a statue of Andrew
> Jackson, riding a horse with one of the most beautiful tails in the world.
> —Wallace Stevens, *The Necessary Angel*

What great nation would have in the principal square of its capital city five statues to national heroes of whom only one was native born? Only in America. The
square itself and the park that fills it are even named for an adopted citizen, the
marquis de Lafayette. For half a century the statue of Andrew Jackson, erected
in 1853, stood alone in the seven-acre park marking the terminus of 16th Street,
whose axis accords to the White House the address of 1600 Pennsylvania Avenue. The Jackson statue was later framed by those of four other generals from
France, Germany, and Poland who provided the rebellious colonies with military
expertise in their War of Independence; they are Lafayette, Rochambeau, Steu-
ben, and Kosciuszko—all 20th-century additions to the park still dominated by
Old Hickory.

Andrew Jackson was the first president born in a log cabin. It was an image
that would become the envy of all their successors. Jackson was the first president to come from the frontier; he was the first populist—a man from the New
West—and he despised Great Britain and Old World traditions. He first fought
the British at the age of 13 and defeated them at New Orleans in the company
of federal troops who had not gotten the word that the War of 1812 had been
concluded in a peace treaty signed several days before.

A British historian of a later generation was to describe Jackson as "violent,
quarrelsome, vigorous, brusque, and uncouth"—a characterization that would
not have disturbed him in the least as he had no pretensions to being an intellec-

Georgian style. It is set in an 18-acre park, and the vista on its south axis is terminated on the Jefferson Memorial and its reflection in the Tidal Basin, as may be seen with some difficulty through a narrow clearing of the trees of the Mall. The north portico faces Lafayette Square and the axis of 16th Street; as viewed on a clear morning from the rise of Meridian Hill down the dead center of 16th Street, the dome of the Jefferson Memorial looks as if it rested on the White House's north porch. The dignity of the house derives from its symmetry at all elevations; it is not ostentatious in scale or decoration, and the chief effect is one of graceful domesticity.

The exterior fabric of the house is of Virginia Aquia Creek sandstone painted white. Although it was known familiarly as the White House since before the British burned it in 1812, L'Enfant described it as the President's House, the District commissioners called it the President's Palace, and Madison called it the Executive Mansion. It has since been formally designated as the White House by an act of Congress of 1902. Its stationery bears the simple legend "The White House, Washington," unsullied by even the initials D.C. or a zip code.

A competition for the original design of the house was held by the District Commissioners. The entry of Thomas Jefferson (under a pseudonym) was rejected, and the award of $500 was won by James Hoban, an Irish-American and self-taught master builder. The cornerstone was laid on 13 October 1792, on the exact 300th anniversary of Columbus's discovery of America. When Jefferson took up residence in the house he was able to add the east and west terraces of his original design. In 1806 America's first professional architect, Benjamin H. Latrobe, rendered a harsh judgment on the results of Hoban's efforts: "George Washington knew how to give liberty to his country, but was wholly ignorant of art. It was therefore not to be wondered that the design . . . of a carpenter [was adopted] for the President's House. . . . it is not even original, but a mutilated copy of a badly designed original near Dublin."

The presidents who lived in the White House were men of strong personal taste which they did not hesitate to indulge. Almost every tenant has left some kind of a trace that survives. John Adams, who liked to bathe in Tiber Creek (where Constitution Avenue is today), installed bellpulls and the first furnishings. Thomas Jefferson, who introduced the custom of shaking hands (instead of bowing) at public receptions, collaborated with Latrobe to add the east and west terraces. James Monroe installed chandeliers and French furniture and decorative objects. John Quincy Adams redesigned the garden and added a billiard table. Andrew Jackson piped in the first running water; Martin Van Buren added gold table service; James K. Polk banned dancing and card playing but brought in gas lighting; Millard Fillmore added a library; and Franklin Pierce introduced central heating.

The White House

After Abraham Lincoln's assassination most of the valuable furnishings vanished. But today, under a 1961 law, all furnishings are part of a permanent collection, and any First Family wanting to dispose of an object must present it to the Smithsonian. Andrew Johnson put in the wrought iron fence; Ulysses S. Grant added the East Room chandeliers; Rutherford B. Hayes installed the first bathroom and the first telephone; James Garfield, the elevator; Benjamin Harrison, electric lights; Theodore Roosevelt, a moose head in the dining room; William Howard Taft, giant bathtubs; and Herbert Hoover, air conditioning.

Although Franklin D. Roosevelt and his family were occupants of the White House for the longest time, they were not too much concerned with the decor and amenities, and left the whole shebang pretty much the way they found it. Roosevelt's chief legacy was the swimming pool he added to provide the only exercise available to him; the funds for it had been contributed by schoolchildren throughout the land. Franklin D. Roosevelt was the last occupant of the White House to speak with an upper-class accent. (Adlai Stevenson might have been, but he never made it. Roosevelt's way of talking was not resented by his common man constituency, only by members of his own class who felt betrayed. An aristocratic accent has all but disappeared from American speech; his successors speak with regional but not social characteristics.)

When Harry S Truman added a second-story porch to the south front, the purists were outraged: it didn't look right, the old ante-bellum houses sometimes had balconies but not full porches. But the front porch (or back, as the case may be) is quintessentially an American invention,* and people have finally gotten used to it.

When I first visited Washington—before World War II—anybody could walk right through West Executive Avenue, and you could see members of the cabinet coming and going from the president's office in the West Wing. Now the whole street is a security enclave. The days when President Woodrow Wilson and his wife would drive over without escort to Keith's Theater on 15th Street after dinner are gone forever. Now the bane of life in the White House has become the merciless invasion of privacy of its occupants. Since the advent of television that bane has grown to monstrous proportions. The north portico is permanently floodlit in a courtship of the nightly news on television. Writing in the *Washington Post* of 28 September 1980, Ben J. Wattenberg dramatizes the problem: "The incompetency myth about presidents stems, it seems to me, in large part from intense press concentrations on the White House. Imagine how you (and your associates) would sound if 100 crack reporters scrutinized every-

_____
* John F. Kennedy introduced a conspicuous rocking chair to the Oval Office. There are said to be no porches or rocking chairs in France.

thing you said, did and thought and then wrote in detail and in particular about every bonehead play, gaffe and misstatement." The White House still awaits an occupant—and perhaps we should be in no hurry—who can employ television with the same kind of mastery with which Franklin D. Roosevelt used radio.

President Nixon's contribution to the style of the White House was as short-lived as it was misguided. He commissioned for the White House guards a set of 130 new uniforms consisting of high-necked white tunics with fancy gold aiguilettes and tall military caps with blue and gold visors. They all looked like members of a Ruritarian guards regiment out of a musical comedy by Victor Herbert. The guards were so embarrassed, and greeted with such gales of laughter, that the uniforms were retired after the first week; they have since been sold as surplus government property to a band of high school musicians in Iowa.

Guarding the White House is no musical comedy affair: three different police agencies with three different uniforms are involved. The uniform division of the Secret Service, a division of the Department of the Treasury, is responsible for patroling the *grounds* of the White House. The policing of the *sidewalks* around the White House is the responsibility of the Park Police of the National Park Service, a division of the Department of the Interior. Pennsylvania Avenue in front of the White House is under the jurisdiction of the Metropolitan Police of the District of Columbia.

The Park Police has the onerous task of issuing up to 1,000 permits a year to the many individual and group demonstrators who have adopted the White House's Pennsylvania Avenue sidewalk as a court of last resort, ranging from solemn and earnest candlelight vigils to a Hyde Park Corner of crazy lost causes. Individuals do not need a permit; they can just show up with their tennis shoes or shopping carts—the normal run of pigeon feeders and picket sign carriers. There was one woman wearing sandwich boards which were totally blank; when asked about the nature of her cause, she would snap, "None of your business." In recent years group petitioners have ranged from Strippers for Christ to Dykes with Tykes (a group of radical lesbian mothers).

St. John's Church   *Lafayette Square, 16th Street at H Street, NW*

> My greatest and dearest personal ambition is to conquer Manila and to be allowed to live in order that I may return to pass the plate at St. John's.
> —Admiral George Dewey

St. John's is not the oldest Episcopal church in Washington but its parish has become the city's veriest citadel of WASP respectability. The oldest Episcopal churches are Christ Church on Capital Hill, St. John's in Georgetown, and Rock

Creek Church, which was out in the country off North Capitol Street; these parishes were far apart and it was only logical for some of their members to break away and establish a new church downtown, destined eventually to become "the Church of the Presidents." President James Madison was a charter parishioner of St. John's (and Dolley Madison was baptized and confirmed there), and every president since Madison has at least attended occasional services there.

The founding vestrymen of St. John's were among the city's richest and most respected citizens. In 1815, after the dust had settled from the brief War of 1812, they subscribed the money, bought the plot of land on the President's Square—as Lafayette Square was then called—and commissioned Benjamin H. Latrobe as architect, all with a fervor that did not wait on formal approval from the head of their diocese, the bishop of Maryland.

Latrobe designed the original church as a Greek cross in plan with its emphasis on the congregation rather than the altar; the altar was not visible from every pew, but the pulpit was. (St. John's has never been very high church.) Latrobe's original entrance was on H Street, but he later extended the west wing in the plan of a Latin cross to accommodate more pews, to terminate in a portico on 16th Street, and to provide a west front in accordance with church tradition. Latrobe refused any commission for his services, and he also served as organist and choirmaster without salary. There is no record of who designed the fine wooden steeple containing the bell cast from a cannon captured from the British. The bell tolls for the death of every president who dies in office—and to celebrate victory: when the Japanese surrendered in 1945 the eager ringers broke the bell rope.

In 1883 the church narrowly escaped reconstruction in the Victorian style. James Renwick was engaged to enlarge the seating capacity and remodel the interior. Renwick was willing to preserve the demilune windows which are the essential features of Latrobe's interior, but he wanted to remove the steeple and add a campanile on the northwest corner. The vestry has always had a number of conservative admirals and generals, and they balked at removing the steeple. Renwick was permitted to add to the seating ingeniously, to extend the chancel to the east, and to add a Palladian window over the altar. (The Palladian window was later furnished with stained glass made by the curator of Chartres Cathedral.)

The sale of church pews had long been one of the most conservative features of St. John's. A few "free pews" were endowed to accommodate strangers at services. And the church has a remarkable record of keeping its doors open from 7 A.M. to 7 P.M. By 1938 there were 13 free pews and by 1948 the rental of pews was dispensed with altogether, although some of the elderly parishioners said they felt like castaways.

Most of the British ministers to the United States attended St. John's, and in 1895 Mary Leiter, the daughter of Levi Z. Leiter of Chicago, was married there to George Nathaniel Curzon, later viceroy of India, with the British minister, Cecil Spring Rice, serving as an usher. In her history of the church Constance McLaughlin Green observes that "St. John's inevitably became Washington's most fashionable church.* If not everyone came to worship God, a great many did."

But St. John's has a long record of initiatives in help to the less fortunate. It founded St. Mary's parish for blacks on 23rd Street, and over the years it has maintained an orphanage, a low-price coal yard for the poor, a boys' club in the inner city, and support to a much poorer parish in Anacostia.

St. John's title as "the Church of the Presidents" seems now to be well beyond the challenge. James Madison, James Monroe, Martin Van Buren, William Henry Harrison, John Tyler, Zachary Taylor, Franklin A. Pierce, and Chester A. Arthur were all parishioners. After Arthur, the nation languished with no Episcopalians in the White House for half a century until the election of Franklin D. Roosevelt. Roosevelt was a member of St. Thomas's, but he attended services at St. John's at the beginning of each of his new terms before World War II. Although President Lincoln has been described as "a Christian without a creed,"† he regularly attended New York Avenue Presbyterian Church, but without ever becoming a member. Lincoln also attended services at St. John's, but he would invariably sit unobtrusively in a back pew rather than in the seat reserved for the president. When Lincoln died, St. John's had a six-months' period of mourning; the church was draped in black and every member of the vestry wore a black armband.

As a Catholic, President Kennedy did not come to St. John's for services, but he put in an appearance to congratulate John Harper on his installation as rector in March of 1963 and he signed the President's Prayer Book before leaving by a side door when the service began. The morning after Kennedy's assassination, President Johnson came quietly to St. John's for private prayers.

In 1954 the church acquired, for use as a parish house, the old brownstone house next door at 1525 H Street. The house was designed by its owner, St. Clair Clarke, and in the 1840s served as the British minister's residence. The new passageway linking the church with its new parish hall was designed by Horace Peaslee.

* When Oliver James Hart was installed as the new rector in 1934, he asked the church secretary for the parish list. He was handed a copy of the *Social Register* with the explanation, "This is what we always use."

† Thomas Jefferson was not a member of any church, but his interest in Christianity was sufficient to prompt him to edit a bible.

Sixteenth Street

Sixteenth Street is laid out on the north-south center line of the White House and it stretches for six and a half miles from Lafayette Square to its north portal at the Maryland line in Silver Spring. It is the most prominent of the numbered streets in the District and it was intended in the automobile age—before freeways—to provide the kind of ceremonial approach to the city for motorists that Union Station afforded the railroads.

It is a street of hotels, apartment houses, impressive mansions, and a variety of churches exceeding even that of Massachusetts Avenue. The range of its domestic architecture rivals that of any street in America in presenting a gamut of house styles, from the most pretentious Renaissance palace to the humblest split level rambler complete with front-yard flamingoes.

First Baptist Church   *16th Street at O Street, NW*
In 1890, on the corner of 16th and O Streets, the First Baptist Church built a very handsome church designed by W. Bruce Gray in a combination of the then voguish Italian Renaissance and Romanesque styles. The rusticated brownstone and red brick facade of the nave loomed six stories high, while a campanile tower at the northeast corner reached to 140 feet. This was the home church of President Harry S Truman, who customarily walked to services, seven blocks up 16th Street from the White House, in the company of a couple of men from the Secret Service. On one occasion Mr. Truman, having arrived unannounced, gave an impromptu commencement address to the Sunday school graduating class.

But fashions change. In 1953 the First Baptists tore down their Romanesque temple and in 1955 completed another handsome church designed by Harold E. Wagoner in the newly revived Neo-Gothic style. The buttresses are severely abstracted and without decoration; the main entrance is flanked by an interlocking setback of masses—eight receding levels like a ziggurat—in a manner suggesting the influence of Frank Lloyd Wright. In a gesture of complexity and contradiction, the granite parapet over the main door to the nave is severely truncated, forcing the eye to search for a steeple that isn't there. This became the home church of President Jimmy Carter, who customarily drove to services in a limousine accompanied by several station wagons full of Secret Service men. For additional security, closed-circuit TV monitors peer down from the roof of the Australian chancery office building next door. On several occasions Mr. Carter conducted Sunday school classes himself.

The Baptists have more churches in Washington than any other denomination. First Baptist is one of eight Baptist churches on 16th Street alone, and it is almost high church in spirit: the minister is even styled *rector*. The elaborate stained glass windows are devoted to specific liturgical symbols as well as the familiar Old Testament themes. In a becomingly ecumenical gesture, all of the dozen or so stained glass windows at the clerestory level celebrate the founders of other churches of the Christian faith—not just Protestant divines like George Fox the Quaker and John Wesley the Methodist, but Orthodox and Catholic leaders as well.

Built at a cost of over $2 million it is the most expensive Protestant parish church in the city.

Foundry United Methodist Church   *1500 16th Street, NW*
This Gothic Revival church in robust, rusticated gray granite was designed by the Washington architect Appleton P. Clark. It is the third church of the name, dedicated in 1904, when the congregation moved northward from its earlier home at 14th and G Streets, NW, to escape an area of increasing commercialization.

Foundry Church was founded by Henry Foxall in 1814 as a thank offering for the providential thunderstorm that helped his foundry, located in a ravine just above Georgetown, escape the fire that swept the city during the British attack on Washington in the War of 1812. His foundry processed iron ore brought down the Potomac from Harpers Ferry, and since it had produced the cannons used by Commodore Perry at Lake Erie, there was reason to believe that it was high on the British list of targets. The name is also an echo of John Wesley's association with the Old Foundry Church in London.

Foundry Methodist enjoys a legendary reputation for its superb acoustics. The main body of the church slopes toward the chancel under a shallow dome with fan-vaulted pendentives. (*Pendentives* are those spherical triangular areas that fill the space between a round dome and its four square corner supports.)

The pews curve in a gentle arc under the fan vaults, providing a remarkable feeling of intimacy for such a large chamber.

The sixth pew on the right is marked by a small brass plate which reads, "In this pew, side by side, sat President Franklin D. Roosevelt and Prime Minister Winston Churchill at the National Christmas Service in 1941." Those were fearful days, just three weeks after the Japanese attack on Pearl Harbor, and the church swarmed not only with men from the Secret Service but with soldiers with armed bayonets.

First Baptist Church

In the years after World War II the environment of 16th Street experienced many demographic stresses and strains as the black population grew and many of the rich moved away. But Foundry Methodist had a socially active congregation responsive to the needs of a changing community, and it survives today as a large city church even though many of its members actually live in the suburbs. (This is in marked contrast to the shameful way in which the National Presbyterian Church abandoned its H. H. Richardson building on Connecticut Avenue—demolished for an office building—in favor of a new candy-box, parking-mall cathedral on Nebraska Avenue.)

Church of the Holy City, Swedenborgian *1611 16th Street, NW*

"The church is within man, and not without him," wrote the Swedish theologian Emanuel Swedenborg (1688–1772), who made no move himself to found a church. Thus for his disciples, the primary stress is on the spiritual growth of the individual and the church as an institution is only secondary. But none of this deterred the Swedenborgians from erecting a building in the very Gothic epitome of ecclesiastical architecture. It was dedicated in 1896 as "the Church of the New Jerusalem."

The architect of the church was Professor H. Langford Warren, founder of the School of Architecture at Harvard and its first dean. So much of his time was taken up with teaching and writing that this is one of the few buildings associated with his name. The Washington architect Paul Pelz supervised the construction.

The style chosen for this church is Early English Decorated Gothic, with the decorated tower vaguely derivative of Magdalen College tower at Oxford. It was originally designed to be capped by a hexagonal pyramidal spire, but funds to finish it were never available. The interior of the church has an exposed hammer beam ceiling, and the nave and chancel are more austere than the exterior decoration might suggest—despite the stained glass windows from the Tiffany Studios. The tower door to the vestibule (facing Corcoran Street) boasts a gargoyle in the form of a devil, a mild heretical indulgence, a relic of the Middle Ages when devils were everywhere.

The Swedenborgians attracted an intellectual following much broader than their formal membership. Henry and William James were the sons of a Swedenborgian minister. In 1928 Helen Keller delivered remarks to the national convention of the church meeting at the Church of the Holy City.

House of the Temple, Scottish Rite   *1773 16th Street at S Street, NW*
Open weekdays 9–4, last tour at 2, free.

> Monarchs themselves have not thought it derogatory from their dignity
> to exchange the sceptre for the trowel.
> —An old Masonic *Charge* to initiates

Inside and out this is a great building for symbol mongers and insignia buffs.
The Masons have gone far with their emblems; they put the rayed triangle with
an eye inside it on the Great Seal of the United States and thus on the back of
every dollar bill.

The full name of this place is "The Supreme Council (Mother Council of the
World) of the Inspectors General Knights Commanders of the House of the
Temple of Solomon of the Thirty-third Degree of the Ancient and Accepted
Scottish Rite of Free Masonry of the Southern Jurisdiction of the United States
of America." No storefront church could be less succinct. The council has jurisdiction "in the countries of China and Japan, and all the states south of the Ohio
and west of the Mississippi rivers," a definition of *southern* exceeding the wildest
dreams of a Jefferson Davis.

What is a Mason? The origins of Freemasonry are lost in the mists of time. It
incorporates a universal humanitarian philosophy of world brotherhood and
self-improvement. From the insights of its original stonemasons it divines and
celebrates the secret harmonies of mathematical relationships. It professes "an
unalterable belief in the Great Architect of the Universe," a concept of the
Deity with broad enough latitude to welcome Christian, Jew, Buddhist, and
Muslim. When Pierre, the hero of Tolstoy's *War and Peace,* joined the Masons
in 1812, his newborn exaltation was the 19th-century equivalent of Esalen or *est.*
Today it is largely a fraternal organization with few zealots but some quirky
causes—for example opposition to bilingual schooling.

What is the Scottish Rite? The wisdom and mysteries of Freemasonry are
presented in a system of 33 progressive degrees of instruction. Freemasonry
flourished in Scotland more than in England; Sir Walter Scott and Robert Burns
were Masons. The Scottish Rite—with today more than a million members recorded in its basement computer—has the chief (but not exclusive) jurisdiction
of the fourth through the thirty-second Masonic degrees.

John Russell Pope's House of the Temple on 16th Street, completed in 1910,
is a reincarnation of one of the Seven Wonders of the Ancient World, the long-
since ruined Mausoleum of Halicarnassus in Turkey, the most famous of all
tombs. Pliny's description of the Mausoleum is sufficiently ambiguous to afford
the reconstructing architect latitude for creative improvisation. Pope was good
at tombs and he made the most of this opportunity. The Scottish Rite Temple is

and the discreet mansard roof is almost concealed behind a balustraded parapet. A strong flavor of continental Europe is provided by the canopy of pollarded Spanish linden trees set in a graveled garden. (*Pollarding* involves severely pruning back the tree limbs to the trunk to promote a density of foliage each spring;

Meridian House

in a similar sense, dehorned ox and sheep are called *pollarded.*) The structure and decoration and setting are integrated with a symmetry of design and a unity of scale to achieve an effect that may be described as architectonic.

In Meridian House, John Russell Pope has avoided the excessive monumentality to which his work is prone. The composition has a restrained finesse; it is a perfectly scaled period piece, an exercise in good taste. The result is refined rather than elegant, elegance being by definition bare boned; refinement is a lesser attribute as it permits less daring. Good taste dotes on nicety and discrimination. Under the pollarded trees, the cobblestones and graveled walks exclude all other vegetation. The effect verges on the effete. You can't be both effete and sexy too; good taste is a fragile value in any context.

Since 1960 the Meridian International Center has maintained 1630 Crescent Place as a hospitality center for diplomats and other foreign visitors; it also conducts an international program of cultural exchange. Despite the new institutional role, most of the original architectural character of the house has been preserved. Some of the sculptural adornments have been removed due to the threat of destruction by air pollution. Stone cupids no longer gambol at the parapet cornices. Terra-cotta sphinxes with faces of young maidens have been carried off to Dumbarton Oaks from their former perch atop two limestone pylons.

The once fine view of the city from the south elevation has since been spoiled by an unlovely complex of crudely designed town houses.

Meridian Hill Park
16th Street between Florida Avenue and Euclid Street, NW
Meridian Hill Park marks the intersection of one of the earliest surveyed north-south meridian lines* of the city and the fall line. The fall line represents the drop from the Piedmont Plateau to the Atlantic coastal plain (see p. 8). The western part of Florida Avenue (formerly called Boundary Street) from 7th to 23rd Streets follows the base of the fall line across the city. It is the program and function of this park to dramatize this single geological feature in a scheme that combines the natural topographical features with a series of formal garden designs.

At the north end of the park is a 900-foot esplanade in which high retaining walls support a broad grass mall—a *tapis vert.* This plateau ends in a terrace with a sweeping view of the coastal plain to the southeast; the terrace in turn ends in a sheer wall with a grotto leading down through a cascade of 13 graduated curved

* The meridian was surveyed in 1816 in the vain hope of establishing a new prime meridian to free American navigators from dependence on that of Greenwich.

fountains down to a pool and promenade with balustrades. The concept is partly that of a park and partly that of a formal garden: it combines features of 17th-century landscape architecture as developed in settings for French chateaux and Italian palazzi. Since funds for the project were limited, the architect devised a special kind of exposed concrete to give an inexpensive but decorative rocaille effect to the walls, sidewalks, niches, and even urns. The chief trouble with this grand scheme is that the once-sweeping view was irrevocably obliterated in 1964 with the erection of a high-rise apartment at the corner of Florida and New Hampshire Avenues.

The statue of Joan of Arc, a gift from the women of France to the women of the United States, is too small to serve as the cynosure that its site demands at the crest of the cascade. The park is now unofficially known as Malcolm X Park, by resolution of the D.C. government, but the Interior Department, which operates the site as part of the National Capital Region Parks, questions the authority of the District to rename federal property.

Only in Washington do parallel lines converge: the park narrows as it rises between 15th and 16th Streets, and at Irving Street, a few blocks to the north, the two numbered streets actually intersect.

Meridian Hill Park

Unification Church   *16th Street at Columbia Road, NW*

There are rich Mormons now: O Pioneers!
—Mahonri Sharp Young, 1970

The persecutions, the wanderings, the hardships, and the ultimate peace and prosperity of the Mormon experience are here epitomized and abandoned. America has religious sects in wild profusion: Shakers, Jehovah's Witnesses, and storefront churches, but few—except Mormons—are distinguished for their architecture. The Mormons were always abstemious but non-Puritanical. Their temple in Salt Lake City, at the heart of the valley where Brigham Young said, "This is the place," is an exuberant celebration of their faith that "God has evolved from man and that men might evolve into gods."

This former Mormon church at the corner of Columbia Road has to take the palm as the most exotic religious edifice on all of 16th Street as it stretches out in one long Salvation Boulevard from Lafayette Square to the Maryland border. It was designed by a grandson of Brigham Young as a refined and delicate echo of the many-spired tabernacle in Salt Lake City. When it was completed in 1933, the papers reported that it incorporated 16,000 pieces of mottled stone cut in the mountains of Utah and shipped to Washington on 32 railroad cars. The result is a pale, taffy-colored marble fabric with attenuated windows, extreme emphasis on verticality—and no deference whatsoever to Anglo-Saxon cultural models.

The sanctuary of what the Mormons then called their Washington Chapel—formerly open to visitors on regular tours—is a high square room with an organ, a choir loft, and excellent acoustics. The dark mahogany pews are arrayed in ample curves and furnished with tufted cushions of red plush. In both their symbolic and decorative elements, the stained glass windows are restrained, filtering their light through predominantly pale earth tones of glass.

Having outgrown their chapel, the Mormons in 1974 built a spectacular new Washington Temple, just off the Beltway near Kensington, Maryland: it is a Disneyland wedding cake of white icing, a suburban Camelot, inaccessible except by automobile. At night this ribbed marble monolith capped by six gold-plated spires looms over a curve of the Beltway so unexpectedly as to present a hazard to approaching drivers unprepared for its dazzling floodlit magnificence.

The old temple on 16th Street had to be abandoned as sadly superfluous, and from its 176-foot spire the Mormons removed the figure of the Angel Moroni. They regard Moroni as a prophet of ancient America, and he plays a role similar to that assigned to Gabriel by other Christians. In the new Beltway temple a twice larger than life-size Moroni blows his trumpet steadfastly on a perch 300 feet above the ground. The new temple is closed to the public—proscribed to the Gentiles, as Mormons call nonbelievers.

The 16th Street chapel soon found new owners in the Unification Church of the Reverend Sun Myung Moon. The Mormons had built the church originally to reflect the close relationship of their religious and social life: there is a recreation hall with a stage and projection room, a Scout room, a banquet hall and kitchen, and even a gymnasium. The young people of the Unification Church find these arrangements very congenial, and they have adapted the building into a sort of hostel, accommodating as many as 70 overnight guests.

Sects overlap. Joseph Smith, the founder of the Mormon Church, was a Mason, and he would have felt quite at home in the Scottish Rite Temple next door. The followers of both the Reverend Moon and Joseph Smith are abstemious but not ascetic: they eschew alcohol and coffee and tea, but the Moon followers are more indulgent about tobacco. Some time after the new owners moved in, a preacher at the All Souls Unitarian Church on the opposite corner welcomed them with a sermon entitled, "The Unification Church—Far Out, But Right Across the Street."

All Souls Church   *16th Street at Harvard Street, NW*

In 1721 the English architect James Gibbs, a protégé of Sir Christopher Wren, built the striking new Church of St. Martin's-in-the-Fields in what was to become a corner of Trafalgar Square next to the National Gallery and opposite the Admiralty Arch. That church was to have an enormously widespread and continuing influence. Its design was perpetuated in books on architecture, and in the words of the British antiquarian John Summerson, "It became the type of the Anglican parish church and was imitated wherever in the world English was spoken and Anglican worship upheld."

Exactly 200 years later the Boston architectural firm of Coolidge and Shattuck designed All Souls Church on the corner of 16th and Harvard Streets as a replica of Gibbs's St. Martin's-in-the-Fields. Washington has many churches that echo the bold scheme of Gibbs's original facade, but All Souls is probably the best copy extant, a deliberate and professional attempt to recapture the scale and spirit of the original prototype. There are, of course, some adaptations to the American circumstances. In the five bays of the nave, native red brick has been substituted for the original limestone. In the center of the triangular pediment over the porch the original baroque cartouche survives, but without the heraldic supporters—the Lion and the Unicorn—of the original Anglican model.

Unlike the earlier examples of Wren, Gibbs's scheme incorporates the tower as an interior and integral part of the west wall, and the steeple emerges through the nave roof. (This same attempt to achieve a compact unity of effect may be found in Pope's National City Christian Church and Latrobe's St. John's, Lafayette Square.) The interior of the church displays another bold departure from the Wren prototypes: the eight Corinthian columns are capped not by just the conventional capital but by the whole full entablature including frieze and cornice—a feature of unusual complexity in an otherwise restrained sanctuary and nave.

The firm of Coolidge and Shattuck won the design for the church in a competition juried by Cass Gilbert and Henry Bacon, among others. The drawings for the losing entries, which included versions by Paul Cret and George Oakley Totten, seem to have disappeared.

In the Unitarian tradition the church has none of the usual Christian icons, not even a cross at the chancel—only a very prominent pulpit in dead center under the apse; in this place there can be no doubt that the *sermon* is what counts. How this church got the name of All Souls is a curiosity for a congregation that affirms neither the Trinity nor even the divinity of Christ. The church has always had a distinguished roster of ministers. During the 1940s and 1950s, when the Reverend A. Powell Davies was preaching in his Scots burr, and before the cinder block Unitarian churches had opened in the suburbs, the Sunday services were always crowded to overflowing.

Presidents John Quincy Adams and Millard Fillmore had been worshipers of this congregation at its earlier locations downtown. William Howard Taft, although he retained his membership in the Unitarian Church of Cincinnati, attended services here regularly as both president and as chief justice, but he usually appeared without the company of Mrs. Taft, who was an Episcopalian and for whom Unitarianism may have verged on apostasy. Taft's funeral services were held at All Souls prior to his interment in Arlington Cemetery. Black members of the congregation have been more distinguished than numerous, ranging from Frederick Douglass to the present mayor, Marion Barry. Among other liberal intellectuals who worshiped here were Justice Hugo Black, Senator Paul Douglas, and Governor Adlai Stevenson.

Walter Reed Army Medical Center   *16th Street and Alaska Avenue, NW*
The Walter Reed Army Medical Center (WRAMC) occupies a parklike setting extending about five blocks long and five blocks deep along 16th Street and Alaska Avenue; the main entrance faces Rock Creek Park. It was established as an Army General Hospital in 1898, and gradually all the scattered army medical facilities in the District were concentrated in this one place. It is classified as a *general* hospital to distinguish it from the post hospitals at the various army forts and bases, and because it is a center for research and training, as well as because

patients are admitted from the army at large for specialized treatment. There are commodious VIP suites in the main hospital which have harbored many foreign chiefs of state who have come to this country for special medical attention and which were also the setting for the exquisitely prolonged terminal illnesses of such celebrities as Gen. John J. Pershing, Gen. Douglas MacArthur, Secretary of State John Foster Dulles, and President Dwight D. Eisenhower.

For the first half century of its existence the sprawling red brick hospital with its white-columned portico and the surrounding barracks and outbuildings were arrayed along curving tree-lined streets in a setting of planned harmony. Recent decades have seen the desecration of this tranquil haven by the construction of two huge institutional buildings arbitrarily sited and designed with total disregard for the character and orientation of established neighbors on the hospital grounds—the bombproof Armed Forces Institute of Pathology and a seven-story concrete block of a new hospital, completed in 1979 with no decent prospect from any mode of approach. Unless you go out to Georgia Avenue on the east to re-enter the hospital grounds, the only vehicular access is a service dock for the unloading of trucks.

Patients reporting for admission are screened by what the army calls a *triager,* a term describing the sorting of battle casualties into three classes: those too far gone for treatment, those who will recover without treatment, and the intermediate third group on whom treatment will be best invested. The scale of hospital charges has a broad range: military dependents, $4.65 per day; military officers, $3.25 per day; enlisted personnel, no charge; civilian emergencies and all others, $298.00 per day. (For officers and dependents hospital treatment is an "entitlement" without charge; their fees are to cover meals, for which enlisted personnel are not charged.)

Armed Forces Medical Museum   *14th and Dahlia Streets, within Walter Reed Army Medical Center   Entrance at 6825 16th Street, NW   Open daily 10–5:30, free   Recorded information 576-2348.*
No one should visit the Armed Forces Medical Museum unprepared for a certain loss of innocence. While there is nothing outright grisly, there are objects on display to daunt even the toughest kid on the block. Many of the specimens here are morbid in the extreme, and morbid curiosity is a fact of human nature: here at the Medical Museum visitors of all ages can have that curiosity sated once and for all.

It is not surprising that a generation raised on *M*A*S*H* should trek out to see the medical marvels here at Walter Reed with a loyalty as keen as those who flock to the FBI. Since the place first opened in 1863 it has always attracted not just doctors but laymen and plain folk of all ages. Parents bring infants not yet

---

old enough to talk, and the toddlers may be seen staring in silent communion with fetuses and deformed embryos in bottles shelved at floor level.

The presentation of all these artifacts of our common physiology is straightforward, clinically to the point. ("We don't need fancy brass labels," says Dr. Edward R. White, the museum's first civilian director. "Typed cards are cheaper and easier to read.") The visitor's progress through the rows of well-lit cases is unhurried. In such an atmosphere it is easy to lose your self-consciousness; after the first few minutes you no longer look around to see if anyone is looking at what you're looking at. Here is the museum experience in its purest form; even the most reticent visitor is somehow forced to come to terms with his own mortality.

For almost three-quarters of a century the Army Medical Museum—as it was then called—was housed in its own building down on the Mall, a building designed by Dr. John S. Billings, the museum's curator. Erected in 1887 on the corner of Independence Avenue at 7th Street, SW, it was especially designed to accommodate the museum exhibits and laboratories. It was boldly Victorian in style, with red brick and terra-cotta ornamentation, and similar in spirit to the neighboring Arts and Industries Building of the Smithsonian; the two buildings together were among the city's chief attractions for tourists, especially children.

Within the walls of the old museum Dr. Walter Reed completed his famous studies on the causes of yellow fever. The first typhoid vaccine was developed, tested on staff members, and manufactured there. In 1965 the building was registered as a National Historic Landmark, but less than four years later it was wantonly demolished to make way for the Hirshhorn Museum and Sculpture Garden that occupies the site today. Congress and the Johnson administration wanted to put the new art museum in that particular corner of the Mall, and they were insensitive to the loss of a landmark* and the fate of an institution. (In crazy complicity, the resourceful bureaucrats eased the way for this architectural vandalism by construing the landmark designation as attaching to the collection rather than the building that housed it.) The Medical Museum was forced to close for almost a decade; its collections were dispersed; and most of its handsome cherrywood display cases were lost.

Since its reestablishment at Walter Reed, the Medical Museum has been slowly recapturing its former popularity with the lay public. Schoolchildren come for special morning tours by the busload. Dr. White, the director, says,

* In 1966, one year after directing the demolition of the Medical Museum, Congress, in an act of atonement, passed the National Historic Preservation Act establishing the Advisory Council on Historic Preservation with a limited review power of properties on the National Register.

"These children know more about DNA now than most adults did a few years ago." There are special programs for the handicapped and for drug addicts. The museum policy is pragmatic. Any specimen will be shown if it is instructive; items are not kept in a closet on grounds of prurience. "I don't keep anything stored if it's worth seeing," says Dr. White. (And indeed he doesn't. Where else would you find the pickled remains of a man with elephantiasis who had to haul his testicles around in a wheelbarrow?) In their new setting the exhibits are displayed to good advantage without the reek or color of the old formaldehyde. A few of the case histories seem to have been abbreviated, robbing the specimens of some of their poignancy.

The museum had its beginnings during the Civil War when the army medical services operated primitively as part of the Quartermaster Corps. In 1862 the surgeon general issued instructions to all field medical units to collect and forward to the newly established museum in Washington "specimens of morbid anatomy . . . together with projectiles and foreign bodies removed." There was the implicit and urgent hope that the study of the objects thus collected would be the basis of research leading to the reduction of loss of life and limb by those wounded in battle. As the collection grew, it focused on what came to be called *pathology,* the study of the structural and functional changes in cells, tissues, and organs caused by disease. This kind of research is dependent on the microscopic examination of the affected tissues. Thus the army's medical service developed expertise in the field of microscopy, and the museum today possesses an exhaustive collection of the finest microscopes of their day from the era of Robert Hooke to the most recent scanning electron microscopes.

The museum's scientific collection of pathological tissues and slides has grown into the nation's largest repository of microscopic medical evidence; it serves as a diagnostic center and as a central registry of tissue files and slides, now known as the Armed Forces Institute of Pathology (AFIP). Pathology was once a subordinate branch of the museum; the museum is now a branch of AFIP.

Much of the sad debris of the Civil War battlefields is still on display. (Many of the amputated limbs had been shipped to Washington in barrels of whiskey.) When Maj. Gen. Daniel Sickles caught a 12-pound cannonball in his right leg, he dispatched both ball and bone—the severed tibia—in an improvised coffin to the museum with his calling card attached. (Three months after his amputation was performed in the field, Sickles was back in the saddle. In his later years he is said to have often visited the museum on crutches to commune with his lost limb.)

You can still see part of Lincoln's skull and the lead pellet that was extracted from it, as well as the bullet-pierced neckbones of his assassin John Wilkes Booth. There is the shattered spine of President Garfield. From World War I there is a German helmet punctured by a machine gun, and a shell fragment that passed through a soldier still had a section of overcoat attached. Among the curiosities are the "stone baby," a calcified fetus from a woman who *knowingly* carried such a burden for 55 years, a two-headed baby, a genuine Jivaro shrunken head, a mummified girl from Illinois, and Viet Cong punji sticks that wound rather than kill.

The museum is housed on the lower floors of the vast and bleak AFIP building set in a podium on a hillside—a podium being a plateau or platform at the street level. The AFIP was completed in 1953 to the design of Faulkner, Kingsbury and Stenhouse at a time when the army thought it reasonable and practical to attempt to make its new buildings proof against an attack by atomic bombs. The result is a windowless building with steel and concrete walls six feet thick. It could not have been a very congenial commission; the result is an ugly bland building unrelated in scale or style to any of its more civilized neighbors.

Seventeenth Street

Seventeenth Street rises from its southern anchor at the statue of John Paul Jones in West Potomac Park and runs along the Ellipse to provide a parklike setting for a variety of monumental institutional buildings. When 17th Street reaches Farragut Square at I Street, NW, it takes an abrupt dogleg to resume an interrupted but parallel course north from K Street; here in the 10-story Hibbs Building at the corner of 17th and I Streets are the offices of Edward Bennett Williams, who owns part of the Washington Redskins and all of the Baltimore Orioles and who was one of the first lawyers in town to hang out his shingle at street level with a bronze plaque sporting the firm's name—Williams & Connolly.

OAS Building: Organization of American States   *17th Street at Constitution Avenue, NW   Open Tuesday–Friday 10–5   Tours (20 minutes), free.*

> Despite its more than 1,300 employes and yearly budget of $80 million, OAS rarely plays a decisive role in resolving the serious differences that exist among the 27 member states.
> —Charles A. Krause, *Washington Post,* 25 October 1979

The architecture of the OAS Building, formerly known as the Pan-American Union Building, embodies the resolution of many contrasting themes. It is a country villa in an urban setting. It blends the architectural styles of North and South America, combining the Renaissance influences of France with those of Spain. And the fabric incorporates design motifs from Aztec, Maya, Toltec, and Inca civilizations, while employing the use of both white marble from Georgia and black granite from the Andes.

The three monumental entrance arches have bronze grille gates under high glass fanlights. These central arches are flanked by groups of allegorical statues representing North America by Gutzon Borglum (a draped female figure carrying a torch for an eager and energetic adolescent boy) and South America by Isidore Konti (a more flamboyant female figure sheltering a more vulnerable and contemplative youth). Above them in high relief are, respectively, the American eagle and a panel depicting Washington's Farewell to His Generals, balanced by the South American condor, and a panel depicting the Meeting of Bolívar and San Martín. Despite the weight of symbolism and the elegance of design, the effect of the building on the visitor at pedestrian level is one of invitation; the result is formal but not formidable.

Here is the headquarters of the General Secretariat of the largely bureaucratic and ceremonial Organization of American States (OAS). It was founded in 1890, first as the International Union of American Republics, and is thus—quite appropriately—the oldest international political organization with which the United States has been continuously involved. There are now 27 constituent OAS member states, with the government of Canada and the Holy See maintaining permanent observers. (An observer to the OAS must enjoy one of Washington's least taxing diplomatic assignments . . . like watching a painted ship upon a painted ocean.) Future decades may allow the OAS a more dynamic role than its past nine decades have recorded.

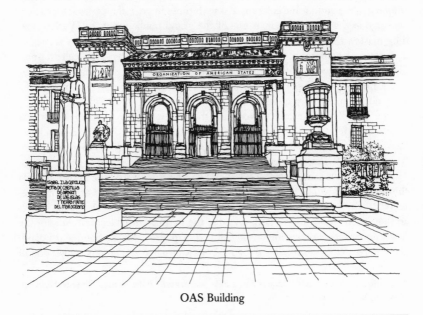

OAS Building

The building was erected in 1910 from the designs of Paul Cret and Albert Kelsey on land donated by the U.S. government and with funds contributed by Andrew Carnegie as supplemented by gifts from the member states. Despite the arbitrary ring of its address on 17th Street, the location of this complex is unique. It is in the exact geographical center of the District of Columbia. If you draw two lines connecting the cardinal points of the District's diamond corners (in effect restoring the lost Arlington County which was retroceded to Virginia), they will cross at the site of the old Van Ness Mansion, which has now become the Aztec Gardens of the OAS.*

The OAS Building—also known as the House of the Americas—has a large interior central courtyard in the Spanish Colonial style. Here is—or was—a fragment of rain forest in a sophisticated urban setting. The sliding glass roof that could be opened to the skies has now been sealed closed in favor of air conditioning. The raucous sounds of the macaws and toucans annoyed the bureaucrats, and these colorful creatures were transferred to the National Zoo. The gently splashing marble fountain remains; it was sculptured by Gertrude Vanderbilt Whitney in various Pre-Columbian motifs.

The courtyard is flanked by broad ceremonial stairs leading (through the Hall of the Heroes) to the hall of the Americas, which, with its barrel-vaulted ceiling supported by paired Ionic columns and with three huge Tiffany glass chandeliers reflected in the parquet floor, is one of the grand public rooms of Washington. The massed flags at the end of the hall have looked down on many scenes of international conferences, concerts, lectures, Pan-American Day celebrations, diplomatic banquets, and, on at least one occasion, a charity ball with Mrs. Marjorie Merriweather Post wearing her famous emerald necklace with a dozen emeralds an inch and a quarter long.

The hall of the Americas overlooks the Aztec Gardens behind which was built a private residence for the secretary general of the OAS. This residence has now been converted—or rather improvised—into the OAS Museum of Modern Art of Latin America, the first such museum anywhere in the world. For much of this century many Latin American artists were little known outside the countries in which they lived. In recent years scores of these artists have received their first international recognition in the OAS Museum group shows and one-man shows and in purchases for the permanent collection. Among the best-known artists represented are Tamayo, Siqueiros, Matta, Soto, and Portinari. There are also examples of Latin American naive art, among which one of

* Washington's Zero Milestone is half a mile away on the edge of the Ellipse at E Street, NW, directly in front of the White House.

the most instructive is Asilia Guillen's rendition of the OAS Building itself recast in an exotic Nicaraguan landscape.

At the back of the site on the corner of 18th and C Streets may be found the stables of the former Van Ness House. This is one of the few surviving works of Benjamin Latrobe; its original wood frame is now covered with a dingy stucco pebble dash.

On 17th Street in the middle of the plaza approach to the OAS Building there is conspicuously installed a stark, handsome, life-size statue of Queen Isabella by Jose Luis Sanchez. The caption translates:

> QUEEN ISABELLA I, CATHOLIC
> QUEEN OF CASTILE
> AND ARAGON,
> AND THE ISLANDS
> AND LANDS
> BEYOND THE OCEAN SEA

That caption is in Spanish with a bit of Spanish hubris, which can be forgiven as Isabella not only financed the voyage of Columbus's first discovery of the New World but her language remains the most common in the Western Hemisphere. The statue was dedicated in February 1966 by the Spanish foreign minister, who presented it as both "a testimony of European past" and "a token of future collaboration." Seldom is a piece of sculpture assigned so overt a polemical mission, such reassertion of a cultural imperative.

Over half of the $80 million OAS budget is funded by the U.S. government.

Daughters of the American Revolution
17th Street between C and D Streets, NW
Museum open weekdays 8:30–4, Sunday 1–5, free. Guided tours 879-3254

> Remember that all of us, you and I especially, are descended from
> immigrants and revolutionists.
> —President Franklin D. Roosevelt to DAR Continental Congress,
>   21 April 1938

Next only to motherhood, patriotism commands the broadest allegiance of any abstract sentiment or popular cause. Motherhood is too universal and perhaps too sacred to require an organized constituency. Patriotism derives from similar deep instincts, but it is apparently more fragile—at times even suspect—requiring a rationale and inspiring membership associations for its support.

It is curious that the caucuses for patriotism in this city are so strictly divided by gender. The Society of the Cincinnati and the Sons of the American Revolution are for men only. The Daughters of the American Revolution, who have made the initials *DAR* a powerful symbol of matronly rectitude and respectability, are staunchly feminine—though not feminist.

When the Sons of the American Revolution held their first national convention in 1890 in Louisville, Kentucky, they voted to exclude women from membership. This act prompted Mrs. Mary S. Lockwood, who was descended from a veteran of the War of Independence, to write a letter to the *Washington Post*. "But were there no mothers of the Revolution?" asked Mrs. Lockwood, ". . . why is not the patriotism of the country broad enough and just enough to commemorate the names of the women also?" This was followed by another letter to the paper from a member of the Sons of the American Revolution offering to help the ladies form a society of their own. (The SAR was later to present to the DAR a bronze flagpole for their new building.)

With three other like-minded and strong-willed descendants of Revolutionary War heroes, Mrs. Lockwood founded the Daughters, under the patronage of Mrs. Benjamin Harrison, then the First Lady. They wasted very little time in overtaking the Sons in importance and influence. Today they number over 200,000 members represented in over 3,000 chapters throughout the country. The DAR is required by the statute of its congressional charter to submit an annual report to the secretary of the Smithsonian Institution, but the secretary's responsibility for review or oversight is not otherwise prescribed.

To be eligible for membership one has to prove descent from a sailor, soldier, or civil officer of the colonies or states who was loyal to the cause of American Independence. To this end the society maintains a free genealogical service—lineage research—to assist potential members in validating their applications, and it publishes a *DAR Patriot Index* listing some 110,790 authenticated patriots (as of 1976).

A married woman has to establish descent through her parents; the credentials of a husband are irrelevant. Nevertheless it has become a curious precedent that the president general of the society must be "a lady prominent in the United States." (Translation: she must be married, and to a person of some respectability if not importance.) All the presidents general to date have been married and they have adopted the use of their husbands'—not their maiden—names. Thus none of the four founding vice-presidents general were eligible to serve as the presiding officer because two of them were widows and two were not even married. The house of woman has many mansions.

The complex of DAR headquarters buildings occupies an entire city block and includes Memorial Continental Hall, a library, a museum, Constitution Hall, and an Administration Building whose address is 1776 D Street, NW. The DAR claims that these constitute the largest group of buildings in the world owned and maintained exclusively by women. Altogether they enshrine the most unabashed monument to patriotism in the nation.

The site the Daughters chose for all this required great foresight and courage. (The nearest streetcar stop was four blocks away.) They moved in across the street from a cow pasture surrounded by a board fence and maintained by the White House.

The history of the DAR as a society is inseparable from the record of the architectural landmarks it erected. At the first organizational meeting a resolution was adopted to build a memorial building "to provide a place for the collection of Historical relics."

Memorial Continental Hall. The Daughters of the American Revolution hold their annual convention every year on the 19th of April, the anniversary of the battle of Lexington—"the shot heard round the world."* They call their annual meeting the Continental Congress—after that of the founding fathers—and that of 1910 was the first one held in their new Memorial Continental Hall. The building was designed in the classic Beaux Arts style by Edward Pearce Casey. Its colossal porte cochere of paired Ionic columns on high pedestals could shelter from the elements a whole regiment on stilts. It asserts a commanding presence over lower 17th Street. On a balustraded terrace to the south is a semicircular porch of 13 columns, which the DAR believes to be the only memorial to the 13 original states in the capital. The door from this porch to the meeting hall within was designed exclusively for the use of the president of the United States on the occasions when he addresses Continental Congresses.

The 17th Street porte cochere gives access to three handsome doors of bronze for use by members of the society and public visitors. It is a sad commentary on the harshness of the times that during Washington's civil rights riots in 1968 (when Martin Luther King, Jr., was assassinated) these doors were locked and they have not since been reopened. Now all access is through the Administration Building.

L'Enfant's original plan for Washington called for the assignment of an individual square to each of the states for them to display their "statues, columns, and memorials" as appropriate. Nothing ever came of this plan, but the DAR complex does have memorials to each of the states and 29 State Rooms occupy four floors of Memorial Continental Hall.

---

* When the DAR Continental Congress of April 1949 passed a resolution against U.S. commitments to international organizations, Herblock of the *Washington Post* drew a cartoon of a beribboned, orchid-bedecked matron firing off a popgun, with the caption, "The Shot Heard Round the Immediate Vicinity."

At the heart of this building is the convention hall, now used to accommodate the DAR's vast library of genealogical records. The skylights of this room tower 60 feet over a cascade of balconies, and it is one of the handsomest architectural spaces in Washington. Except for the convention month of April when the library is reserved only for members, the open-stack collection is generously open to the public for research and reference with the payment of a nominal daily fee of one dollar. This space was skillfully converted to library uses without violence to the grandeur of the original architectural conception. The most conspicuous decorative feature in the hall—above the place where the stage used to be—is the insignia of the society outlined in electric lights: the insignia is a spinning wheel of 13 spokes crossed by a distaff holding flax in its cleft. (It is just as well that the spinning wheel was an obsolete piece of technology by the time it was adopted, because no wheel with an odd number of spokes would long survive in practical use.)

In 1921 the Memorial Continental Hall was used as a site for the historical—and eventually irrelevant—Conference on the Limitation of Armaments.

DAR Museum and State Rooms. Visitors to the DAR Museum are asked to sign a guest register, but the receptionists are unfailingly helpful and hospitable. You can wander alone in the main museum gallery while waiting for a docent to guide you through the State Rooms.

The museum is essentially a history museum emphasizing the domestic arts of hearth and home. It has no pretensions to the esthetic standards of a museum of the decorative arts; this affords it a latitude to display quirky and sentimental and even trivial articles, particularly those associated with historic personages. Here you will find milk skimmers and candle molds, but also much fine Paul Revere silver. There is a tea chest from the Boston Tea Party, and a picture of the battle of Bennington by Grandma Moses (who was a member of the DAR).

The State Rooms—most of which are furnished as period rooms—range from the small and modest to the grand and formal: a California adobe house, a Massachusetts bed chamber, a Kansas Congregational chapel, a Missouri Victorian parlor, a New Hampshire children's attic, a Rhode Island music room, an Oklahoma kitchen, a New Jersey Jacobean council chamber, a New York drawing room, and a Georgia tavern.

Constitution Hall. In the 1920s, as the ranks of the members attending the annual convention swelled to 4,000 delegates, the DAR outgrew its old home on 17th Street and commissioned the premier Beaux Arts architect of the day, John Russell Pope, to design its new assembly hall on its 18th Street site. Constitution Hall was completed in 1929. Its pediment sports the most stylish eagle in the city, clutching a pennant in its beak astride a staff perched on swags of marble drapery, gazing steadfastly to its right, and flanked by the dates, 1776 and 1783, of the American Revolution.

The hall seats 4,001—making it the largest auditorium in Washington—and has entrances on three sides with a broad carriage ramp on the north. Marble corridors lead into a U-shaped amphitheater with a rising tier of open boxes for delegates from each of the states. The walls are of gold vinyl and the stage curtain is of blue silk with gold stars and medallions. A lunette in the proscenium arch portrays in pastel hues the massed colors of eight Revolutionary battle flags. For four decades the DAR provided this hall as a home for the National Symphony Orchestra. The sight lines are excellent, and even Toscanini praised the acoustics. The orchestra has now moved to the Kennedy Center, but Constitution Hall is still home to the annual lecture series of the National Geographic Society.

The chief function of Constitution Hall is to provide a dramatic setting for the annual spring DAR Continental Congresses when the national level officers parade onto the stage flaunting the wide ribbons of their office. They are attended by pages in long white dresses. The Marine Corps Band provides ruffles and flourishes. At exactly 8:30 on the opening Monday night the last figure to enter is the president general herself. At that moment a colossal American flag

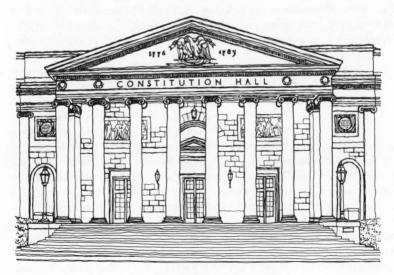

DAR: Constitution Hall

of the sheerest bunting is broken loose to float over the stage, and another convention of the Daughters is in session.

At moments like that it is easy to forget the silly DAR resolutions against the Peace Corps and UNICEF Christmas cards.

American Red Cross   *17th Street between D and E Streets, NW*
Open weekdays 8:30–4, free.

Three white marble buildings with green copper roofs occupying the block between 17th and 18th Streets, at D and E Streets, house the national headquarters of the largest volunteer organization in the country, the American Red Cross. These buildings were built on public land with both federal and private funds in a symbiotic way reflecting our form and philosophy of government. The quasi-official Red Cross is one of the chief ornaments of a capitalist society: it provides essential welfare, relief, and social services on a vast scale and performs them more congenially than could be done by either the private sector or the government acting alone. (Try to imagine the national blood bank program as it might be run by Johnson & Johnson or by the Food and Drug Administration.)

The responsibilities and duties of the organization for disaster relief and support of the armed forces are imposed by congressional charter; the means to carry out these duties derive primarily from the contributions, membership dues, and donated services of American citizens. Although the president of the United States (who serves as honorary chairman) can make available government supplies, communications, and support in times of disaster and need, the organization is governed by volunteers and its planning initiatives rest entirely with civilians.

Preserving the civilian character of the Red Cross is essential to the neutralities and immunities required for assistance to prisoners of war, the care and support of military personnel, and its role as the chosen instrument to carry out U.S. interests in the Geneva Convention and under international law.

The chartering act of Congress has a curious passage requiring the Red Cross to "serve as an independent medium of voluntary relief and communication between the American people and their armed forces." What this means in practice is that the Red Cross can always serve as a compassionate link between soldiers, sailors, and airmen, wherever stationed, and their families at home—without going through the Pentagon or the military chain of command.

The Main Building by architects Breck Trowbridge and Goodhue Livingston was completed in 1917 and is unremarkable in its conventionality. The portico has probably the only marble pediment around to be wired for electricity and sports a big Red Cross light. The attic is towered over by four big chimneys that do not appear to be an integral part of the design. The severity of the effect is softened by stands of flourishing magnolia trees and boxwood. The building is a monument to the women of the Civil War, and an inscription over the ceremonial stairway dedicates it

TO THE WOMEN OF THE NORTH
AND THE WOMEN OF THE SOUTH

in two separate phrases in which the twain have not quite met.

The most notable space in the building is the Assembly Room on the second floor, which is dominated by three prominent memorial stained glass windows by Louis Comfort Tiffany. Their unrelieved sentimentality makes it difficult for the modern visitor to regard them without condescension.* They can be viewed most charitably as period pieces. Here are extracts from an official contemporary description of 1917:

> The window is from the studio of Mr. Louis C. Tiffany, the great American ecclesiastical artist of New York.... The subjects [the Red Cross Knight, Una, and St. Filomena from Spenser's *Faerie Queene*] were suggested by the Hon. Elihu Root. They have been developed in a masterful manner by means of Tiffany Favrille Glass, whose iridescence and opalescence have made possible a presentation of earnest women bent on doing noble deeds, and the beauty of the scene is at its best when the bright sunlight breaks through the indescribable tones of the richly colored glass.... this window covers perhaps a larger area than any other window of modern times.

Corcoran Gallery of Art   *17th Street at New York Avenue, NW*
Open Tuesday–Sunday 10–4:30, Thursday until 9, suggested contribution.

The best designed building in Washington.
—Frank Lloyd Wright

The Corcoran Gallery of Art is the largest and most influential private art museum in the second most important city of art museums in the Western hemisphere. It is a privately endowed nonprofit corporation fulfilling a unique unofficial mission to the city—and even to the nation—in the display and recognition and documentation of American art, "for the encouragement of American genius" in the prescription of its founder.

The Corcoran's modest but long-established endowment funds have afforded it a record of largely conservative but independent esthetic judgment without

---

* The vogue for Tiffany lamps, vases, and stained glass reached its peak around 1900, only to be totally repudiated by the taste of the 1920s; in the 1970s imitation Tiffany lamps were to enjoy a cliché revival in borax motel decor and stripped-brick singles bars.

official interference or restraint. It survives—one hopes forever—outside the Smithsonian family of museums which dominates the capital. Through modest private and voluntary support it is an institution free in its programs of acquisitions and exhibitions to repeat past mistakes, missed opportunities, and not a few victories, untrammeled by even the most indirect deference to the taste of a congressman or a chief justice.

As an art city Washington has been a late bloomer, but it has early antecedents. The Corcoran is not only the oldest surviving art museum in the city but the oldest of the country's first three major art museums. The Metropolitan Museum of Art in New York, the Museum of Fine Arts in Boston, and the Corcoran were all incorporated in the same year, 1870, and served as models for later museums to be founded in Philadelphia, Chicago, and a score of other cities. But the Corcoran—its collection and the building for it—had actually been established before the Civil War, in 1859, as an individual benefaction of the banker William Wilson Corcoran, Washington's first great philanthropist.

W. W. Corcoran has been erroneously described as having lent the U.S. government the money to prosecute the Mexican War of 1847–48, but it was not quite that way. That was an unpopular war and the country did not buy the war bonds the government was trying to sell. What Corcoran did was to gain appointment as exclusive agent for the sale of the bonds in Europe. He was a superb salesman and the entire issue was subscribed to by Europeans, earning him commissions of over a million dollars—much of which went into his art collection and eventual bequest.

The first Corcoran Gallery was built at the corner of 17th Street and Pennsylvania Avenue (now the Renwick Gallery), and it was almost finished when the Civil War broke out. Washington became overnight a northern capital in a southern city, and Corcoran was a southern sympathizer. The museum building was commandeered by the Union Army for use as the corps headquarters for the quartermaster general.

After the war the trustees successfully sued the government for back rent and they opened the new gallery in 1871. The collection and its original School of Art grew steadily under Corcoran's patronage. Popular support for the museum included a working-class clientele who flocked in to see the plaster copies of classic sculptures; it was a surprise that they were willing to pay the 25-cent charge for admission. Shortly after Mr. Corcoran's death the trustees determined that a new and larger home for his bequest would be required.

When Ernest Flagg was commissioned to design the new home for the gallery on 17th Street it had been just a year since he was graduated from the Ecole des Beaux Arts in Paris and his only other commission had been St. Luke's Hospital in New York. This Washington commission was a plum and he almost lost it. Six months after he had completed the drawings, some of the trustees called for an open competition. The invitations had been out for a week when Flagg's patrons on the board succeeded in having the job placed—finally—in his hands.

American millionaires liked to display their art in the rich settings of European aristocracy, and Flagg conceived of his museum in the palatial tradition—a tradition that was later to be culminated (in fact terminated) in Pope's National Gallery of Art of 1941.

Flagg's scheme is a brilliant solution to a difficult trapezoidal site plan with the building to rise close to the sidewalk on a frontage sloping down toward Constitution Avenue. The acute angle of the trapezoid is accommodated by a semicircular amphitheater—one of two asymmetrical pavilions flanking the central block of the main structure. The austerity of the great expanse of white Georgia marble is relieved by elaborate grillwork and cornices under a steep green copper roof.

The building's purpose is declared without ambiguity: the legend DEDICATED TO ART is inscribed above the main portal, as it was in the earlier Renwick

Corcoran Gallery of Art

building. Under the cornice is an inscribed frieze bearing the conspicuous names of eleven artists in high bold letters:

PHIDIAS GIOTTO DÜRER MICHELANGELO RAPHAEL
VELASQUEZ REMBRANDT RUBENS REYNOLDS ALLSTON INGRES

No rationale survives for this arbitrary selection, this random fallout, this dog's breakfast of Great Masters. And what is Allston doing in that grand company? The suspicion that these names were selected by the architect himself, without benefit of committee, is reinforced by the circumstantial fact that Washington Allston (born in Charleston in 1779) was an uncle of Ernest Flagg's mother. Current versions of this frieze appear in monochrome on the covers of the gallery's brochures and publications, but—with a revisionist zeal worthy of the Great Soviet Encyclopedia—the name of Allston has been dropped and the name of DaVinci has been added.

The Corcoran's Conservatism. The charter of the gallery provides for nine life trustees who elect their successors, a dutiful cadre of heirs and collateral descendants of the Corcoran family, mostly bankers and lawyers. In recent years there has been some broader civic participation by the introduction of as many as 15 term trustees who serve for a limited period at the invitation of the charter board; thus the term trustees share in the board's deliberations but not in its legal authority. The William Wilson Corcoran Endowment resulting from the original bequest is still the chief financial trust. The board of trustees has placed the financial management of this endowment in the hands of the Riggs National Bank, under whose guardianship the funds appear to have grown from $1 million in 1900 to $1,047,475.24 by 1954. The conservatism of the board's fiscal policies prevails also in its artistic judgments. In the early 1960s a board member who serves also as a trustee of the Riggs Bank vetoed the acquisition of a Mark Rothko painting with the explanation, "What would my depositors think?"

The Corcoran lacks the kind of commercially based support that have nurtured the more comprehensive collections of its neighboring Virginia Museum of Fine Arts in Richmond and the Baltimore Museum of Art. The federal government agencies have found means of compensating for this deficiency without compromising the gallery's independence: the Institute of Museum Services under the Carter administration initiated modest but unrestricted annual grants; since the Corcoran's building ranks as a Historic Site, the National Park Service helps with janitorial services; and the National Endowment for the Arts has offered program funds on a two-to-one matching basis.

In the period following World War II the directors and the board of the Corcoran mustered considerable detachment from the more radical currents and experiments of the art scene, particularly the ascendance of the New York

School, which was transforming the whole landscape of American art. As a result a few of the Corcoran trustees broke away and joined other sponsors to found in 1962 the short-lived Washington Gallery of Modern Art (WGMA) to provide a showcase for the avant-garde products that would have enjoyed no hospitality elsewhere in the city. In less than five years, as the WGMA was overextending its resources, the Corcoran decided to catch up with what had been going on in New York and elsewhere in the world, and took over the WGMA building on 20th Street and some of its acquisitions, and embraced its increasingly respectable exhibition program.

In 1966 the Corcoran staged the first full survey of American art ever held in Washington, called "Past and Present: 250 Years of American Art." What was so remarkable about the show was not just its scope and scale—more than 700 individual works—but that almost the entire exhibit was drawn from the resources of the gallery's permanent collections.* In the 1970s the board approved a new policy of deaccessioning some of its rarely shown European paintings so that the proceeds could strengthen its holdings of past and present American artists and thereby reinforce its initial and destined field of concentration. The display and documentation of the origins, growth, and continuing ferment of American art are the Corcoran's chief distinction.

This is not to suggest that the Corcoran has a commanding role in American art even in this city. In the field of 18th-century portraiture and 19th-century landscapes and genre painting it is very strong, ranking with the two or three best collections in the country. In the field of contemporary American art it is rivaled where not surpassed by the Hirshhorn Museum and the National Gallery of Art. In both past and present its holdings—and its exhibition programs—supplement those of the National Museum of American Art, only recently emancipated from being a catchall for all kinds of objects relegated to the nation's attic of the Smithsonian. Washington's various art museums might once have been neatly sorted out into complementary pigeonholes with separate fields of artistic and cultural concentration, but the time for that opportunity (or threat) has long since passed. It is now irrevocable that our city's museums will continue to compete and overlap in luxuriant untidiness.

The Clark Collection. The W. A. Clark collection is one of broad artistic and chronological range, a heterogeneous assembly of European paintings, Persian carpets, marble sculpture, bronze statuettes, French boiserie, Tournai tapestries, needlepoint laces, Gothic stained glass, Dutch Masters, Barbizon landscapes, Majolica ceramics, classical antiquities, and an Italian harpsichord. It is

---

* At any given time the gallery is able to display about one-fourth of its American paintings and about one-seventh of its sculptures.

an eclectic conventional sampling of European objects that an American tycoon felt safe to buy when he was impelled more by pride of possession than by the discerning eye of a connoisseur.

The arresting, imperious face of William Andrews Clark staring out from William Merritt Chase's portrait gives little hint of the former Pennsylvania farm boy and Missouri schoolteacher that he was before moving on to Montana to become one of the great robber barons, a king of copper. Clark's connection with Washington was limited to the single term he served as senator after building a great mansion in Butte and before building another on New York's Fifth Avenue.

The collection came to the Corcoran in 1928 by default, only after it was refused by the Metropolitan Museum of Art on grounds not of its quality but of objection to the stipulation that it must be displayed intact as a unit in perpetuity. General survey museums in particular benefit from dispersing individual collections to enhance their various departments, a convenience for curator, scholar, and visitor alike. But Senator Clark (like Mrs. Post in later years) said no: such is the hubris of wealth in imposing an ephemeral taste on defenseless future generations. (Unaccountably, the Metropolitan acceded to identical restrictions in cases of the Lehman, Altman, and other bequests; their quality must have been a factor.)

So the Metropolitan's loss was the Corcoran's gain when its trustees decided to admit the camel into the tent. The very range of this European collection lends a florid resonance to the gallery both as an adjunct to its School of Art and as a counterpoint to the sterner and starker offerings of the American galleries. But the Clark collection survives as an anomaly in a museum whose chief focus is on American art. The heirs of Senator Clark made a graceful accommodation to his second choice of a home; after building the new wing for his treasures (by architect Charles Platt in 1927), they provided endowment funds earmarked for American art programs and purchases.

Assorted Treasures. W. W. Corcoran shared with his Baltimore colleague William Walters (who founded the Walters Art Gallery there and who served on Corcoran's board of trustees) an admiration for the small animal bronzes of Antoine Louis Barye. It was one of his few forays into contemporary European art. The academicians then in power in Paris felt that animals belonged in the background of larger canvases as conventional symbols but were unworthy as subjects for an artist in themselves, so they scorned the scientific and romantic spirit that led Barye to devote to these creatures such detailed and naturalistic treatment.

In America, Audubon had sought out his birds and animals in their natural habitats, but Barye had no such impulses and never ventured further from Paris than the Barbizon pastures of his contemporaries Millet and Corot. Barye studied animals in the Paris zoo and in wandering circuses and menageries, but he would drop all his work to study some newly captured beast not yet broken into captivity.

Since his own countrymen had neglected him, he was particularly touched when he received, at an advanced age, Corcoran's order for a specimen of every bronze he had ever made—107 in all. These small bronzes that now ornament the Corcoran are a product of more than a mastery of naturalistic detail; only their artist's rare and private imagination could have conjured up the juxtaposition of such improbable combats as those between jaguar and hare, tiger and gavial, and lion and serpent.

The Corcoran has had a direct impact on the careers of many Washington artists. Artist Gene Davis has said, "It was to the Corcoran Gallery that I looked for artistic confirmation." Anne Truitt has described the Corcoran as "a tremendous boost . . . an atmosphere in which artists can flourish." Among the better-recognized artists who serve or have served on the Corcoran Art School faculty are Leon Berkowitz, William Christenberry, Robert Newman, Paul Reed, and Ed McGowin. In recent years the gallery has appointed an associate curator with exclusive responsibility for contact with the Washington arts community and who assumes the initiative for mounting shows of local artists. The Corcoran Area Exhibition open to all artists (except photographers) living within a 25-mile radius of the Capitol has afforded many their first critical recognition and even prompted a few to move their studios closer to the city in order to qualify. At a time when many Washington art museums still do not recognize photography as an art form appropriate for study and display, the Corcoran has an active program in photography and has shown a continuing interest in that medium ever since William Wilson Corcoran sat for a portrait by Mathew Brady.

The Corcoran's great double atrium on the first floor and the stepped platforms flanking the grand staircase were designed for the conspicuous display of plaster casts of classical antique sculpture. A relic of that school of museology remains in the South Atrium where there is, at ceiling level just under the balcony, a running frieze of casts of the Elgin marbles, the frieze of the Parthenon transported from Athens to the British Museum by Lord Elgin.

The marble head of *The Veiled Nun* is a favorite with all visitors, but the mystery remains as to how the silken softness of her enigmatic face is achieved in marble. Another mystery is the identity of the anonymous marble cutter from whom W. W. Corcoran himself acquired her in Rome and brought her home in his luggage.

Federal Deposit Insurance Corporation   *550 17th Street, NW*
During the Great Depression following the crash of 1929, a multitude of small depositors lost much of their lifetime savings when banks failed across the nation. That this kind of catastrophe can never happen again is due to the Federal Deposit Insurance Corporation (FDIC). It was established by act of Congress in 1933 to provide mandatory insurance for all depositors in national banks—at first up to a maximum limit of $2,500, a limit which has since been raised to $100,000 for each individual account.

The FDIC headquarters is a severe office building of diamond gray granite from Cold Springs, Minnesota. Its architects were Chatelain, Gauger and Nolan of Washington and Perkins & Will of Chicago. The FDIC claims that its lobby sports the largest seal of the United States on record: 4,000 pounds of bronze, 12 feet in diameter. Speaking at the building's dedication in 1963 as chairman of the House Banking and Currency Committee, Congressman Wright Patman said, "We did not desire nor did we get, a monumental building. We think we did get a modern and useful office building."

Further on in his dedicatory remarks Mr. Patman advanced a surprising argument for the respectability of bank failures. He explained that the purpose of the FDIC was to protect depositors, not to insure that no bank will fail. "Where there is risk taking there are inevitably some failures. . . . When we are tempted to boast of no bank failures, let us remember that several thousand other business firms may have failed because the banks did not take as many reasonable risks as they might have taken."

Executive Office Building/Old State, War, and Navy Building
17th Street and Pennsylvania Avenue, NW   Not open to the public.

> I don't want it torn down. I think it's the greatest monstrosity in America.
> —President Harry S Truman, quoted in the *Washington Star,*
> 4 April 1958

I first ventured up the forbidding steps of the massive south portico of the Old State, War, and Navy Building for an interview with the U.S. Foreign Service in the spring of 1941. At that time the entire Department of State was housed in the lavender labyrinths of this single building. Any pedestrian could then walk through—you could even park your car in—West Executive Avenue, just a few feet from the president's office in the West Wing of the White House. There were no hints of the present white fence barriers and sentry boxes.

You could walk through any of the great front and side porches of the State Department and through any of its two miles of corridors, mostly paved in diamond dominoes of black and white marble. To circulate the summer breezes, office doors were open, barred only by a swinging shutter of white slats; the only room not thus inviting to the visitor had a solid door marked Code Room. Outside, every window sported a green and white striped awning under a bracketed stone hood mold. In summer before air conditioning Washington was a city of awnings, particularly at every western exposure. The touches of color were made more carnival by the pink magnolias (*soulangeana*) in April or the scarlet canna lilies sprouting from urns on pedestals in July. In winter the offices in the State Department were warmed by coal grates burning in working fireplaces.

After the war when I returned to Washington in 1947, the Old State, War, and Navy Building was regarded pretty generally as an embarrassment: we should have known better. People with the gift of taste were ashamed of it as an ostentatious relic of the excesses of the Grant administration; as secondhand corruption of French building styles as rendered by a designer who was more of an engineer and bureaucrat than an architect; a pompous echo of imperial themes more appropriate to the regime of a Napoleon III; a decadent testimony

Executive Office Building

to the overwrought and artificial; and a particular affront to the Neoclassic principles more recently expressed in the buildings of the Federal Triangle.*

Some years after the Civil War, President Grant was said to be still smarting from memory of the shabby makeshift buildings from which the War Department had conducted the Union campaign. (Only the quartermaster general had been housed in suitable style in the requisitioned Corcoran Gallery of Art.) So Grant ordered construction in 1871 of what was to be for decades the biggest office building in the world. It took so long for its construction—17 years—that the French Empire style it embodied had almost gone out of fashion by the time of its completion in 1888. (One reason that it was not built like the Treasury Building in the Greek temple style was that it was hard to make a temple big enough while French mansards and porticoes could be crowded tier upon tier.) The scale of the State, War, and Navy Building was so vast and its cost so great that it constituted an implicit commitment to Washington as the permanent national capital; this building in effect laid to rest recurring schemes to move the capital to St. Louis or elsewhere in the Mississippi Basin. It also provided the first permanent homes for the State Department on the south, the Navy in the east portico, and the War Department on the north.

The architect of the building was Alfred B. Mullett who, as architect of the Treasury, had cornered the post office and custom house business throughout the country. He took on this task both ex officio and as a separate commission in a conflict of interest that was to plague many Washington projects of the type.

What the French architects Visconti and Lefuel had done for the New Louvre in pale limestone,† Mullett recreated here in dark purple-gray Virginia granite. It is an imposing edifice, a massive pile with 566 rooms and no less than 10 acres of floor space. The first floor is of rusticated stone ashlar set back behind a grassy moat; above that ground floor are some 900 free-standing columns arrayed in porticoes and pavilions of setback porches. The first three stories are of the Doric order and the fourth is Ionic; and above that are two levels of mansard roof attics. All of the windows are crowned by gables on brackets, but they differ on each floor, ranging from peaked pediments to lintels to curved segments with crowned hemicycles for the attic dormers. The copper mansard roofs, long since turned the palest of greens, are accented by huge chimneys capped by oversize chimney pots.

* For Romanesque rather than French Empire reasons the Old Post Office on Pennsylvania Avenue suffered at the time the same uncharitable judgment; both buildings narrowly escaped demolition.
† President Grant himself had inspected the new wing of the Louvre on one of his visits to Europe.

The Site. In the original L'Enfant Plan, New York Avenue was to provide an uninterrupted vista from the Potomac River to the south front of the White House. But this building—now called the Executive Office Building, EOB in bureaucratic jargon—effectively blocks the view of the White House much as the Treasury Building, its pendant to the east, blocks the view to the Capitol down Pennsylvania Avenue. But that is the only view the EOB blocks; its grand facades are on the axis of no route of approach save one, New York Avenue, which is perversely one way the wrong way. The only good view of the EOB from the proper distance to take in its full scale is from the middle of New York Avenue; one should approach it from 18th Street going toward 17th, a hazardous enterprise against four lanes of traffic even if it's not rush hour. The best we can get is a receding glimpse from the back window of a car or taxi.

The Gilded Age. The flush of Civil War victory had brought Washington an urge for memorials on a monumental—even gargantuan—scale. The result is a legacy of opulent buildings with an elaboration of decoration and workmanship and with innovations of stone and brick construction that could never be reproduced in a later age: the Library of Congress, Healy Hall at Georgetown University, the Pension Building, and the Arts and Industries Building of the Smithsonian, like the EOB itself, all express a self-confidence and vigor and robustness that the city has not since seen equaled.

Beginning in the 1870s the spirit of French design swept the country. Surviving monuments of this ephemeral rage include Renwick's Vassar College, the State Capitol in Albany, Philadelphia's City Hall, and our own EOB, which the architectural historian Henry-Russell Hitchcock salutes as "perhaps the best extant example in America of the Second Empire."*

Many of New York's first skyscrapers had mansard roofs, but they are almost all gone now. In robustness is vulnerability. Alfred Mullett had designed many post offices, court houses, and federal buildings in the French Renaissance style throughout the country. Some of the smaller works survive, but the larger ones were torn down with only two exceptions—the Post Office and Custom House in St. Louis and the EOB here. When they tore down Mullett's New York Court House and Post Office in 1939, it shattered the wrecking balls.

Even in the first flush of enthusiasm Americans never felt quite at ease with the French style. Why would a new addition to the Louvre be a suitable model

---

* Hitchcock wrote that in 1958, but appreciation of the Gilded Age was slow in coming. As late as 1934 the architectural historian Charles H. Whittaker described this same list of Victorian buildings in America as "a cacophonous medley. One can hardly believe that good white paper was ever so wasted, or that the stuff was really built." Mansard roofs, said Whittaker, were "ugly . . . frightful."

presidential press conferences, new cafeterias, and a ceremonial motor court to receive and despatch exalted visitors under cover from the weather.

Military Trophy in North Pediment. The earliest trophies were memorials of captured arms and booty hung from a tree at the scene of victory on the field of battle. Later the Romans began the practice of displaying the booty in memorials in the capital in Rome. It is in this tradition that we find such a trophy above the north portico of that part of the EOB housing the old War Department.

This one is metal, a huge looming gray sculptured trophy of cast iron, sanded and painted with gray enamel with a crested eagle helmet and flags and tasseled flagstaffs bursting flamboyantly from the curved French Empire pediment that frames it. The centerpiece of the composition is an empty heroic torso of a medieval suit of armor with the gaping visor above it revealing not a face but an upended, double-bladed sword. That bold figure is bracketed by cannon, cannonballs, a pikestaff, a battle axe, and frozen torches: the effect is somber in the extreme, barely relieved by branches of laurel and oak leaves the size of palm fronds.

It is the work of Richard von Ezdorf, an Austrian born in Venice and educated in Stuttgart. He was hired to work on this building at the age of 25 and spent the major part of his 47-year government career as a resident sculptor to the army and navy, designing the building's lamps, hardware, doorknobs, skylights, and mantels, most of which survive as his chief monument, but, except for this trophy, sadly hidden from public view.

Alfred B. Mullett. The taste of the Gilded Age was for massiveness; people liked bold effects and did not mind risking pomposity. It is sad to reflect that after creating his masterpiece in the State, War, and Navy Building, Mullett ended his career in litigation and suicide. Mullett's suit against the government claimed that he had devoted "time, taste, and skill" to the project quite beyond his normal obligations as architect of the treasury, often requiring him to work "until two or three in the morning." Soon after the suit was denied, he shot himself.

Mullett's demise brings to mind the cruel epitaph that Alexander Pope wrote for Sir John Vanbrugh, the architect of the duke of Marlborough's Blenheim Palace, a monument of comparable pretentiousness. Pope's couplet ran,

> Lie heavy on him earth: for he
> Laid many a heavy load on thee!

Winder Building   *604 17th Street, NW*

This stark five-story building was Washington's largest office building in its day. It was built by William H. Winder in 1848 as the capital's first high-rise speculative office building, a precursor of the bleak anonymous buildings that have been housing government agencies ever since.

The architect is unknown and the original facade has been restored. The building pioneered in the use of structural cast iron and a central heating system. Four years after its completion it was bought by the government for the use of the War Department. A brass plaque claiming that President Lincoln visited the Winder Building to receive direct telegraphic reports on the progress of Civil War battles was recently removed for lack of historical evidence. The building is usually at the disposal of the White House, often for such ephemeral institutions as the Carter administration's Council on Wage and Price Stability.

Federal Home Loan Bank Board Building   *G Street at 17th Street, NW*
This splendid new headquarters of the Federal Home Loan Bank Board (FHLBB) is the first federal office building with spaces specifically designated for public and commercial use. In 1976 Congress, which has its own way with words, passed the Public Buildings Cooperative Use Act providing, in effect, that Uncle Sam can "live over the store." Urban planners call this *mixed use;* it is an effort to bring in round-the-clock activity to office areas and to avoid the scene of desolation that prompts office workers in the Federal Triangle not just to go home at night but to *flee.*

Executive Office Building: Military Trophy in North Pediment

By engaging the most fashionable architect of the day Corcoran wanted to create a splash, and he did. Renwick was a self-trained virtuoso architect. He was also wealthy, urbane, and precocious; he earned his degree in engineering from Columbia while he was still 17. He gained his first commission by winning the competition for New York's Grace Church at the age of 22. His churches were mainly Gothic revivals, but in the same eclectic spirit he sprinkled the landscape of New York and New England with Swiss cottage mansions and Tuscan villas. His Smithsonian on the Mall was in the style of a Norman castle.

For their new art gallery Renwick and his client wanted a building in the palatial tradition and in the avant-garde of taste. The result is an imitation of the Tuileries addition to the new Louvre as done for the Paris Exposition of 1855. The gallery's first handbook labeled the style as "Louis the Thirteenth," but it was later to become known as French Renaissance or Second Empire. In introducing mansard roofs of gray slate, filigree ironwork on the roof ridges, and curved pediments capping pilastered bays, the new gallery was to influence much architecture that followed—including the State, War, and Navy Building that rose two decades later on the site directly across Pennsylvania Avenue to the south.

The first story of the gallery is characterized by the massive use of vermiculate quoins—those worm-eaten blocks in a European tradition of morbid rustication. But elsewhere on the exterior Renwick introduced strictly American motifs in the employment of plain red brick for the walls (unknown in France at the time) and in the sculptured capitals of the columns flanking the main entrance in which the conventional acanthus leaves have been abandoned in favor of fronds of tobacco and half-shucked ears of sweet corn. The benefactor is memorialized in a medallion profile and in elaborate monograms of his interwoven initials surrounded by garlanded swags.

In the entrance bay the purpose of the building is symbolized by reliefs of an artist's palette and a sculptor's hammer and chisel; any lingering uncertainty that may remain is dispelled by the explicit legend DEDICATED TO ART.

Architectural critics describe Renwick's gallery in characteristically idiosyncratic ways. Ada Louise Huxtable of the *New York Times* says it is "an ornate Technicolor pastry. . . . Humility hadn't yet been invented for the rich." The *Washington Post*'s Wolf Von Eckardt regards it as an example of "charming phony French Renaissance." In the *Pelican History of Art* (1958) Henry-Russell Hitchcock deplores "a rich but muddled facade still rather flatly conceived."

During the Civil War the building was occupied by the Union Army, and Mr. Corcoran had to wait 14 years to install his collection. The period when the Corcoran Gallery was to enjoy its new home was brief but glorious. In 1871 the gallery was opened with a grand ball for the benefit of the Washington Monument building fund. President and Mrs. Grant walked over from the White House. The white-gloved guests climbed the steep staircase—described as an architectural rolling of drums—to the Great Salon lit by gaslight and decked with cages of singing canaries under which Mr. Corcoran received his guests assisted by General Sherman and Admiral Porter.

This Grand Salon—the color of crushed mulberries—served as the main picture gallery in which the paintings were hung high above the line of sight in the manner known as *skying*, the frames stacked as close together as practicable from the wainscoting to the ceiling cove. Originally the cove had scrolls and

Renwick Gallery: Vermiculate Quoins

stenciled medallions celebrating the names of artists admired by Mr. Corcoran. The Octagon Room opposite was designed for the display of Hiram Powers's notorious nude statue, *The Greek Slave*. Only Mr. Corcoran's conspicuous rectitude reconciled the public to the nude figure at a time when men and women visitors had separate visiting hours. The admission fee to the gallery was 25 cents—not a small amount then—and no one under 16 was admitted under any circumstances.

Downstairs the picture galleries were devoted to the decorative arts and plaster casts of classical sculptures. There were cast copies of the Parthenon's Elgin Marbles from the British Museum; these have since been removed to the south atrium of the new Corcoran at the corner of New York Avenue. The building also accommodated the first Corcoran School of Art, patronized largely by women as the study of art was regarded as more of a hobby than a profession.

As the Grand Salon is restored today there are only three paintings on loan from the original Corcoran collection: the life-size portrait of W. W. Corcoran by William O. Stone, the genre picture of the young Dutch girl helping an old man pull the oar of a rowboat (this is called *The Helping Hand* and reproductions of it were very popular around the turn of the century), and a vast canvas of a cardinal's levee too big to move. All of the other pictures belong to the National Museum of American Art under control of the Smithsonian; they include two handsome Puvis de Chavannes landscapes and a smirky cartoon of two monks giving the connoisseur eye to a torso of Venus de Milo. The salon also has huge wooden cabinets for the display of porcelain and ceramics; they are in the style of Eastlake and were removed here from the old Smithsonian Castle. Tufted velvet island settees provide an ample setting for the two 10-foot Limoges faience urns given by the government of France to the Philadelphia Exposition in 1876. They have been on extended loan to the Arts and Industries retrospective of that centennial, but one hopes they will be returned to the Grand Salon setting for which New York's Metropolitan Museum relinquished them.

From 1899 to 1964, the Renwick building was assigned as the temporary home of the U.S. Court of Claims. In the early 1960s there were plans afoot in the General Services Administration and on Capitol Hill to demolish it as an eyesore and firetrap. As in so many cases, President Kennedy's administration initiated the salvage and President Johnson survived to sign the authorizing legislation (although he had previously sponsored a bill for its demolition). As a result the building was painstakingly restored on the basis of old drawings and Mathew Brady photographs; stone molders had to be imported from Italy and craftsmen had to be retrained in the lost skills of glass etching and marbleized painting. Molds were made of surviving carved fragments, and broken stones were ground up and recast with epoxy. Thus a monument to Victorian taste was recreated not just in the authenticity of detail but in the tone and spirit of the era. Hugh Newell Jacobsen was the architect for the restoration of the interior.

In its present reincarnation the Renwick Gallery, rechristened for the architect who conceived it, operates as a subordinate branch of the National Museum of American Art, which is an element of the Smithsonian Institution. The gallery is not a museum in the conventional sense as it has no permanent historical collections nor any program of acquisitions. (This is in contrast to the Smithsonian's Cooper-Hewitt National Museum of Design in New York, which is amassing a permanent survey collection.) Rather the Renwick serves as a relic of the old Corcoran and the decorative era of General Grant, and as a host to changing temporary exhibitions in the fields of design, crafts, and the decorative arts.

When the Renwick Gallery was opened it did not fully anticipate the renewal of interest in decoration and pattern—not just in crafts but in studio art as well. For decades the word *decorative* had been a term of contempt. Had not Picasso told us in 1944 that art is an instrument of war . . . and that "painting is not made to decorate apartments"?

The curatorial staff at the Renwick still tends to disdain the term *decorative* as "suggesting that which is added on or is frivolous." Both the Renwick and New York's Cooper-Hewitt National Museum of Design seem to emphasize *design* as a concept more esthetically and philosophically respectable. Despite all this, the Renwick in 1976 presented the most original and brilliantly critical Bicentennial exhibit of any art institution in the nation: Venturi and Rauch's "Signs of Life: Symbols in the American City," documenting the popular tastes of the sprawl, the strip, the suburbs, and the city with department store displays of living rooms furnished in "Comfortable Chippendale" and "Colonial Convivial" and "Regency Gazebo"—decoration pure and simple.

Metropolitan Club   *H Street at 17th Street, NW   Private club.*
In 1908 the Metropolitan Club commissioned the architectural firm of Heins and LaFarge—which had previously completed St. Matthews Cathedral five blocks to the north off Connecticut Avenue—to design its new clubhouse at the corner of 17th and H Street in the form of a Florentine Renaissance palace. In a remarkable exercise in participatory design the architects provided copies of their floor plans and elevations for circulation and comment by each of the club's members; more than 80 of them replied with specific design suggestions which the architects were charitable enough to characterize as useful. The result is an imposing edifice in buff face brick with limestone trim. As an afterthought, in

the course of construction limestone balusters were added at the second-story windows and at the roof line.

The Metropolitan Club is chiefly a men's social institution where the cave dwellers habitually open the ranks to newcomers who are willing to wait a decade or so to be asked to join. There is a high ratio of nonresident members, including many American diplomats who serve abroad and use the clubhouse as a temporary pied-à-terre. Social life at the club blossoms chiefly at lunchtime, when the lobby and bar and dining rooms are teeming with important and busy and cheerful people in a hurry; it provides a convenient meeting place between the business community and government officials, between lawyers and politicians.

It is of course bad form to talk shop, and members have occasionally received letters of admonition from the secretary when they have failed to check their business papers in the cloak room. Ladies are not admitted into the dining room at lunch, not even professional women or cabinet members, though they may be entertained in a private dining room or at dinner—by which time the place has become a deserted cavern.

Persons who become president of the United States without being members of the club are customarily invited to join.*

Inter-American Development Bank   *808 17th Street, NW*

The standard Washington glass box office building and the equally nondescript offices directly across the street house the Inter-American Development Bank (IADB), which functions as a regional counterpart to the neighboring World Bank and as an economic development adjunct to the Organization of American States—although it has no legal or organizational relationship to either. The IADB exemplifies the growing role of Washington as a seat of international finance. The bank's charter prescribes that its headquarters shall be in the District of Columbia. In its brief two decades of existence the bank's resources have risen to close to $30 billion, with an annual lending volume of over $2 billion for the kind of social programs in health, sanitation, housing, and rural development beyond the capacity of private banking systems to underwrite.

The ground floor lobby windows of both IADB office buildings contain changing displays of Latin American arts and crafts.

---

* In her *Washington,* Constance McLaughlin Green reports that "President-elect Wilson . . . declined membership in the Chevy Chase Club, which he looked upon as . . . people with more money than good sense. Annoyance increased at his playing nine holes now and again at the unpretentious Congressional Country Club. For the first time since the founding of the Metropolitan Club in the 1870's, its officers extended no invitation to the President of the United States to join that select body."

Barr Building   *910 17th Street, NW*

This office building is a 20th-century version of a high-rise building in the English Perpendicular Gothic style. The rich ornamentation of its facade survives as a rebuke to the boring borax banality of the computer-designed structures which adjoin it at either side. The architect was Stanley Simmons, and it was completed in 1930.

International Union of Operating Engineers   *1125 17th Street, NW*

This is the national headquarters for those union men who operate bulldozers, backhoes, steam shovels, tower and boom cranes, and pile drivers—an industrial elite who earn just about the top hourly pay in the construction industry. These highly skilled laborers are the star attraction for sidewalk superintendents at every building site; they call themselves *operating engineers* on an analogy with professional engineers—the former run the equipment while the latter just design it.

When the International Union of Operating Engineers moved its headquarters from Chicago to Washington in 1957, it brought in a traditional old-line Chicago architectural firm, Holabird and Root and Burgee, to design its new building. This firm had contributed greatly to the development of the steel frame office building and survives into its third generation of partners. For its first project in the nation's capital, it decided to introduce the glass and steel curtain wall which had just made its first spectacular appearance in New York's Lever House on Park Avenue in 1952. Holabird and Root and Burgee employed a similar blue green glass, with window frames, mullions, and sills of costly stainless steel. The entrance is of white Georgia marble with black trim, while the large open lobby is embellished with green Cardiff and Listavena marbles.

The intervening years have brought to downtown Washington many cheap copies of the curtain wall building, none of which live up to the standards of this handsome prototype.

National Geographic Society   *17th Street at M Street, NW*
Explorers Hall open weekdays and Saturdays 9–5, Sunday 10–5, free.

I grew up with the Bible in one hand and the National Geographic in the other.
—President Lyndon B. Johnson, 26 January 1964

This unshabby headquarters building of the National Geographic Society houses the oldest and the most prestigious of Washington's proliferating nonprofit organizations. Nonprofit—but with a handsome and carefully monitored excess of receipts over expenditures. Its 11 million loyal members renew their subscriptions to the society's magazine (that is, their memberships in the society) at a rate close to 90 percent. The circulation of the *National Geographic* is exceeded only by *Reader's Digest* and *TV Guide,* and it still describes itself as the nation's largest magazine "of original content."

When the magazine was founded in 1888 it had to compete with *Century, McClure's,* and *Munsey.* (Where are they now?) Mr. S. S. McClure was retained as a consultant to help the new journal build its circulation. His advice was, first, to move the magazine to New York since "it is impossible to establish a popular magazine in Washington"; second, he said change the name to something simpler and never mention the name of the society since people abhor geography; third, abandon the plan to build circulation by membership.

Shortly after receiving this advice the president of the society, Alexander Graham Bell, the inventor of the telephone, appointed his son-in-law Gilbert H. Grosvenor to the editorship. Grosvenor started out as editor in 1899 when he was 23 years old, when the circulation of the magazine was 1,000, and he personally addressed all the wrappers for the first issue he edited. He paid absolutely no attention to the expert from New York City, and he survived to edit 660 issues of the magazine over a period of 55 years. From the outset he said he "thought of geography in terms of its Greek root *geographia*—a description of the world. It thus became the most catholic of subjects, universal in appeal and embracing nations, people, plants, animals, birds, fish." He perceived the tradition of the first-person eyewitness account as the key to the success of the classics by Herodotus, Darwin, and Dana; he introduced this first-person principle as a style rule for every *National Geographic* article, a practice that survives to this day.

In 1914 Gilbert Grosvenor submitted to the board of trustees his formula for a successful magazine. He had seven rules:

1. The first principle is absolute accuracy
2. Abundance of beautiful, instructive, and artistic illustrations
3. Everything printed in the magazine must have permanent value and be so planned that each magazine will be as valuable and pertinent one year, five years, or ten years after publication as it is on the day of publication
4. All personalities and notes of a trivial character are to be avoided
5. Nothing of a partisan or a controversial character is to be printed
6. Only what is of kindly nature is printed about any country or people
7. The content of each number is planned with a view of being timely

Rule no. 3 explains why the magazine has retained its 7-by-10-inch format, easily held in the hand by young and old alike, but, more important, convenient for stacking in standard bookshelves so the titles of articles can be read along the flat spine; thus it came to clutter the attics and basements of houses in every street and county in the nation.

The National Geographic Society was founded in 1888 by Gardiner Greene Hubbard who was succeeded as its president by his son-in-law Alexander Graham Bell. Bell was succeeded by *his* son-in-law Gilbert Hovey Grosvenor. Gilbert's 67-year reign was succeeded by that of his son Melville Bell Grosvenor. The current president is Melville's son Gilbert Melville Grosvenor. In a series of begats rivaling the Book of Numbers this seigneurial tradition flaunts three names, three-piece suits, and the courtly habits of the gentleman-explorer in a perpetual safari in which the camera has replaced the rifle.

The National Geographic Society's board of trustees is quintessentially establishment. It is composed of the president of George Washington University, a dean from MIT, a retired four-star general, a former governor of the Federal Reserve System, the presidents of two of America's largest foundations, the wife of a former president, the chief justice of the United States, and the board chairmen of four of America's largest corporations—not to mention the president of the American Red Cross and the director of the National Gallery of Art. This virtually ex officio assembly of industrialists, academics, and government officials possibly comes as close as anything in America to Britain's royal privy council. It is one of the nation's chief founts of honor and patriotism, and the sheer clout of its board could probably be relied upon to preserve the republic as a shadow government through any constitutional crisis.

The society is not chartered by Congress, and unlike most Washington institutions it is unburdened by outside auditors and issues no annual financial report. Since it has no stockholders, it pays no dividends; and since it is educational, it pays no taxes. It is nonprofit—but the phenomenal success of its magazine and its book programs yields a staggering income from subscriptions, advertising revenues,* and from investments. Eleven million loyal readers renew their memberships to get the magazine for annual dues of $11.50. (You can subscribe to the magazine without joining the society, but that costs $13.00.)

Partly because the National Geographic Society does not participate in direct government grants, it has no obligation to reveal what it spends on expeditions and research projects, nor does it publish an annual budget. It pays all of its own bills and—through an imaginative ($2 million) program of research grants, both large and small, many of them ending up as grist for magazine articles—it pays

---

* In recent years the tax code has required it to pay taxes on advertising revenues as "unrelated business income." The balance of its operations are educational and tax exempt.

the bills of a great many others besides. Thus it enjoys the indirect government immunities afforded a quasi-official eleemosynary organization combined with the individual enterprise of a devoted staff with the incentive of conspicuous fringe benefits. In a mixed society it is an economic sanctuary, a peculiar ornament to the best of both capitalist and bureaucratic virtues. The society's substantial real estate and investment assets are owned by its members and managed predominantly by the latest generations of the talented and industrious Grosvenor dynasty.

In this institution the photographer is the man in the saddle; story assignments go to the photographers, the pictures tell the story, and hirelings can be found to write the subordinate captions (known as *legends*). The history of color photography is inseparable from that of the technical and production developments first introduced by the magazine. The photographers have their own floors of laboratories, their individual walk-in camera lockers, their free issue cameras, their expense accounts to call home nightly from the Antipodes. Here is the home of an army of photojournalists for whom no event is complete until it has first been recorded in a photographic image.

The society has a sense of self-regard and ceremony appropriate to the semi-official scope of its journalistic and educational mission. It has its own flag, its own heraldry of awards and medals, and its own china dinner service. It even got Calvin Coolidge into white tie and tails for the annual official banquet.

The *National Geographic* started taking advertising in 1906—with an absolute ban on all alcoholic beverages, tobacco, and self-administered medicines. Since the crash of 1929 it has instituted a ban as well on investment and financial advertising. The advertising pages are separated from the text and restricted to the front and back of the book. Dr. Grosvenor explained that this was "in the interest of the advertisers themselves": not just to facilitate the removal of the ads for permanent binding but so that the advertising copy "will not have to compete with the magazine's renowned pictures for the eye of the reader."

Many Washingtonians were surprised when the conservative Grosvenors selected the modernist architect Edward Durell Stone to design their new headquarters building on 17th Street. Stone's chief achievement had been New York's Museum of Modern Art (with Philip L. Goodwin, 1939), executed in the boldest international style and marking him then as a member of the avant-garde. In the early 1960s the city was just getting used to the radical new Dulles International Airport Terminal of Eero Saarinen (1962) and the new "post-modern" wing of Dumbarton Oaks by Philip Johnson (1963). Mr. Stone's headquarters building was to be the most striking new modern office building in Washington since William Lescaze's Longfellow Building of 1940. The architect's successful blend of modern technology with the local demands of monumentality earned him instant popular and critical approval.

When the headquarters building was under construction it was characteristic of the society to install a time-lapse movie camera across from the site on 17th Street where an operator could push a button once a day to expose a few frames—so that the new steel and glass structure could be shown sprouting organically from the ground like a mushroom to be clad finally in marble veneer. This preoccupation with the camera, the impulse to record reality on film, reveals the most direct route to the institutional psyche—through its darkroom, with pictures that emerge strictly on the sunny side of the street.

Sumner School   *M Street at 17th Street, NW*
This florid red brick building with ornate stone trimming around its doors and windows was designed by Adolph Cluss. It was erected seven years after the close of the Civil War for the education of the black children of the District and Georgetown. It later became the headquarters for the Colored Schools of Washington, and it was to house the city's first high school for blacks. The structure survives precariously because neither the school board nor the city government has found a permanent function for it and so the demolished cap of the clock tower and collapsed main roof remain unrestored.

The school was named for Senator Charles Sumner, a prominent abolitionist from Massachusetts who in 1856 was savagely caned on the floor of the Senate after delivering an oration against slavery.

American Psychological Association   *1200 17th Street, NW*
This headquarters of the American Psychological Association, completed in 1964, was designed by downtown Washington's most prolific architect of office buildings, Vlastimil Koubek, who shares the top floor of the building for his own offices. The floors are supported by exterior bearing walls of precast concrete columns, eliminating the need for interior columns. According to the architect it is modeled on the Banque Lambert Building in Brussels and the John Hancock Insurance Building in Chicago.

A Ph.D. in psychology is a requisite for membership in the American Psychological Association (APA). The APA is not to be confused with the American Psychiatric Association which, with a museum and library, is to be found at 1700 18th Street, N.W.

B'nai B'rith International   *Rhode Island Avenue at 17th Street, NW*
Klutznick Museum open Sunday–Friday 10–5, free.
This headquarters of B'nai B'rith looks almost too much in harmony with the pastel plastic veneers of the neighboring motels. The site is imposing. The client

occupants might appreciate the fact that their cast iron hero's audacity was not lacking an element of prudence. He said "Damn the torpedoes! Full speed ahead!" all right, but he was in his flagship and it was not the lead ship of the column.

Mayflower Hotel   *Connecticut Avenue at De Sales Street, NW*

On an Easter morning in 1933 the Mayflower Hotel was the scene of my first encounter with grand luxury. At the age of 13 I was on a visit to the capital, and I can remember seeing, parked outside the Mayflower coffee shop on De Sales Street—right there in the clear morning sunlight—a Rolls Royce, a Duesenberg, and a Hispano-Suiza. I was fairly certain that the first two makes of cars existed, but until I actually saw the Hispano-Suiza, I thought it was just a name that someone had made up. What a concentration of mechanical splendor! In those Depression years before motels only the poor and the very rich traveled by car—except that the rich called it *motoring.*

The Mayflower Hotel was designed by the New York architectural firm of Warren and Wetmore, whose masterpiece is Grand Central Station in New York. The Mayflower was completed in 1924, and for over half a century its two great curved bays have given a special cachet to the city's main shopping street, which they overlook. On the ground floor a 475-foot-long lobby—really an interior street—leads from Connecticut Avenue through to 17th Street. Warren and Wetmore worked in the Beaux Arts tradition and decked out the yellow brick and limestone-trimmed facades with vaguely Louis-Katooey details like parapet urns, heraldic medallions, and carved swags. When the Mayflower opened, rates were from $5 to $12 per day, and that was not considered cheap.

President Calvin Coolidge's gala inaugural ball of 1925 marked the hotel's formal opening. It was all white tie and tails. Miss Ailsa Mellon took a ballroom box for friends from Pittsburgh. (Washington was becoming sort of a suburb of Pittsburgh in those days.) Vice-President Dawes disliked crowds and put in only a brief appearance. The favorite tunes played by Vincent Lopez were "Rose Marie" and "Indian Love Call."

During World War II the place was an unofficial headquarters for war contractors. It was so crowded that even when they could get a room, it was never available till late in the day. So the management set up an Interval Club, where businessmen could wait through the day with makeshift use of showers, lockers, and writing desks. For 20 years J. Edgar Hoover had lunch every working day at the Mayflower; when he died in 1972 his regular table was draped in red, white, and blue for a week of mourning.

The hotel has always been very public relations conscious. For 40 years, it sponsored a monthly magazine covering the capital's social scene. Brass labels document the celebrities who slept there. For instance, a plaque outside Rooms 776 and 781 indicate that they were the temporary home for Franklin D. Roosevelt and his family in 1932 before the Hoovers moved out of the White House. A brief stalk of the corridors memorializes Charles A. Lindbergh (1927), Will Rogers (1933), Gen. Charles de Gaulle (1944), King Farouk (1951), and Nikita Khrushchev (1959).

Since the building has been designated a Historic Site, alterations have to be approved by the Joint Committee on Landmarks. In a profligate way, the hotel (even with 800 rooms) is 35 percent smaller than zoning regulations now allow; with the committee's approval, expansions are planned to remedy this intolerable condition. Coincidentally with the arrival of the Reagan administration in

Mayflower Hotel

Shoreham Hotel *2500 Calvert Street, NW*
You hear people say that the Shoreham Hotel is the ugliest building in town,*
and at first glance it isn't very ingratiating. But it has a glitzy Hollywood character all of its own with its brutal buff brick geometry rising above the tree line,
devoid of decoration and unfussy in the extreme. And few inland cities could
provide a more dramatic site for a hotel nestling in its own hilly sector of Rock
Creek Park looking out over the Massachusetts Avenue and Connecticut Avenue bridges.

Washington builder Harry Bralove built the Shoreham as a rival to the older
Wardman-Park (now reincarnated as the Sheraton Washington) one block to
the north. It was designed by Joseph Abel, whose horizontal windows and bal-

* It isn't, not by a long shot. The ugliest buildings in town are the office buildings on the
southeast and southwest corners of 19th and M Streets, NW, Blackie's House of Beef at
22nd and M Streets, NW, and the Soldiers' Home Domiciliary Building on North Capitol Street above Irving Street, NW.

Lothrop House

cony shadow lines suggest a debt to Frank Lloyd Wright. The public rooms descend expansively on a central axis from the broad entrance porte cochere to a terrace and pool overlooking Rock Creek Park. If the outside is severe, the interior is futuristic Frenchified Renaissance with indirect lighting on pastel walls. There was a Palm Court with hanging ferns, a Salon de Bal Moderne, a soda fountain with decorative Lalique glass canopies, and a pipe organ in the lobby. There was even an outdoor miniature golf course—one of the rages of the day. The hotel was opened with a gala ball on Halloween Night 1930, and for the occasion Rudy Vallee and his band were flown down from New York in a specially chartered Ford trimotor plane.

For the past two decades the Marquee Lounge of the Shoreham has served as home base for Washington's favorite stand-up comedian, Mark Russell. It is a Russell dictum that "Washington without lawyers would be like Rome without priests," and he provides solace to true natives with the explanation that many of the town's worst political misfortunes have a broad geographical provenance:

> It seems that everything blessed, pure, and beautiful is found in Kansas, or
> Georgia, or Iowa, or anywhere but the source of everything evil and nasty,
> Washington. . . . But if there is horrid corruption, bungling, chicanery,

Shoreham Hotel

and stupidity (and there is), where did all those boobs come from? They came from Kansas, Georgia and Iowa, that's where. And the reason everything is so pure in the rest of the country is because you sent all your scoundrels to Washington. They're not from here; they're from *there.**

Connecticut Avenue Bridge over Klingle Valley
Connecticut Avenue between Devonshire Place and Macomb Street, NW
This bridge is one of architect Paul Cret's lasting but least familiar contributions to the Washington urban landscape.

An earlier bridge of 1891 had been built to carry the street car route out Connecticut Avenue, opening up the whole area from the National Zoo to Chevy Chase to suburban development with apartments lining the main route

* Mark Russell, *Presenting Mark Russell* (New York: Everest House, 1980).

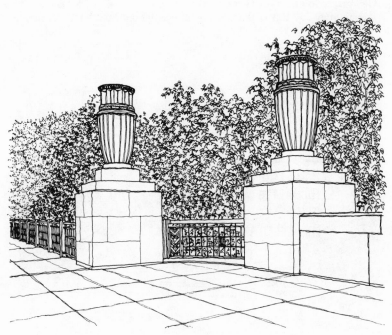

Connecticut Avenue Bridge: Monumental Urns

and houses along the side streets. In 1931 this obsolete trolley bridge was replaced by a single steel arch span between piers faced with random stone. The structure is so unobtrusive that it is scarcely noticeable from Klingle Road below, and at the level of Connecticut Avenue motorists are hardly aware that they are crossing a bridge except for Paul Cret's eight monumental Art Moderne urns with lanterns at their rims capping the stone abutments of the steel arch, an unusually graceful note of street architecture in an automotive age.

A report of the Commission of Fine Arts (1974) describes the bridge as "at once anonymous, proper, and subservient to the city plan around it."

Hillwood *4155 Linnean Avenue NW   Tours (2 hours) daily except Mondays and Sundays, $10, reservations required (686-5807). Children under 12 not admitted.*
Hillwood is a large red brick, vaguely Georgian, suburban house in the middle of the city. Its south entrance opens on a sloping lawn and alley through the trees on the exact axis of the Washington Monument—six miles to the south—clearly seen in the distance. The official brochure of the Marjorie Merriweather Post Foundation, which administers the museum and its 25 acres of grounds, describes the gardens as "lovely," in one of those rare cases where that is perhaps the mot juste.

Under the terms of Mrs. Post's will when she died in 1973, the estate and the opulent Hillwood collection of Russian and French decorative art of the 18th and 19th centuries were offered to the Smithsonian Institution together with an endowment of funds for their maintenance. In the past the Smithsonian has displayed great resourcefulness, even cunning, in rationales for the acceptance of large bequests, however tangential to its purposes; but in this case it demurred, and I think the uncharacteristic reticence was justified.

The institutional homelessness of Hillwood is ironic, as its owner designed it to function both as a palatial residence for entertaining and as a museum for the display of decorative arts; it cannot be called a success in either aspect, although it undoubtedly provided Mrs. Post with just what she wanted. In addition to a large domestic staff of butler, chef, footmen, and two women whose sole assignment was to wash china, the house had a resident curator. A picture survives of Mrs. Post inspecting her gardens with her head gardener: he is wearing a dark suit, white shirt, and pocket handkerchief; she is wearing pearls, white satin shoes, and long white gloves, and carrying a handbag.

Mrs. Post liked to entertain formally at dinner parties and less formally with square dancing or movies in the ballroom (equipped with a balcony from which off-duty staff could watch the movies). She had enough independence of mind to dispense with the tennis court and swimming pool considered de rigeur in large Washington houses. She did not—with celebrated exceptions—relish overnight guests, and there are not many bedrooms. Every room displays objets d'art indirectly lit behind glass cases, and some rooms consist of only glass cases, but the scale is so domestic and the entrances so narrow that visitors in the tour must be limited to groups of no more than eight at a time. This was all right for dinner guests and square dancers, but as a museum it requires a prohibitively high ratio of guards and guides to visitors—a ratio the Smithsonian felt it could not maintain by the endowment proffered.

The current guards are walking arsenals, a joyless group who look as if they might have been imported from Russia in the 1930s along with the samovars and icons. The docents are enthusiastic and conscientious suburban matrons of conspicuous—even blood-curdling—refinement.

The gardens at Hillwood are distinguished chiefly by the profusion of azaleas, rhododendrons, dogwoods, fruit trees, and holly in a natural hilly setting. The formal gardens are less successful; the elements have no clear relationship to each other. The formal terrace is marred by tables with blue and white metal umbrellas. The Japanese garden echoes the roof garden of the old Ritz. The general character of sentimentality culminates in the Friendship Walk, a present to Mrs. Post on her 80th birthday from 113 of her friends whose names are conspicuously recorded in a series of obtrusive low pillars.

Mrs. Post's will contained a stipulation—at which the Smithsonian, to its credit, apparently balked—that the entire Hillwood collection had to be kept perpetually intact and just as displayed by her—including all the antique lace lampshades, the jade snuffboxes, the dozens of pairs of every hue of satin shoes in her closet, the locked glass shelves of china and silver in the pantry, the half dozen large oil portraits of the regally beautiful chatelaine herself, and presumably also the dog cemetery with headstones memorializing Cafe au Lait and Creme de Cocoa—with dates of birth and demise—guarded by stone statues of sejant poodles. (The poodles are heraldic; *sejant* means "seated" in the language of heraldry.) The dog cemetery is ringed by weeping dogwoods and planted with beds of dogtooth violets, the funereal theme being further embroidered with forget-me-nots, bleeding hearts, and pansies.

Narcissus has many mirrors. Mrs. Post could wake up in her bedroom with her first glance falling on a large oil portrait of herself by Douglas Chandor. (In the navy at sea on my ship there was a yeoman second class who kept a framed photograph of himself at the foot of his bunk.)

Mrs. Post was a woman of usually exemplary philanthropic instincts: for many years she single-handedly made up the deficits of the National Symphony Orchestra, and her support of the Boy Scouts of America was legendary. But it is a common failing of the wealthy to impose on succeeding generations the transient tastes of a single individual in one time and place in history.

Marjorie Merriweather Post Close Hutton Davies May was the only child and heir of C. W. Post of Illinois, Texas, and Battle Creek, Michigan. (Fortunes were spent in Washington, but they were never earned here.) Post introduced Americans to their first commercial health food: Grape Nuts. The company flourished, branching out from its own form of corn flakes, called Post Toasties, into Jell-O, Postum, Sanka, Baker's Chocolate, and other staples of the national diet. Mrs. Post's father trained his beautiful and bright daughter in all aspects of his factories and finances, and she developed into the shrewd businesswoman who persuaded the Post company to buy up Mr. Clarence Birdseye's frozen food business. (When she was Mrs. Hutton she had successfully served his frozen duck on the world's largest private yacht, the *Sea Cloud*.) Though she owned the company, the resistance to a woman playing a role in business affairs was so great that it was many years before the corporation—which eventually became General Foods—even admitted her to a seat on its board of directors.

Of her four marriages the longest—20 years—was to Joseph E. Davies, who was Franklin D. Roosevelt's first ambassador to the Soviet Union. To pave the way for this union Mrs. Post* settled $2 million on the previous Mrs. Davies. At the time of her wedding they purchased the 27-acre Tregaron estate which, like Hillwood, bordered on a branch of Rock Creek Park. On their return from Moscow it was in Tregaron that the Davieses first installed their great booty of icons, paintings, and porcelain, and even a *dacha*—then probably the most representative collection of Russian art outside of Russia.

When she divorced Mr. Davies in 1955 it was disclosed that title to Tregaron was solely in her husband's name and he had no intention of relinquishing it. She bought Hillwood in revenge and proceeded to remodel it to reinstall all the art collection from Tregaron. The art was released amicably, but the collection of shrubs and prize azaleas were harder to come by; she had to steal them in the dead of night with an army of gardeners.

The royal porcelain dinner services used by Catherine the Great are the crown of the Hillwood collection, and they could hardly be displayed to better advantage. The four largest services are in homage to the Imperial Orders of Russia's four patron saints, with the ribbons of the several orders decorating not only the plates and cups but the china handles of the knives and forks to great dramatic style and effect. While the Russian porcelain tends to the bold, the French furnishings throughout the house tend to the more delicate: on the mantel of the drawing room fireplace may be found a pair of small twin candela-

* After having been styled as Marjorie Merriweather Post Close Hutton Davies May she reverted to her maiden name of Post.

ings in that formal stretch are the old Public Health Service building, the Federal Reserve Bank, and the National Academy of Sciences—sometimes identified by tourist guides as "Healthy, Wealthy, and Wise."

The Federal Triangle is defined with its apex at the junction of Constitution and Pennsylvania Avenues: together they are the city's two ceremonial ways. Pennsylvania Avenue is reserved for inaugural parades, celebrations of military victory, and for state funerals such as those of Presidents Eisenhower and Kennedy. The parades on Constitution Avenue are just as traditional but less weighty in theme: the Cherry Blossom Festival (with commercial floats), the school safety patrols, the high school band competitions—the usual route being from 4th Street to 18th Street.

Viewed from the terrace of the west front of the Capitol, Constitution Avenue and the parallel Independence Avenue to the south distinctly bracket the Mall with boundaries clear through to the Potomac. At the river end Constitution Avenue has no terminus; it just peters out in an amorphous labyrinth of approaches to Theodore Roosevelt Bridge. That bridge is the utilitarian handiwork of the D.C. Highway Department, built at the height of the freeway era and unassisted by any impulse to register scale or ornament or relationship to its topographical setting. It is merely a network of freeways joining in midstream with no feeling from either shore of an approach and no sense of a middle that—as you get on Memorial, Key, and Chain Bridges—spans a great view. The Roosevelt Bridge is ugly because it is engineered for a high speed inappropriate to its urban function—not that this prevents it from being stalled bumper-to-bumper in rush hours. Transportation yes; transports of ecstasy no.

Across the river high on the Arlington shore are the green trees of the National Cemetery, framed by conspicuous high-rise apartment houses and office buildings which are being deplored by many as a desecration of the landscape. (Since Rosslyn and the Virginia hinterland are beyond the District, they are not within the purview of the Commission of Fine Arts.) The apartments, motels, and office buildings obtrude on an otherwise bucolic scene, but not without some compensating merit in providing a focus and scale for the eye and a reminder that we are living in a city and not some endless park.

Departmental Auditorium
Constitution Avenue between 12th and 14th Streets, NW
This great temple of government, with its splendid Doric portico and pediment looming over Constitution Avenue, links the U.S. Customs Service (originally built for the Department of Labor) on the left and the Interstate Commerce Commission on the right. It was designed by Arthur Brown, Jr., who had cut his teeth in the Beaux Arts style with his San Francisco Opera House, and it is the

apotheosis of the Correct Neoclassic Federal style. The entire complex—completed in 1935 as the center base of the Federal Triangle—provided the avenue with its single largest expanse of monumental classical architecture. It was conceived in part as an echo of Paris's Ministry of the Marine on the Place de la Concorde, and it represents the kind of extravagant use of sculpture and free-standing columns, and the skilled workmanship they require, that we will never again have the talent or the inclination to employ.

Hardly anyone knows the name of the place, and people invited to the Departmental Auditorium—for invariably ceremonial functions—often have trouble in placing it. The building was first called the Interdepartmental Auditorium (suggesting its bureaucratic homelessness); then described as the Connecting Link (with unfortunate evolutionary implications); and it is now simply called the Departmental Auditorium (despite the fact that it has no particular relationship to any particular government department).

The auditorium chamber is high and square and surrounded by ornate columns and pilasters like the peristyle of a pagan temple turned inside out. The exuberant decoration rivals some of the grander movie theater lobbies of the period, though carried out with much finer materials. Gilded bas-reliefs, golden curtains at the windows, and rows of metal and crystal chandeliers in the mod-

Departmental Auditorium

ernistic style shimmer under a light blue ceiling. There is no stage proper, but a podium in the center under a monumental niche coffered in asymmetrical pentagons and flanked by huge panels of conventionalized gilded trophies of armor and banners. The place is incurably ceremonial, not appropriate for budget hearings.

The Departmental Auditorium normally seats 1,300 people, but 4 times that number crowded in, in October 1940, to witness President Franklin D. Roosevelt presiding over the Selective Service lottery in anticipation of World War II. The North Atlantic (NATO) Treaty was signed here in 1949 in the presence of President Harry S Truman, Secretary of State Dean Acheson, and the foreign ministers of 11 European nations. In more recent years the auditorium has been used by the National Endowment for the Humanities for its annual Jefferson Lecture; in past Christmasses it has been the scene of massed band concerts by some of the capital's military bands.

Many of Washington's large pediments are filled with allegorical sculpture groups that are static and academic in the extreme (as at the National Archives and the Supreme Court), but all the five pediments along this 940-foot facade are full of life and action. Over the entrance to the auditorium itself is Edgar Walter's depiction of Columbia flanked by a nude warrior on a steed (National Defense) and a nude female seated bravely on a bull while holding a sheaf of wheat (National Resources); beasts and figures alike have an energy that is barely confined within the triangular tympanum frame. The statues have projecting white points connected by wires charged with electricity to ward off the damage caused by roosting pigeons; in 1979 the current was turned off to save on the power bills—an invitation to irreversible damage.

Granite Fountains *Constitution Avenue at the Ellipse, NW*

One of the most elusive axes of L'Enfant's grand plan is that between the White House and the Jefferson Memorial directly to the south. The vista is partially obscured by a hill rising on the Mall just south of the Washington Monument. When Lady Bird Johnson was First Lady, she suggested that the view from the White House balcony would be enhanced with some kind of an architectural or sculptural accent at the point on this axis where the Ellipse becomes tangent to Constitution Avenue. She asked Nathaniel Owings to be the architect for such a scheme, and since he was then serving with the Pennsylvania Avenue Development Commission on leave from his firm of Skidmore, Owings & Merrill, he graciously agreed.

With his partner David Childs, Mr. Owings in 1967 designed a pair of shallow monolithic basins with twin shafts of white foam rising as fountains on either side of the Constitution Avenue entrance to the Ellipse. In his autobiography,

The Spaces in Between, the architect gives an account of some of the logistical problems the fountain entailed:

I sent John Galston to ask John R. Alexander, the owner of the greatest granite quarry in the world, for two samples of a certain special vein of granite. "Why certainly," said the unwary quarry head. "How large would you like them to be?" "Well, Mr. Owings thinks two pieces about twenty feet square and two feet thick would be just fine."

Pieces of granite that size hadn't been handled in one piece since the Pharaohs. Mr. Alexander was intrigued. He granted Galston's request and found rail cars strong enough to carry the monoliths—which, he explained, might wreck any tunnels encountered along the way, although he quickly reassured us the tunnels wouldn't do the granite any harm.

The two-foot thick, twenty-foot square, rough-hewn slabs, tops prepolished, shallow basins routed out, were gently freed from their billion-year-

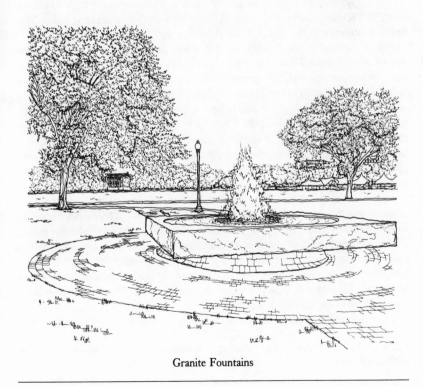

Granite Fountains

old resting place by the slow, horizontal cutting of sand and water. All honor to Alexander's name, he did not suggest—as a lesser man might have—that we cut the granite into pieces.

Those slabs finally arrived in Washington, D.C., after a two-week journey stretching from Minnesota to Florida on seven different railroads. Trucked at night over D.C. bridges, the two great blocks of granite were put in place. Standing up well under the student demonstrations in Washington as hordes of young people happily bathed in the tall spray, dancing and rejoicing in the two shallow basins, the great blocks seemed to belong there.*

Federal Reserve Building

Constitution Avenue between 20th and 21st Streets, NW
Public tour every Thursday 2:30   Group tours (45 minutes) by arrangement
(452-3149), free   Entrance on C Street, NW.

Economics is a process reinforced by mythology and symbols. Banks are designed as emblems of security and stability. The system, we are told, works on trust. In Washington the Federal Reserve is the very Valhalla of the dollar: fostering confidence in the dollar is the chief objective of its monetary policy.

When the building was designed, the Commission of Fine Arts prescribed that its esthetic appeal should be "through dignity of conception" and "purity of line, proportion and scale." The result—in harmonious scale with its neighbors along Constitution Avenue—is an edifice of conspicuous dignity, genuinely grand in effect, its starkness modified by refinement of detail. The deliberate effect is more than human in scale. The facade is set back almost 200 feet from the avenue. People look small climbing the marble steps. There is a bold central bronze door capped by a marble pediment set back in a central opening bracketed by four severe pilasters supporting a plain architrave surmounted by a stylized marble eagle with half-spread wings.

In November 1978 that front door of the central bank of the richest nation on earth was "permanently closed for budgetary reasons." The money changers were not driven from the temple; they just locked themselves in. The governors of the Federal Reserve System were advised that not enough people used the main entrance to justify maintaining a guard. You may enter through the back door on C Street, but be prepared to state your business to the security guard and sign in his logbook. The governors themselves drive, or are driven, unceremoniously into the basement garage.

The Federal Reserve System headquarters is not a bank and it has no money.

* Nathaniel Owings, *The Spaces in Between: An Architect's Journey* (Boston: Houghton Mifflin, 1973).

Most of the gold in the system is in Fort Knox and at the Federal Reserve Bank of New York. Visitors from abroad are sometimes shocked to learn that the only money in the imposing headquarters building is at the employee's credit union and petty cash for the cafeteria. Since Washington is within the boundaries of the Fifth Federal Reserve District, its governors and employees are paid by check from the Federal Reserve Bank of Richmond.

"The Fed" operates in a sort of governmental limbo halfway between Washington and Wall Street. Although the *U.S. Government Manual* lists it as an independent agency, it is not properly a part of the executive branch. Its financial statements are audited by a private accounting firm (Arthur Anderson & Company) rather than by the General Accounting Office, which audits most government activities on behalf of the Congress. The chairman of the Board of Governors submits his annual report not to the president but to the speaker of the House of Representatives. The Fed has no direct relations with the Treasury Department. Congress wanted to make the system independent of day-to-day political pressures, free from presidential temptations to turn on easy money at

Federal Reserve Building

election time. Board members are appointed by the president, but their 14-year terms of office are staggered and they may not be reappointed; from their ranks the president appoints a chairman for a term of four years. This overlapping tenure guarantees the board considerable independence from the White House, if not from the banking industry from which its candidates are recruited. Professor David Bazelon of SUNY Buffalo has put it more cynically: "We in America are so pleased with our separation of powers, whereby public government retains its monopoly of force, while most of the major lying is carried out by the private corporations, with the expert assistance of Madison Avenue and other publicists" (*Times Literary Supplement*, 11 August 1980).

As in the cases of the Federal National Mortgage Association and Comsat, the government abhors close association with any institution that makes a profit. In the capitalist ethic, profits are for the private sector. Congressional committees are familiar with deficit operations; they become distinctly uncomfortable when faced with responsibility for break-even—or worse, profitable—entities.

The Federal Reserve System operates exclusively through its 12 constituent member banks, which are all privately owned (by the individual commercial banks) and limited to a nominal profit (6 percent). There is nothing like this in Europe: a unique blend of public and private domains. All that happens here on Constitution Avenue is the invisible function of making policy: turning the valves of monetary intervention and restraint; fine tuning the discount rates (at which banks borrow from banks) and the reserve and margin requirements (at which banks lend to others); and maintaining the Federal Open Market Committee (which meets in secret) to buy and sell federal securities at the market. These are arcane and technical functions generally unfamiliar to the public. But The Fed does two broad tasks of direct popular concern: (1) it acts as a central clearing house to collect and exchange the vast quantities of individual bank checks between all banks; and (2) it issues dollar bills in the form of Federal Reserve notes that make up 90 percent of the nation's pocket money. The currency itself is printed at the Treasury Department's Bureau of Engraving and Printing, but it is The Fed that backs the paper money with the full collateral of government securities and gold certificates.

Take a dollar bill from your pocket and you will find on the left face of the note (within a black circular seal of the Federal Reserve) one of the letters *A* through *L* indicating which of the 12 banks has issued the note: *A* for Boston, *B* for New York, *C* for Philadelphia, *D* for Cleveland, *E* for Richmond, *F* for Atlanta, *G* for Chicago, *H* for St. Louis, *I* for Minneapolis, *J* for Kansas City, *K* for Dallas, and *L* for San Francisco. (Note that Missouri, curiously, is the only state with two such banks.)

In the center of the H-shaped Federal Reserve Building is a large marble atrium with ceremonial stairs leading up to a second-floor gallery with six rooms on each side designated for resident representatives of each of the 12 banks by the large low-relief letters, *A* through *L,* in gilded paneled ceiling soffits. These rooms, though conspicuous, are not now so used, as such permanent representatives proved unnecessary.

The Board Room where the governors meet is dominated by a fireplace of baronial proportions which, though never used, could accommodate small redwoods. There is a mural map of the Federal Reserve System by Ezra Winter. The high windows to the south are so heavily draped by silk curtains that artificial lighting has to be used even in midsummer. The furnishings, sideboards, chairs, and light sconces were all designed by the building's architect, Paul Phillipe Cret, but the furniture lacks the elegance of his architectural decoration, inside and out. The heavy golden pile carpet picks up the room's Greek key motif; if it were any thicker it would need mowing. The Sunshine Act of 1978 opened up some of the board's meetings to the public (usually at 10 A.M. with seven days' advance notice in the *Federal Register*), and coincidentally the table around which the governors meet was made shorter and more intimate to allow room for three rows of chairs for the public at one end.

Off the Board Room visitors may see a conference room of unrelieved uncoziness. The walls are lined by portraits of embarrassingly flattering realism, displaying a kind of amateurism with which bankers apparently feel more at home.

The Neoclassic Federal style characterizing the architecture of Washington during the first half of this century reaches its apogee in Paul Cret's Federal Reserve Building of 1937. Both as a practicing architect with four major Washington commissions to his credit and through his service on various boards and juries, Cret was the prototypical architect of the period and the Federal Reserve is his masterpiece.

The dazzling white palaces of Chicago's Columbian Exposition had created an opulent model for the revival of classical symbols, a taste that was to dominate urban planning in Washington and other cities—with emphasis on symmetry, axiality, and the formal design of public open spaces. Seven years after graduating from Paris's Ecole des Beaux Arts, Cret designed his first Washington building, the Pan American Union in pure Beaux Arts style. In 1932 he did the Folger Shakespeare Library in Art Moderne. His Federal Reserve of 1937 is the epitome of *starved classicism.* And in 1940 he did his valedictory design of the National Naval Medical Center in Bethesda in high-rise *modernistic.*

Cret's work is chaste, borrowing stripped classical elements and setting them in severe blank masses. His particular hallmark evident in all four examples is the use of darker vertical strips of windows set within planar walls or between flat columns without ornament.

The American Institute of Architects' *Guide to the Architecture of Washington* in its first edition, of 1965, omitted the Federal Reserve, presumably because it did not conform to the *Guide*'s declared esthetic that "structures erected with proficiency but which reflect an architectural philosophy of a former historical period are for the most part not included."

Cret wrote his answer to that dogma in 1933: "We must no more be hypnotized by the desire to be original than by the complex to be archaeologically correct" (*The Federal Architect*, July 1933).

American Pharmaceutical Association   *Constitution Avenue between 22nd and 23rd Streets, NW   Open 8:30–5 by arrangement (628–4410, ext. 41).*
This austere shrinelike temple—to, guess what? drugs—was designed by the ubiquitous John Russell Pope and was opened in 1934. It is the last building before the river and the only nongovernment building on the whole of Constitution Avenue. At the very apex of the Federal Triangle to the east, the Federal Trade Commission polices the advertising claims of the drug manufacturers; here at this serene end of the avenue are housed the several organizations dedicated to the advancement of pharmacology as a discipline of the biological sciences and of pharmacy as a profession in the service of public health.

This conventional monument is the epitome of the white marble building in the green parklike setting prescribed by the Beaux Arts formalism of the McMillan Plan. A former chairman of the Commission of Fine Arts, Charles Moore, described the building as "a vital portion of the frame of the Lincoln Memorial picture." Urban planners like to see the parts in relation to the whole, but the Mall is so wide and the Lincoln Memorial is so far away that only the rare visitor will perceive the relationship that Mr. Moore regarded as so vital.

The front of the building facing Constitution Avenue features four highly stylized Neoclassic pilasters (a *pilaster* is a flattened column set into a wall) that bracket two sculptured relief panels and a central arch framing a bronze door. This severe facade with its high attic parapet (a *parapet* is a wall at the edge of a roof) is partially enfolded by a terrace with marble balustrade rails terminating in two marble urns.

If ever an architect designed a building with a *front door,* here it is. But don't bother to climb the steps, as the doors are permanently locked; they are not even opened for the convention that meets once every decade to amend the *U.S. Pharmacopeia.* The front door of the association's near neighbor two blocks away, the Federal Reserve Building, is also permanently locked; this is what happens when ceremonial buildings are adopted for essentially prosaic purposes—like the regulation of drug standards and the money supply, functions that can apparently be carried out more conveniently through the back door.

The two panels of the facade in high relief were carved by Ulysses A. Ricci with inscriptions in Greek (as are those of the National Academy of Sciences next door). PHARMAKEUTIKE is self-explanatory, but PHOS KAI ELPIS means "Light and Hope."

For many years the association had a gaping unfinished backside of yellow brick showing a loading dock and service area to the main entrance of the State Department across C Street. In 1961 this eyesore was happily obscured by the construction of a stone-faced annex complementary to Pope's original building—this time having no entrance at all on the street it faces. Access to the building now is only through parking lots on either side off 22nd or 23rd Street: the Beaux Arts can ill accommodate the drive-in age.

In 1976 there were newspaper stories of efforts by the government of Saudi Arabia to buy the building for use as its embassy. (The envoys could just walk across the street to the State Department without getting in their big black limousines.) The drug people were somewhat tempted by the offer, as the District Government had been pressing Congress to remove the tax exemption for this nonprofit institution.

In the 1930s, shortly before the trustees of the institute had accorded their final approval to John Russell Pope's design for their new headquarters, they learned from the architect's office that the whole scheme was a virtual replica of one Pope had drawn up some time before for a commission that had not yet materialized: to shelter in perpetuity the log cabin that Abraham Lincoln was born in, just off what is now Interstate 65 in Hodgenville, Kentucky.

Thus we see the indifference of practitioners of the classic Beaux Arts style to organizational function or ceremonial theme: it affords an all-purpose, all-weather symbolism; one model fits all sizes; a building for all reasons and seasons—drug trade association lobbyists in business suits, Arab diplomats in flowing white robes, or gawking tourists in slacks and shorts.

This is a tribute to Ulysses S. Grant not as a president but as a general—the only pursuit at which he was a success. The theme of the entire 252-foot-long composition is relentlessly martial. To the north is the Cavalry Group of seven horsemen of the color guard in full charge on the field of battle; to the south is the Artillery Group of three horses pulling a two-wheeled caisson with cannon through the mud and mire, wheeling through a turn as the rein of the lead horse breaks. In the center is the mounted figure of Grant high on a pedestal guarded by four disdainful lions. In contrast to the violent action of the flanking tableaux of soldiers and horses, Grant's mount, the Kentucky thoroughbred Cincinnatus, stands motionless with nostrils and ears catching the scent and sound of distant battle. The reins are loose. The general slouches in the saddle; he wears a battered old hat and an overcoat like a cape; he doesn't bother to carry a sword. His pose and expression convey serene withdrawal; he is somberly brooding over the fate of a desperate struggle. He was a man of action not words: the sole inscription in the whole composition is the single word GRANT.

Congress authorized a memorial to Grant in 1901, and the New York sculptor Henry Merwin Shrady was commissioned to design it. The project was to be the crown of Shrady's career, and he prepared for it by taking on the role of a soldier; he joined the New York National Guard and embarked on a meticulous study of Civil War military history. The secretary of war provided him with authentic uniforms, and the commandant at West Point had the cadets stage cavalry drills for him to observe. He had live horses as models and would have water hosed on their haunches to reveal the rippling of their muscles in action.

But the project was plagued with setbacks and disasters. The payments from the government didn't begin to cover Shrady's costs. The truck carrying the plaster figures to the foundry caught fire. Then when the bronze was being cast, the foundry caught fire and it was only by a miracle that the castings came unscathed out of the smoldering embers. After struggling on the commission for 21 years, Shrady was to die of strain and exhaustion two weeks before the memorial was dedicated on the centennial of Grant's birth, 27 April 1922.

From the end of the Civil War to the first years of the 20th-century the art of sculpture was popularly identified with the creation of public statues. An academy of sculptors was enlisted in creating public statues devoted to moral themes and the personification of abstract virtues. Ethics and esthetics were inextricable. (Can you imagine commissioning a sculptor today to portray the spiritual values of government?) Despite the sentiments of the times, Daniel Chester French with his Lincoln and Henry Merwin Shrady with his Grant Memorial escaped the impulse for symbolism. They were among the first of the new realists, and they were both obsessed with the correctness of anatomical proportion.

(Shrady depicts war as hell; his view is not romanticized as in the Iwo Jima memorial, which shows the heroism without the horror.)

James M. Goode in his *Outdoor Sculpture of Washington, D.C.* has given us this description of the Cavalry Group:

> This group of seven horsemen of the color squad of a cavalry regiment making a charge onto the field of battle possesses more dramatic interest and suspense than any sculpture in the city and, indeed, in the Nation. The lead horse carries the commanding officer who, with drawn sword, is giving the command to charge. One almost expects to hear the bugle notes from the bugler who has just caught the command to charge. His chest is expanded and his position tense. The viewer is immediately struck with the impending tragedy of the cavalryman who with his horse has suddenly fallen to the ground. Only the rider to the immediate rear of the fallen soldier is aware of the plight of his comrade. He has instinctively thrown back his arm while he is desperately pulling up his horse to avoid the fallen horse and rider ahead. Shrady himself posed as a model for the fallen trooper, using a mirror to capture his own features as he worked. The faces of the other men in the group are modeled from Shrady's friends, such as Edward Penfield, Ernest Thompson Seton, Maxfield Parrish, and Jerry Bogardus. Shrady so strived for accuracy with these figures that he modeled the lead horse, carrying the officer with drawn sword, nine times before he was satisfied. It is interesting to note the thumb prints of Shrady preserved on this bronze lead horse.

National Gallery of Art, West Building   *The Mall, Constitution Avenue between 4th and 7th Streets, NW   Open weekdays and Saturday 10–5, Sunday 11–6, free*

> From architecture that has dignity, splendor, permanence, people seem
> to gain an enhancement of their own personalities.
> —John Walker, second director of NGA

John Russell Pope's National Gallery is the city's last great edifice in the classical mold and probably the country's last art museum conceived on the aristocratic model of a princely palace. Pope was to design 14 buildings* in Washington, and they were all impervious to the notion that modern technology of steel and concrete construction should have any effect on traditional concepts of how a building's plan and facade should be expressed. Louis Sullivan had prophesied that the reactionary impact of Chicago's Columbian Exposition of 1893 would

---

* Twelve of which survive as of 1981.

"endure for half a century." As the last of the monumental buildings to be commissioned by the government before the coming of World War II, Pope's Jefferson Memorial (1943) and National Gallery (1941) confirm Sullivan's prophecy that the urge for eclectic revivalism would take a long time to run its course. Unless some unpredictable Roman spring reoccurs in architectural taste, these two buildings—both echoes of the Pantheon—are quite possibly the last marble domes to be erected in the city.

When Pope's new gallery was dedicated, it won the instant approval of popular taste; people liked the magnificent and sumptuous effect for which it strove, and which it achieved. The modesty of Mellon's gift, in proscribing the use of his name, had made a monument for Everyman more becoming. But professional architects of the day were less comfortable with the results, finding them out of step with the esthetics of modernism, and the official *AIA Journal* disparaged the building as platitudinous.

Even a quarter century after the West Building was finished, architectural critics withheld their enthusiasm. The architectural historians John Burchard and Albert Bush-Brown in a history sponsored by the American Institute of Architects, show their disdain in this judgment:

> Many architects escaped the challenges altogether. There were lingering classicists . . . like Cass Gilbert and John Russell Pope, who kept on grinding out classic monuments at Washington; the Supreme Court and the National Gallery of Art—buildings of a hollow and pompous cast, despite materials so rich that any modernist envied them the opportunity. . . .
>
> It might have been hoped that a new National Gallery would lead the way; but Pope's confection of 1939–1941 was an outdated extravaganza of multiple-returned cornices, pilasters and entablatures intended to provide genteel backgrounds for fine Italian primitives but not really well suited for the exhibition of any art, architecture or sculpture, ancient or modern.*

Whatever the unresolved doubts about matters of style—and they persist—there are no questions about the excellence of what is now called the West Building in terms of the suitability of its scale to the site and the quality of its materials.

Pope's severely symmetrical plan presents an austere horizontal building with a central rotunda on the 6th Street axis and two windowless wings stretching a total of 780 feet. (His first rendering had called for a columned portico and pediment at the east and west fronts, but these were later eliminated in favor of au-

* *The Architecture of America,* abridged ed. (Boston: Little Brown, 1966), pp. 379, 419.

dacious, heroic-scale bronze doors set into the podium at ground level.) The facades of both the Mall and the Constitution Avenue fronts of the building place exclusive emphasis on the *piano nobile,* for which London's National Gallery appears to have been a model. (The *piano nobile* is an Italian term for the principal and important floor—but not the ground floor—whether in a country villa or in a brownstone parlor; it is conceived as a noble floor for noble architectural purposes.) Pope gave no thought to the public use of the ground-floor spaces, though they were later pressed into service for temporary exhibitions not contemplated in the client's original program.

The basic masonry structure of the gallery consists of bearing walls of brick covered by an articulated cladding of marble blocks in modules of two feet by five feet and in varying shades of pink. When the architect inspected the first shipments of marble as they arrived from the quarries in Tennessee, he was distressed to observe that there were five different gradations in the shades of pink. He prescribed that the darkest pink should be used and the balance rejected. But the quarry reported that there was not enough of the marble in any one shade to fill the full order. And here arose one of those fortuitous accidents which talented architects have the wit to exploit. Pope prescribed that the darker pink marble should go into the podium at the bottom with the lighter gradations being employed in turn up to the nearly white dome. These color nuances enhance the exterior and are best appreciated when the marble is still wet after a light rain.

Whether the visitor enters from the ground-level vestibule on Constitution Avenue or up the sweep of steps leading to the high portico òverlooking the Mall, he must, before encountering any of the 100 rooms full of paintings, traverse the rotunda under the central dome which divides the *piano nobile* into two wings (each ending in a garden court), and which serves as a central focus for all further explorations.

This circular hall is 100 feet in diameter, covered by a coffered dome with a circular oculus window. There are 24 huge green black columns capped by white Ionic capitals, arrayed to support the drum of the dome without obstructing the entrances at the four cardinal points of the compass. These columns are of brecciated Carrara marble, *brecciated* meaning a kind of conglomerate rock imbedded with angular fragments, in these examples like large chunks of white confetti in a predominantly black ground. They are from quarries near Lucca in Italy, but before being installed here, they were shipped to Vermont for cutting and polishing. The floor of the hall is of Vermont verde antique marble. And elsewhere in the gallery we can find examples of stone, marble, and granite from 40 different quarries: limestone interior walls from Alabama, travertine fountains from the Ozarks, marble from Missouri in the rest rooms, as well as rarer varieties of Istrian Nuage from Italy and Radio Black from Vermont.

The floodlit bronze figure of Mercury hovers over the fountain like a small ballet figure over a great chalice, providing this otherwise static chamber with a grace note of light and movement. Mercury was the messenger of the pagan gods, bearer of news and protector of the travel weary; he wears a winged hat and winged sandals and carries a staff with the intertwined serpents of the caduceus. This bronze statue is a Flemish version of the original sculpture by Giovanni Bologna, and it is the sole iconographic figure in a profane grove of marble columns—a great circular empty space richly furnished but otherwise devoid of symbolism.

We can recall that Rome's original Pantheon (which was half again larger than this variation on the theme) has survived since it was first built in the uninterrupted service of religion, first as a pantheon to the heathen gods, but since the 7th century as a reliquary for the bones of Christian martyrs from the catacombs rededicated as S. Maria Rotunda. In the National Gallery architectural splendor has become an end in itself. The rotunda has sometimes been pressed into ceremonial service for presidential inaugurations as a reception hall for the wife of the president to receive the wives of visiting dignitaries.

The gallery's first curator, John Walker, has said that "the building was intended to satisfy an often unrecognized desire on the part of the public. In this country there is a lack of the magnificent churches, public buildings and palaces of Europe; Americans living for the most part in apartments and small houses feel the need for buildings more sumptuous, more spacious·and less utilitarian than their everyday surroundings."

When the British art critic Kenneth Clark first visited the gallery he found the rotunda "oppressively grandiose," but more recently he has softened his judgment: "In this age art has taken the place of religion, and what Mr. Mellon envisaged was really a sort of cathedral. Now that the National Gallery is always full of eager and appreciative people I can share their admiration for the central rotunda." Hugh Thomas in *A History of the World* goes further: "It has, sometimes, seemed in the nineteenth or twentieth centuries, as if art had been a substitute for God." If such is the case, John Russell Pope has given us a temple for the profane.

Immediately to the east of the Mall entrance is the large Founders Room of painted oak (one of the few where smoking is permitted) containing 10 portraits of the founding benefactors. As a survey of the art of portraiture it displays more concentrated variety than can be found in any room of the National Portrait Gallery. It is a good place to test the truism that a portrait has to be disqualified as a likeness—or perhaps even a work of art—if the sitter is pleased with the result.* Above the fireplace mantel Andrew Mellon is exuberantly canonized by Oswald Birley. Chester Dale, another founder, frequently commissioned pictures from artists who were his friends and whose works he collected; among these were George Bellows, who did the fine portraits of Dale and his wife Maud. There is a De Laszlo of Ailsa Mellon Bruce, and Leopold Seyffert did the two Kresses. The best delineations of character, the most striking figures, are those of Joseph Widener by John Singer Sargent and his son Peter A. B. Widener by Augustus John. The most recent portraits, those of Paul Mellon by William F. Draper and Lessing Rosenwald by Oscar Cox, seem the most dated.

Andrew Mellon began and ended his career as a collector with an almost exclusive concentration on his taste for Old Masters—oil paintings by artists of established reputation in 16th-, 17th-, and early 18th-century Europe, the cream of pictorial art of Western civilization. He made his first purchases at the age of 27 when he accepted the invitation of another young Pittsburgh millionaire—the 30-year-old Henry Clay Frick—to make a joint grand tour of the art capitals of Europe. By the time Mellon came to Washington in 1921 as secretary of the treasury under President Harding, he had picked up enough Rembrandts here and Van Dykes there to furnish his 15-room apartment richly. In fact, for visitors from abroad, a dinner invitation to Mr. Mellon's offered the only opportunity in Washington to see the kind of Old Masters on view in their own capitals.

By the time Mellon went to London as ambassador in 1932, his collection had become truly notable. He was not without competition from other American collectors, but he made the most of the rare opportunities that political events in Europe were creating to acquire the kind of exceptional works that seldom come on the market. When Knoedler and Company and Colnaghi, the art dealers of New York and London, learned that the Soviet government was prepared to surrender some of the masterpieces from the collection established by Catherine the Great in the Hermitage, they suggested that if Mellon would advance them $7 million—together with an indication of his personal preferences—they could assure him first choice of anything they were able to acquire. He agreed, and as it turned out ended up buying—sight unseen—everything they wrested from the Hermitage, including Botticelli's *Adoration of the Magi* and two stunning Raphaels, *St. George and the Dragon* and *The Alba Madonna*—the latter being the first picture for which anyone ever paid more than $1 million. Mellon's purchase of 21 Hermitage pictures in 1931 made up one-third of the value of Soviet

* Of his portrait of her, Gertrude Stein protested to Picasso that she didn't look like that. "No, but you will," he replied—and eventually she did.

exports to America in that year; the financing of the five-year plan in Stalin's view was much more important than nurturing the national treasury of art. Mellon was rather circumspect about these purchases, partly out of secrecy over his eventual intentions, partly out of sensitivity to the general distress of unemployment and bank failures of the day.

Mellon's gift of the gallery to the nation was not to be consummated without a sordid wrangle over tax evasion—the fate of many other collectors since. A weekly magazine accused him of "dangling a huge sugar plum before the United States people." Mellon filed with the Internal Revenue Service a retrospective claim to have bestowed the pictures in question to the "A.W. Mellon Educational and Charitable Trust." His case was tainted by failure to make any public disclosure of his plans at the time of the alleged gift to the trust, by his failure to claim a deduction for the gift on his tax return for the year in which it was claimed, and by the circumstance that only Andrew Mellon and not his trust held the key to the storage rooms in the basement of the Corcoran where most of the collection was kept. Mellon disparaged the affair—initiated by the first Democratic administration in 12 years—as "politics of the crudest sort." His art dealer Lord Duveen testified in the Board of Tax Appeals hearing that the controversy was unworthy of his client's collection, which he described quite simply as "the finest in the universe." The board was strongly influenced by the art dealer's eloquence and eventually ruled in his client's favor.

Olympian, Andrew Mellon may have been, but the fact remains that acting solely as an individual entrepreneur of great taste, determination, and daring, he assembled a collection deserving to be called a *national gallery,* one that could never have been put together by a committee, a foundation, or a philanthropic bureaucracy.

When Mellon was serving as secretary of the treasury, that department had jurisdiction over the construction of federal buildings; this afforded him an ex officio vantage point as well as a literal one—looking down the Mall out of the window of his treasury office—to select and reserve the best remaining site for the structure, which he never lived to see.

During his tour as ambassador to the Court of St. James's, Mellon studied how the National Gallery in London was governed; he queried its director Kenneth Clark closely about how its trustees functioned as a mixture of private collectors and high public officials appointed by the prime minister but free of political interference. He proposed, and gained, congressional sanction for a similar formula to administer his new gallery in Washington. The NGA board of trustees is composed of four ex officio members prescribed by statute (the chief justice of the United States, the secretaries of state and treasury, and the secretary of the Smithsonian Institution), who are outnumbered by five private citizen suc-

National Gallery of Art, West Building

cessor trustees—usually including a number of art collectors and patrons. The chief justice of the United States had always served as chairman, until recently when Chief Justice Burger complained of the press of other duties. The board is now presided over by John R. Stevenson, a managing partner of Sullivan and Cromwell—not a chief justice but something like the next best thing. The prestige of its independent board and its separate endowment afford it a high degree of autonomy.

The advantage of having a chief justice on the board was well illustrated at the time of the bequest of P.A.B. Widener, the Philadelphia traction magnate. Philadelphians wanted to keep the collection in their city and the state of Pennsylvania was demanding an inheritance tax of $195,000, knowing that Widener's will stipulated that if his pictures were to be given to the public no inheritance tax should be paid by the estate. Chief Justice Harlan Stone explained the matter to President Franklin D. Roosevelt, and the two of them persuaded Congress to appropriate the entire sum due the state of Pennsylvania—the first and probably the last time the Congress ever appropriated money to pay the state tax of a private citizen.

As an official of the treasury Mellon had also learned about civil service regulations and discovered some of the limitations of bureaucratic organizations. Thus he established a separate endowment so that the gallery's six top officers could be paid from private rather than official funds. It is characteristic of the founder's self-confidence that when the new National Gallery first opened neither any of the trustees nor any of the new staff had had any previous experience in running a museum (except for Duncan Phillips, who was still in the process of teaching himself). The first director was David E. Finley, Mr. Mellon's lawyer and former aide at treasury. The term *museology* had not then been invented, and there were no apologies for an implicit elitism of the collection's major focus on Old Masters—with a limited but specific charter for inclusion of American works of art of the highest quality. No works of art were to be accepted except from artists who had been dead for more than 20 years. Mr. Mellon's letter of gift to the president prescribed that "future acquisitions . . . shall be limited to objects of the highest standard of quality, so that the collection shall not be marred by the introduction of art that is not the best of its type." As a result the new National Gallery became certainly the youngest museum and possibly the last to achieve world-class "eminence as a summary of the history of art through superior examples."*

Mellon's gift of 121 Old Masters was the largest gift of any individual to any

* John Canaday, writing in the *New York Times* on the gallery's 25th anniversary, 20 March 1966.

government. When his apartment overflowed, the latest acquisitions from the Kremlin were stored in the basement of the Corcoran Gallery where he would inspect them in cramped and solitary circumstances. During his lifetime the collection was never assembled together in one place. When the paintings were finally displayed in the new gallery in 1941, they filled only a few crannies, leaving most of the five and a half acres of gallery space empty and with no certain prospect of how it would be filled. There were about 24 works of art to the acre, and in one cavernous gallery a basketball court was set up for the guards.

Despite all the initial emptiness of the building, Mellon had had the foresight to stipulate that the Mall site to the east should be reserved for the gallery's future expansion—a reservation affirmed by Congress in accepting the gift. At that time there could have been no faint inkling of the splendid bequests to come from the Kress, Widener, Dale, and Rosenwald collections, no prospect that the gallery would have to expand into its site to the east after the passage of little more than three decades. This expansion has relegated to John Russell Pope's original gallery the revised and prosaic title of West Building, which for all its great scale now contains less display space than the new addition.

The change in title to West Building symbolizes more than the need for an expanded area for the physical display of objects of art. The current director of the gallery, J. Carter Brown, concedes that "the definition of an Old Master changes with the perspective of history." But the art historian Hans Tietze in his review of the great national galleries of the world assesses the Mellon pictures as of "such quality that they are above the normal fluctuations of taste." Be that as it may, what has changed at the National Gallery of Art is not so much a relaxation of the rigidity of its initial standards as a redefinition of its function as an institution. It began as essentially a custodial museum for the conservation and display of works of art from past history. The obligation to educate public taste was largely passive—just showing the pictures to a few scholars and the occasional Sunday visitors was enough; the role was expository rather than critical or heuristic.

With a recent high water mark of 6 million visitors a year, the gallery has acquired—like museums everywhere—an unprecedented popular constituency, and along with it a new role. It has greatly expanded its educational services and exhibition programs to schools and libraries throughout the country, and sales of publications and reproductions have grown accordingly. Scholarly research has increased in the field of conservation as well as in curatorial areas. The gallery's program now fully embraces the recognition of contemporary art and American artists to an extent not anticipated at the time it was founded. A university level of scholarship was established with the new Center for Advanced Studies in the Visual Arts. The narrow concept of *fine arts,* suggestive of an area beyond popular grasp, has indeed been outmoded.

The NGA has no presumption or possibility of rivaling the comprehensive scope of survey museums like the Metropolitan or the Louvre. As a matter of curatorial policy its collections focus on American art and on the art of Western Europe from the period of the Middle Ages to the present. Nevertheless the gallery's Center for Advanced Studies in the Visual Arts (CASVA) embraces universal aspects of art in all fields—including architecture and photography.

The antipathy between curators of paintings and architects of public buildings is almost inevitable; curators want nothing in the room or on the wall that competes with the picture for the eye of the spectator; architects cannot suppress an urge to create a setting that is an object of regard in its own right. There is a competition between the container and the thing contained. An article on "Museums and Galleries" in the *Encyclopedia Britannica* of 1947 describes the problem as if it had been solved once and for all: "No longer is a lavishly decorated Renaissance palace the best home for art, because it distracts the visitor's attention. Better by far a plain box-like structure with no decoration whatever in which superb works of art become the absorbing interest."

Well, it hasn't quite worked out that way in either Pope's West Building or I. M. Pei's East Building—they are both powerful frames that compete boldly with the treasures they contain for the attention of the beholder. Scarcely a generation separates the contrasting esthetic approaches of the two buildings, yet they both struck a resonant chord in popular taste; if anything, Pei's building of today has been received with even wilder public enthusiasm than that accorded to Pope for his gallery of 1941.

National Gallery of Art, East Building   *The Mall, Constitution Avenue between 3rd and 4th Streets, NW   Same hours as West Building.*

The conception of the National Gallery's expanding program . . . is going to alter the way we think about museums for generations to come.
—Hilton Kramer, *New York Times,* 9 June 1974

Washington had to wait until the last quarter of the century to get, in I. M. Pei's East Building of the National Gallery of Art, its first unmistakable example of 20th-century architecture. The city has very few buildings that express the philosophy of modern architecture; the monumentality of its most important buildings is itself anti-modernist in spirit. That the East Building, completed in 1978, is both modern and monumental is but one of its many distinctions. Most of the capital's monumental buildings could function quite as well on one site as another, but the complex conception of the East Building is inseparable from its site—an awkward trapezoid, one of the last and most prominent unused plots of

L'Enfant's city plan. When Andrew Mellon presented the National Gallery of Art (now known as the West Building) to the nation in 1937, his deed of gift stipulated that the site immediately to the east should be reserved for future expansion; it was not in vain that his office as secretary of the treasury gave him a fine view down Pennsylvania Avenue of the sites where the West and East Buildings now stand.

When the National Gallery of Art (NGA) opened in 1941 with half-empty galleries, no one could have dreamt that it would run out of space in just 30 years' time; but the gallery's expanding collections as well as its greatly broadened institutional program brought an urgency to the need for expansion and dictated full use of the available site envelope. There is a rule of thumb that two-thirds of a museum's space goes to the support of what the public sees—storage, documentation, conservation, and so forth. Pope's West Building had given no thought to public use of the ground floor spaces; they were soon pressed into service for the unanticipated acccommodation of temporary shows. In addition to more exhibition space, the new building had to provide facilities for the museum's expanded role in education and scholarship, a larger library, file areas for 2 million photographs, a larger auditorium (seating 450), and a whole newly established Center for Advanced Study in the Visual Arts.

There was hardly any choice except to call the new building the East Building, although one of the less felicitous consequences is that the Sunday evening concerts now take place in "the East Garden Court of the West Building." It is all one single institution with an interlocking complex of collections and purposes. The old NGA had long since abandoned its initial embargo on the acquisition of works of living artists, but there was never any thought of building a new *modern* building to house the new *modern* paintings. A Picasso should be as at home in the old building as a Rembrandt in the new—or at least *almost* as much at home. The parts of the buildings are interchangeable; it is not a wing or a pavilion. And Paul Mellon was no more willing than his father before him to have his magnificent gift named after him. So East Building it is.

Most of the operating expenses and overhead of the National Gallery of Art comes as its own line item in the federal budget separate from the budget of the affiliated Smithsonian Institution. (Congress doesn't like homeless institutions and attached the NGA to the Smithsonian as it did the Kennedy Center—both of which have separate boards of trustees and separate budgets.) Not a cent of federal taxes went into the construction of either of its museum buildings. (And for that matter, there is not a single picture in the NGA purchased with government funds.) The East Building was a present of Paul Mellon and his associated family foundation. Instead of demanding a budget for it, he simply volunteered to underwrite whatever the project ended up costing—which turned out to be just a shade under $95 million. I. M. Pei has said that he had the ideal clients for the gallery, not just in terms of money but because he could deal directly with men of taste and authority instead of with a committee. His clients were three knowledgeable people: Mr. Mellon, J. Carter Brown, the gallery's director, and David M. Scott, who was in charge of program requirements; they could make decisions confidently and without lengthy waits for approvals. Mr. Pei says that Mr. Mellon's only injunction to him was, "Don't forget the West Building"—in other words, he should be sensitive to the merits of the older structure and take pains not to upstage it.

The existence of Pope's original gallery mandated the use of marble for the new building, and the old quarry in Tennessee was reopened to provide the same pink marble—this time in three different shades instead of the original five. Both buildings have blocks of the same two-foot by five-foot modules, except that in the old building they make up solid articulating walls while in the new they are a thin veneer. To create monumentality and to vary the scale, the architect employed sheer polygonal towers rather than conventional pediments. He was told he could not build higher than the old gallery of 1941, so his towers all rise 108 feet above the ground elevation, or one foot less than the 109-foot height of the West Building dome parapet and cornice line.

Pei's inspired strategy reconciled symmetry with asymmetry by dividing the trapezoidal plan into two triangles, accommodating optimum use of the site with axial balance and harmony. The central axis of the old building lines up directly with the midpoint of the base of the isosceles triangle that forms the main block of the new building. The main street facade faces the angular confluence of Constitution and Pennsylvania Avenues, with the latter chosen as the chief point of reference; a low marble wall, on which wisteria is beginning to grow, shields the interior from the visual clutter of automobile traffic at this busy intersection. The boldness and dynamic complexity of the scheme was further justified by the unrelieved static blandness of its neighbors; the intricacy of the East Building's interlocking polygons entangles the eye of the observer against the barren landscape of the uniformly conventional facades of the U.S. Court House, the Department of Labor, and the Carpenters' Union.

The craftsmanship of the building is nothing less than exquisite in its sensitive blend of disparate materials—marble, concrete, glass, and stainless steel—joined together to extraordinary tolerances of 1/16th of an inch. I. M. Pei and his patron have achieved an effect of polish without varnish. All the door and window spans are bridged by monolithic concrete lintels, but so carefully cast in cement mixed with marble dust in forms made by cabinetmakers that the joints between the bearing members and the marble veneer are structurally exposed but barely noticeable to the eye. The uncluttered effect of the interior is enhanced by the ingenious concealment of heating and ventilating ducts, for instance, behind marble stair risers and planters for ficus trees.

The large interior atrium is clearly designed to take care of big crowds—including those standing in lines for the special exhibitions area on the lower level. The atrium has been disparaged as resembling a suburban shopping mall; perhaps it does, but it sorts out the crowds far more hospitably than the cold Roman temple lobby of the West Building. People tell Mr. Pei that his building is sexy, and he answers that if that is the case, it is perhaps due to the fact that every area—open or closed—has not two but three triangular axes, three vanishing points, whose interplay produces a constant sense of movement. (The effect is one of distraction—at least subliminally—in a room whose main purpose is to display objects of art.) Another feature that has been called sexy is the acute dihedral edge, the vertical apex of the triangular grid—like a ship's prow—that people seem to find exhilarating. The blade-sharp 19-degree edge at the southwest corner of the building has already compelled so many visitors to reach out and touch that it is becoming as worn as the toe of St. Peter in Rome.

Such a striking museum as the East Building presents an inescapable paradox—the esthetic dilemma of the extent to which the frame of a picture should be allowed to compete with the picture itself for the attention and delight of the viewer. Museum people—directors and curators of art—tend to be distrustful of architects, suspicious that they will be tempted to go too far in producing, in the most public of the arts, an architectural object as an end in itself. The opposite extreme would be to filter out all formal and decorative elements, reducing the setting for art to that of laboratory sterility. In the East Building, no matter how much the smaller galleries are screened off from the atrium complex, no matter how muted the fine materials, the polygonal galleries with their alternation of acute and obtuse angles impose on the viewer a sense of movement and involution of which he can never be oblivious. This may be partly because the act of observation is innately conservative, the result of reflexes conditioned to the norms of orthogonality, the comfortable finite reassurance of square floors and straight walls. Whether the East or West Buildings ever become models of their genre or not, they provide no more justification for the hypothesis of museums as square boxes than the argument that pictures should be hung without frames.

What the East Building signals is the opening up of a museum's function to the broadest possible spectrum of popular participation and support. It is no accident that the big atrium rivals the main hall of the National Air and Space Museum; they both will keep an awful lot of people out of the rain. When the old NGA opened in 1941 it had two narrow clienteles: the informed connoisseur and the casual tourist in an act of conscientious homage. Those two categories have now vanished, along with the term *fine arts*. The East Building is more than additional space to show more pictures; it is the setting for an expanded program to attract and educate a whole new lay public to increasing involvement in visual arts, while at the same time advancing curatorial and scholarship standards. In terms of capital and current accounting one could figure that it costs about three dollars for every visitor who walks—at no charge—through the revolving doors of the NGA. In a television age, the museum phenomenon has apparently not yet peaked.

National Air and Space Museum, Smithsonian Institution
The Mall, Independence Avenue between 4th and 7th Streets, SW
Open daily 10–5:30, free.

> Orville Wright was still alive in 1947, the year Capt. Charles Yeager
> broke the sound barrier.
> —C. D. B. Bryan, 1979

Since the National Air and Space Museum (NASM) opened in 1976, it has become the world's most popular museum, attracting 10 million visitors a year—more than the Lincoln Memorial, the Washington Monument, the White House, and the U.S. Capitol combined. Michael Collins, the astronaut who orbited the moon in Apollo–11, was the museum's first director, and he attributes this phenomenal popularity to the fact that the museum's collections represent historical events that even the youngest visitors can recall as part of their—perhaps vicarious, but personal—experience.

The museum stretches for three city blocks—it is 685 feet long by 225 feet wide—and presents its best face to the Mall, where its main entrance is on the axis of John Russell Pope's National Gallery of Art (West Building). The Mall facade is divided into seven bays: four sheer boxes clad in a thin veneer of marble separated by three bays of tinted glass covered by acrylic bubble skylights. At the request of the Commission of Fine Arts, the space museum employs the same Tennessee pink marble as was used 35 years earlier for the art gallery. The two buildings resonate with each other across the greensward, and the inevitable vast bulk of NASM helps redeem and justify the overscale topography of the Mall.

The museum was conceived and its design was executed by experts, but they were experts who had no experience in the field of museology. The director Michael Collins was an aviator and astronaut. The architects Hellmuth, Obata and Kassabaum—with Gyo Obata as partner-in-charge—had no previous experience with museums. Collins's deputy Melvin Zisfein, who was in charge of designing the exhibits, was an aeronautical engineer whose previous museum experience was limited to research. Together, they all brought in a novel building on schedule and under cost estimates—itself a tribute to how the General Services

Administration's bureaucratic practices could be tempered by aerospace design strategies. The result is a building as much of a popular magnet as Paris's Centre Pompidou, but much better articulated in its interior.

The structural system is a very simple one consisting of steel framing and tubular trusses; the exposed trusses span the glass-enclosed bays and support many of the airplanes on display in a manner suggestive of a giant hangar. The glass bays give people outside a hint of what goes on within, while from inside they open the museum to wide views of the Mall and the Capitol, which almost become part of the display. The concept is a soaring one, a system that works both as structure and as symbolism. The largest object suspended from the tubular trussed roof is a classic Douglas DC-3, a veteran of decades of transport service.

The visitor enters NASM directly into its main exhibit hall, captioned "Milestones of Flight" in the manner of the National Geographic. This great room captures, epitomizes, and enshrines the greatest original artifacts of 66 years of air age technological progress from Kitty Hawk to the landing on the moon—a peculiarly American adventure. Here is the plane first flown by Wilbur and Orville Wright, a dour pair who skimmed the dunes in business suits and stiff collars; the longest of their four flights on 17 December 1903 was 59 seconds. (Newspapers in the Wrights' home city of Dayton did not mention the event, and the first complete description appeared the following March in a periodical called *Gleanings in Bee Culture*.) The centerpiece of the hall is *The Spirit of St. Louis*. When Charles A. Lindbergh took off in it for Paris, his cockpit was so loaded with extra gas tanks that they blocked all frontal vision and he had to turn and bank to see out of the sides of the cockpit. Here also are the Bell X-1 that broke the sound barrier in 1947, the Apollo-11 space capsule, and an actual piece of moon rock that triggers the imagination more than all the neighboring objects made by man.

It was not until 1966 that Congress expanded the charter of the National Air Museum to include space exploration and applications. As the machines progress from Kitty Hawk to the Apollo program, the combined teamwork of scientists and engineers tends to supplant the role of the individual, and the machines come to seem less and less like airplanes and more and more like devices. The newest acquisition, the man-powered *Gossamer Albatross* that was pedaled across the English Channel in 1979, helps return matters to the human scale.

NASM has two unique theaters. Its motion picture theater has a screen five stories high, designed to accommodate nine synchronized slide and movie projectors; the total effect presents a new kind of sense experience, sometimes putting the viewer dizzyingly into the driver's seat. The museum planetarium is called the Albert Einstein "Spacearium," and its Zeiss instruments and control system, a Bicentennial gift to the United States from the Federal Republic of

Germany, make it the most technically advanced planetarium extant—but one hopes it is not too late to find for this magnificent installation a worthier and more euphonious name.

Hirshhorn Museum and Sculpture Garden, Smithsonian Institution
The Mall, Independence Avenue at 8th Street, SW
Open daily, 10–5:30, free.

> I could not have done what I did in any other country. My collection belongs here.
> —Joseph H. Hirshhorn

It took a lot of artistic and professional chutzpah—of which Gordon Bunshaft has never been in short supply—to toss this monumental doughnut on the *tapis vert* of the Mall, but the circumstances of his commission in terms of the self-esteem of the client and the difficulty of the site, invited—indeed demanded—audacity.

The exigencies of the site were particularly vexing. The architect had to fill a two-block area between (1) the nostalgic 19th-century Arts and Industries Building, a fairy tale castle of polychrome brick, and (2) the huge rectangular stone and glass hangar of the National Air and Space Museum, without doing offense to (3) the Neoclassic National Gallery of Art across the Mall to the northeast, while providing an anchor for (4) a new axis to be developed across the Mall with its opposite focus at (5) the National Archives, at the same time having to suffer—and perhaps even accommodate—the banal streetscape environment created by (6) the Federal Office Building No. 10 (FOB 10) housing the Federal Aviation Administration across Independence Avenue.

Critics lamented that Bunshaft's doughnut had destroyed the Mall. Well the museum is obtrusive, but it still fits into the Mall scheme much better (for instance) than the Housing and Urban Development Building fits into L'Enfant Plaza, or than the Kennedy Center fits into the Potomac waterfront. Besides, the Mall is much too big to be offended by a building like the Hirshhorn, which has kept well within the bounds of its site. (The Mall is too big anyway—far greater than the street-level sight lines prescribed by L'Enfant, far too big for a pedestrian scale, while paradoxically being increasingly barred to vehicular traffic.)

If we are going to have an art museum in the round—a form that has its own rationale vindicated in Bunshaft's example—it will go quite as well on the Mall as anywhere else in town. I would not trade that doughnut for a conventional granite temple with columns or for a sleek glass box like its many neighbors on Independence Avenue.

Gordon Bunshaft practices architecture as managing partner of the firm of Skidmore, Owings & Merrill. He is a giver of new forms, as his many expensive monuments in New York testify. Most of his great buildings are on stilts and most of them do not "fit" the scale of their neighbors. His Lever House is on stilts; it pioneered a new open ground-floor plan and it gave Park Avenue its first glass-walled skyscraper. His Chase Manhattan Bank, on stilts, gave Wall Street its first tower in the International style. At 9 West 57th Street he gave New York its first sloping front office building, also on stilts, mirroring the sedate Plaza Hotel from one of its curving facades and offending all pedestrians at street level.

I think Bunshaft has given Washington what we deserve; it is at least what we could have expected when compared to his other major commissions. Being more daring than most of its contemporaries of the Washington architectural landscape of the 1970s, the Hirshhorn Museum may age faster than they do, but it will become—however dated—a favorite period piece at worst and a classic at best.

Once you walk past the monumental Henry Moore bronze—an almost ritual entrance artifact—you enter the glass lobby to take the escalator, and you forget about your surroundings. With great restraint every architectural function is muted and subordinated to the display of works of art. Doorways and enclosing rooms are dispensed with. The Hirshhorn does not even need a floor plan for the visitor. Wall areas flow in an easy and inviting pedestrian circuit. The circular arc of the walls is sufficiently broad to show the largest of canvases without distraction. None of the galleries for paintings have windows or skylights; they rely entirely on artificial light. All the smaller sculptures, on the other hand, are displayed in an interior ambulatory gallery flooded with daylight from the eccentrically sited circular court. Until you look down at the elliptical fountain, you forget that the building is round.

The museum's solid pink aggregate cylindrical wall is punctured by only one window, a third-floor balcony overlooking the Mall, usually described as a blockhouse or turret. But the view from this balcony is one of the finest in the city. The conventional and rather monotonous facades of the Federal Triangle and Mall buildings are relieved and bracketed by the I. M. Pei East Building complex to the right and the discordant eaves of the FBI Building to the left, exchanging a brutalistic resonance—as if drawing a bead on the Hirshhorn turret.

Five years after its opening, the Sculpture Garden is being relandscaped to provide barrier-free access as well as to introduce textures with more contrast than the bland gravel underfoot. It would be better, both from inside and out, if the solid high walls could be replaced with handsome iron grilles. And much of the sculpture would show off to better effect against the green grass of a lawn.

Perhaps ivy and other vines can eventually provide more contrasts of texture and shade.

There was an American ambassador to Rome who was an heir to the founders of the Procter & Gamble Company; he had the engaging habit upon meeting a new acquaintance of suspected affluence of inquiring, "What's yours? Mine's soap." By that standard the Mall's benefactors could say Freer's was freight cars, Kress's was 10-cent stores, Widener's was streetcars, and Hirshhorn's is uranium.

At the age of six Joseph Hirshhorn arrived at Ellis Island with his widowed mother and her family of 11 as immigrants from a Latvian ghetto. At 17 he entered the New York curb market and parlayed $225 into $168,000 in 10 months. At 28, several weeks before the crash of 1929, he sold his holdings for $4 million. At 33 he took a full-page advertisement in a Canadian newspaper announcing "My Name Is Opportunity and I Am Paging Canada." At 52 he gained control of the biggest uranium deposits ever discovered, around Blind River, Ontario, not far from the American border, and bearing more ores than all the 635 existing uranium mines in the United States. As chairman of the Rio Tinto conglomerate in Canada, he admitted the Rothschilds to a minority interest. (Take that, Lorenzo the Magnificent.)

And what did he do with all that money? He was not the first American millionaire to put the bulk of it into art. But no one before him—not even J. Pierpont Morgan or William Randolph Hearst—had done so on such a personal and wholesale scale. No one before him had bought in such quantity, on such quick impulse, and with such ravenous assurance. He never paid anybody to buy pictures and sculptures for him; no acquiring curator, no exclusive dealer or agent, no Duveen in the background.

At the time Mr. Hirshhorn presented his collection to the government it was quite possibly the largest collection ever amassed by a single private individual. His 4,000 paintings and 2,000 sculptures were twice the number that New York's Museum of Modern Art had acquired in its half-century lifetime. Most of them had never been publicly exhibited. The Hirshhorn was an "instant museum."

In the period following the Second World War, New York City for the first time snatched the palm from Paris and became the world capital of art productivity. It was a period of great ferment for dealers and art critics in Manhattan, and Mr. Hirshhorn succeeded in acquiring such a variety and profusion of the output of so many artists that his collection virtually encapsulates the art market of the time—if not like an insect caught in amber at least like a living archive of two decades of the marketplace. Thus in addition to its artistic range, the collection takes on a certain sociological or economic dimension.

On the day the U.S. government accepted the Joseph H. Hirshhorn Museum and Sculpture Garden on the donor's terms—12 May 1966—Duncan Phillips, the founder and director of the Phillips Collection, died. Seldom does one land-mark chapter of art collecting succeed another with such chronological precision.

A pioneer collector of modern art, Duncan Phillips had broken new ground as a patron of young artists as they came on the scene; but he was guided primarily by the principle of that indefinable quality called *taste,* a highly personal discrimi-nation, particularly of how pictures would show off to advantage displayed grouped together in the domestic setting of a gallery. Joseph Hirshhorn's col-lecting seemed to be free of aspirations to the taste of angels, free of preoccupa-tions with ensemble display. He was more visceral; he bought a picture when he could say, "It knocks me cold!" Phillips had the monocle of the connoisseur, Hirshhorn the wide-angle lens. Neither of their collections is comprehensive, but they are happily complementary as reflections of overlapping periods of art and different esthetic strategies.

Two decades before the opening of the Hirshhorn Museum on the Mall the art critic Aline B. Saarinen had, in her book *The Proud Possessors,* this prescient appraisal of its benefactor:

> He has never sold any of his American paintings. . . . He has never bought American art for either investment or speculation. He finds his satisfaction by seeing his judgment vindicated, not in the rise of market values, but in the subsequent approval of his "comers" by museum men and art critics.
>
> Predilection for the strong statement is the only discernible line of taste in this vast catholic enthusiasm. . . . Hirshhorn will pick the one with maximum emotional impact. His method of buying, like panning for gold, results in a large amount of dross for every few nuggets. His best things are splendid and unsurpassed; some of the rest is mediocre. . . . The con-sensus is that in sculpture his eye is almost infallible.

There were almost a dozen other contenders for the Hirshhorn collection be-fore Hirshhorn and his attorneys and the U.S. Congress finally agreed on a compact granting him almost certain recognition in the nation's capital in perpe-tuity. There are those who think he bought posterity too cheap. But not more than three blocks away the Freer Gallery provided a precedent for a memorial museum named for its donor on federal land; Freer paid for the construction of his building; Hirshhorn did not. Hirshhorn agreed to the sale or exchange of any items in his collection—deaccessioning; Freer would not even permit loans.

The negotiations for such an opulent bequest bred inevitable intrigue and ma-neuver. As secretary of the Smithsonian, Dillon Ripley was surely involved in enlisting the enthusiastic initiative of President Lyndon Johnson and Lady Bird Johnson in their ultimately effective overtures to Mr. Hirshhorn. When the congressional committee having oversight of the Smithsonian felt it had been presented with a fait accompli on the issue, one can muster a certain sympathy with Mr. Ripley in his plea that he could not be in the position of second-guessing a gift that had already been accepted by the president.

How should the vast, and increasing, holdings of the collection be reassessed in the refining experience of the passing years? Should the mediocre be winnowed away; should all the lacunae be filled in? Should, for instance, large new chunks of Jackson Pollock and Isamu Noguchi be acquired? If so, as the museum became more comprehensive, might it not also risk homogenization?

Perhaps it is providential that a round building—especially a doughnut in a walled garden—does not lend itself to incremental wings as a collection might grow. The genius of the Hirshhorn collection was that its wholesale acquisitive strategy guaranteed an almost inadvertent hospitality to a wide range of trends and movements—as compounded by money plus enthusiasm.

In his review of the Hirshhorn opening (one of his valedictory essays), the most influential art critic of his time, Harold Rosenberg, offered this appraisal:

> Had he been more respectful of the critical dogmas current during the many years of his acquisition, his collection could never have achieved its present range. . . . [it] reflects the art of our era with the neutrality of time itself. . .

And this prescription:

> If refining the Hirshhorn's Collection is to entail the "de-accessioning" of the benefactor's "mistakes," I should prefer to see the inventory remain as it stands. Since everything must reach a limit . . . it may as well be the life, taste, and time of Joseph Hirshhorn.

Arts and Industries Building, Smithsonian Institution *The Mall, Jefferson Drive at 9th Street, SW Open daily 10–5:30, free.*

Victorian architectural styles appear in a variety of subcategories with various names—romantic or mildly disparaging, depending on your point of view—of which the Smithsonian's Arts and Industries Building has been described as "bastard Swiss bellringer." The architects themselves, Adolph Cluss and Paul Schulze, describe the style as "modernized Romanesque," which they chose to harmonize with the Norman Gothic of James Renwick's neighboring Castle and to provide more practical standards of safety and efficiency. When it was completed in 1881 it was the most modern museum building in the United States.

The building is conceived in the exposition style, derived from earlier examples of the Dresden Museum and the Paris Exhibition of 1867. Its engineering functions are vigorously exposed and the place is filled with airiness and light. It is a building made to fly banners. And indeed contemporary lithographs show pennants streaming from every turret, heralding a place to savor the multiplicity of things. One half expects to find a merry-go-round in the rotunda; there is no carousel, but there is a working steam calliope which sounds forth in occasional noontime concerts. The public got its first view of the new building when it was the scene of President Garfield's inaugural ball; the newspapers described it as a crystal palace in which the contrast of the white electric lights and the thousands of yellow gas burners produced a fine effect as seen from outside through the many windows.

To a certain extent the successive buildings of the Smithsonian Institution reflect the organizational role it perceives for itself in the community as one generation yields to the next. The first building, the Castle, suggests an introspective role of medieval scholasticism. The Arts and Industries Building transmits a sense of gaiety, confidence, and celebration. The National Museum of Natural History across the Mall, completed in 1910, projects an effect of academic monumentality. And the National Museum of American History of 1964 abandons any known style and represents to many observers a simple confusion of values.

The Arts and Industries Building was erected as the National Museum in circumstances of some urgency, as it had to house some 60 freight car loads of exhibits left over from the Philadelphia Centennial of 1876. That was a six-months' World's Fair, and when it was over, 38 of the 41 foreign exhibitors and many of the state agencies, to save the expense of shipping home the objects they had on display, simply presented them to the federal government. When these trainloads of indiscriminate exhibits arrived in Washington they immediately precipitated a housekeeping crisis at the Smithsonian, which was regarded as the obvious repository. The Smithsonian's secretary, Joseph Henry, rebelled; he had always been interested in using the collections primarily for study and scientific research and he did not envision the institution as becoming either the national library or a great public museum. As usual, Congress had the final say; it simply overruled the secretary and appropriated $250,000 for a new National Museum—the name that survives over the front door today.

This was the event that won for the Smithsonian the accolade of "the Nation's Attic." It was to become, perhaps inevitably, an omnium gatherum, a cemetery of bric-a-brac, a miscellany of all sorts of things in all sorts of conditions and with little regard to their suitability or order for purposes of scientific or esthetic contemplation. Cultural artifacts of any kind were to find a home here. What began with Gatling's machine gun mounted on a camel ended up with a collection that was to include Teddy Roosevelt's personal teddy bear and the worn upholstered armchair of Edith and Archie Bunker. What began as *arts and industries* has since been subsumed in a variety of competing disciplines—anthropology, technology, and history.

Though all this may sound trivial, the consequences were far-reaching and enduring. Overnight the bequest from Philadelphia produced a fourfold increase in the size of the Smithsonian's holdings, and it brought the fields of history and technology into the mainstream of what had been the institution's previous concentration on natural history. Moreover, it completely reversed the ratio of congressional support: up to that time 90 percent of the Smithsonian income had come from the endowment and private sources, with only 5 percent from government appropriations. That 5 percent of government support for the annual budget has now grown to about 80 percent. And not the least consequence of the Philadelphia deluge has been that, in all subsequent World's Fairs held on these shores, foreign exhibitors have been proscribed from making presents to the host government and have been required to guarantee the costs of dismantling and dispersal.

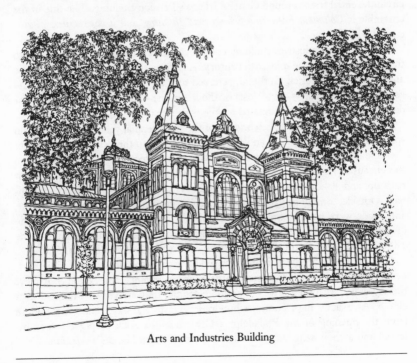

Arts and Industries Building

The building that Congress got for its quarter of a million dollars is an economic and artistic tour de force. Cluss and Schulze as architects must share part of the credit with the virtuoso Gen. Montgomery C. Meigs of the U.S. Army Corps of Engineers who drew up the original concept of the building: a square, one-story main floor with no basement, with trussed shed roofs over meandering iron balconies. Part of the rationale of its four-square plan was to allow for all of its design elements to be duplicated at least four times: four naves leading to a central rotunda describe the interior plan of circulation. The exterior is characterized by the polychromatic use of brick, tile, and slate that juxtaposes contrasting colors and textures under a maze of angular turrets and gables. The interior is flooded with light from the angles and slopes of its various roofs. Extravagant as all that looks, the result is nevertheless almost certainly the least expensive permanent building ever erected by the U.S. government. It was completed in less than 15 months for $250,000 at a net cost of six cents per cubic foot (less than three dollars per square foot of floor area).

Above the high gable end of the north nave, the museum's main entrance, is a statuary group of three female figures by Casper Buberl, the sculptor of the long circumferential frieze around General Meigs's Pension Building. The title of the ensemble is *Columbia Protecting Science and Industry,* and it is executed in zinc coated with plaster.

The Arts and Industries Building epitomized a style particularly repugnant to the popular taste of the mid-20th century. As late as 1964 the Washington critic and historian, Frederick Gutheim, referred to it as "the unhandy atrocity" and reported contendedly—or at least without protest—that it was scheduled for demolition. Why are we ashamed to live with our past?

As the centerpiece of its celebration of the Bicentennial year, the Smithsonian splendidly restored the Arts and Industries Building to the pristine condition of the time it was founded. Under the direction of architect Hugh Newell Jacobsen the encaustic floor tiles were replaced, the tin-shaded electric lights were put back up, and elaborate wall stencils were newly created in the spirit of the originals. Outside, a modern variation of Victorian garden was installed to the west, and inside were placed pots of verbena shrubs and banana trees. Many of the original objects from Philadelphia were displayed in cases and furnishings of the 1876 period. The exhibit halls were festooned with flags and bunting.

On 10 May 1976 the building was rededicated in the presence of Chief Justice Warren E. Burger, chairman of the board of regents, and Dillon S. Ripley, the secretary; with their wives in period costume, they arrived in a horse-drawn chaise. At exactly high noon—a hundred years to the day, hour, and minute from the opening of the Philadelphia Centennial—a flock of pigeons was released and a choir sang the "Hallelujah Chorus" from Handel's *Messiah.*

Freer Gallery of Art, Smithsonian Institution
The Mall, Jefferson Drive at 12th Street, SW   Open daily 10–5:30, free.

From the time it was established, the Smithsonian had included art within the range of its interests. The art objects it accumulated were not so much a collection with a sustaining theme as a casual amassment of miscellanea acquired with the easy criteria by which family treasures find their way to the attic. Paintings were hung over cases of beetles and statues loomed over glass shelves of fossils. But that all changed with the advent of the Freer Gallery in 1923; for the first time the Smithsonian got a collection of the first rank, and for the first time it got a building designed exclusively for the preservation and display of works of art. And for 40 years it was the only art museum the Smithsonian had; it now has six, not counting the National Gallery of Art.

The Freer Gallery is devoted primarily to the study and display of Oriental art, the fine arts of the Near East and the Far East. For instance, in the field of Chinese art it has no less than 42 centuries of Chinese paintings in albums and on scrolls, panels, and screens; it excels in bronzes, jade sculptures, lacquers, and porcelain of the Classic period, the Tang and Sung dynasties.

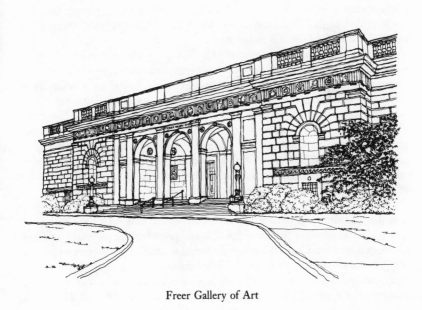

Freer Gallery of Art

Just as the term *fine arts* is itself in decline, so are the designations *Near East* and *Far East* because of their parochial implication of Western ethnocentrism. The less pejorative terms are (culturally) *Oriental* and (geographically) *East Asian*. Whatever the terminology, the art of these cultures is not everybody's dish, which is one of the reasons why the Freer Gallery, even at the height of the tourist season, is one of the most peaceful places in the city, a refuge conducive to the solitary and contemplative regard of exotic complexity. The Freer is a haven of exquisiteness, a treasure house of somber wit.

Most people, at least most Westerners, find it difficult to appreciate fully the art of the Orient without some detailed background knowledge of the historical and cultural context from which the particular work derives. This is true of all art, but especially so of artifacts from ancient and alien cultures, and the art of East Asia is apt to be inaccessible to those not initiated in its complexities. Do not look for easy abstractions; expect no inviting nudes. When you visit the Freer, it helps if you have some familiarity with the vocabulary of calligraphy or the symbolism of Oriental philosophy and religion or even the relation of art to class structure—objects commissioned by a courtly patron are different in kind from those of the scholarly amateur. A vase or urn or scroll can reveal much deeper beauties to those with a knowledge of the precise social and historical circumstances of the particular dynasty involved. It is an art for connoisseurs. Perhaps this is the reason why the Freer, though the casual visiting tourist is made to feel entirely welcome, seems like a university museum designed primarily for the purposes of scholarship.

Among the outstanding museums of Oriental art in North America the Freer is not only the foremost—its director is generally acknowledged as near the pinnacle of his profession in our country—but one of the few to enjoy a wholly independent architectural setting. At the chief survey museums—Boston, Cleveland, the Metropolitan in New York, and the Royal Ontario Museum in Toronto—one walks through long galleries of irrelevance to find the Oriental treasures. Other comparable collections of Oriental art are the Avery Brundage collection in San Francisco, the William Rockhill Nelson-Atkins Gallery in Kansas City, and the Fuller collections in the Seattle Art Museum—all housed as adjuncts to local museums of broader scope.

Charles Freer commissioned the Beaux Arts architect Charles A. Platt to design the Florentine Renaissance palazzo to house his collection, and he had exacting specifications for the amenities it should provide. The exterior is of Stony Creek granite from Connecticut and the inside court is of Tennessee white marble. The main entrance faces the Mall and consists of a central loggia of three arches accented by Doric pilasters. (A more modest entrance on Independence Avenue is kept locked.) The building is one and a half stories, with a high basement for storage and service functions and a main floor for the exhibit galleries, capped by a parapet railing above a frieze and cornice. The basement level is separated from the main floor by a horizontal band or string course decorated by a Vitruvian *wave scroll,* a continuous line that starts as a spiral and then reverses its curve in a concave sweep to start the next wave of the series; the effect is to relieve the otherwise static elements of design.

Smithsonian buildings tend to reflect the perceived role of the institution in the changing values of successive decades. Contrast the introvert Freer (1923) with its forbidding privacy of an Italian palace—a little elitist—with the inviting openness of the National Gallery of Art's extrovert East Building (1978).

Mr. Freer liked to show his treasures to friends in small doses, displaying just a few at a time; in the same spirit Platt's galleries—and the exhibit cases that he also designed—can accommodate less than 10 percent of the holdings. The rest

Freer Gallery: Wave-Scroll Decoration

of the collection is permanently reserved in storage vaults and stacks where scholars spend their time describing, analyzing, and dating the objects. In the workrooms for ceramics the floors are heavily carpeted and the tables padded with cork. Freer had no pretensions to scholarship, and he deferred to scholars on all questions of attribution. At the Freer it is not unusual for scholars to come from Japan to study Japanese screens. Individuals may bring items to curators for authentication, but appointments should be made well in advance.

The Freer bequest is one of the most restrictive on record. None of the items may be removed even for loan to similar institutions, and the building may not shelter items borrowed from elsewhere. (But the museum is generous in providing color transparencies on request.) No items may be deaccessioned; the endowment provides about a quarter of a million dollars a year for acquisition—sometimes for a dozen objects, sometimes for just one, but each having to be approved by the secretary of the Smithsonian, a practice virtually ruling out acquisitions from auctions. Frames may be sent out for repair or restoration; paintings may not.

Charles Freer was born in Kingston, New York, of a family so poor that he had to leave school after the seventh grade to work in a cement factory and later as a clerk in a general store. His forte was accounting and he soon became accomplished in the myriad resources of double-entry bookkeeping. He worked as an accountant for the Eel River Railroad until it was bought out by the Wabash, when he moved to Detroit to start—at the age of 24—a company to manufacture railroad cars. The railroad industry was just at the point of converting from the old wooden cars to steel rolling stock for both freight and passengers. Freer was to make the most of this kind of manufacturing opportunity, but he was interested chiefly in the financial controls rather than in the engineering or production aspects.

In 1899 he organized the merger of 13 railroad car manufacturing companies into what was to become the American Car and Foundry Company. One year later, at the age of 44, he retired from business to devote his full time to the collecting of art.

Freer was a fastidious bachelor of delicate stature. He wore a Vandyke beard and pince-nez glasses. In *The Proud Possessors,* Aline B. Saarinen describes him as follows:

> He could not suffer a chef who knew nothing of "pastry-work." . . . Many of his chefs were returned to New York from his Middle Western home having survived but a single meal. His finicky scrutiny missed no detail from the flat silver and the ivory dishes with gold edges on his table to the size of the monograms embroidered on his sheets and pillow cases by the

nuns of a nearby convent. . . . He was aghast at crude manners . . . and offended at anything but the most chivalrous conduct toward women. . . . Some of the Detroit industrialists complained that "Charley Freer was no good on a picnic," preferring to talk of the tariff on Italian paintings rather than the price of steel.

From his friendship with the New York architect and boulevardier Stanford White, Freer acquired an enthusiasm for the works of those triple-named artists of the turn of the century: Thomas Wilmer Dewing, Abbott Henderson Thayer, Dwight William Tryon, and other members of that virtuous and virginal school who painted self-conscious masterpieces to be hung in imposing gilt frames. This aspect of the Freer collection is incidental and static, not to be added to by Freer's own decree, and it has not merited the attention of a full-time curator.

Freer's friendship with Ernest Fenellosa, the great scholar of Oriental art on the faculties of Harvard and the Fine Arts Academy of Tokyo, afforded him an introduction to the civilizations of East Asia. Fenellosa was a practical guide to the wily traders in the marketplaces of the Orient, and he helped Freer refine his taste without becoming either a dilettante or a scholar.

But Freer's greatest friendship was for that scourge of philistines James Abbott McNeill Whistler, whom he got to know by the reckless expedient of simply knocking on his front door one day in London. Freer's collection of Whistler has been described as virtually monopolistic. He bought 100 paintings and 1,000 graphics and even the famous Peacock Room, which he bought entire in London, installed in his house in Detroit, and finally in the southeast corner of the gallery. Whistler's *Arrangement in Black and White,* better known as *Whistler's Mother,* escaped from Freer's clutches; it was bought in Paris—eventually for the Louvre—for less than $1,000. (A provincial New York lady is said to have observed, "I don't know why they make so much of that picture. She was only a McNeill from Philadelphia.") But Freer did get *Whistler's Father,* a small canvas lacking the artist's usual flair; it has none of the tenderness reserved for mothers.

National Museum of American History, Smithsonian Institution

The Mall, Constitution Avenue at 14th Street, NW   Open daily 10–5:30, April–Labor Day evenings till 9, free.

The National Museum of American History (NMAH)* was completed in 1964 as the first new building to be erected on the Mall since John Russell Pope's

* In October 1980, with congressional approval, the name of the former National Museum of History and Technology was changed to the National Museum of American History.

National Gallery of Art of 1941. The Smithsonian awarded the commission to the last of the great Beaux Arts architectural firms, McKim, Mead and White, and it was completed by the successor firm of Steinmann, Cain and White, with Walker O. Cain as partner-in-charge. Thus the NMAH is professionally and chronologically the end—one might say the dead end—of the Mall's institutional buildings in the Beaux Arts tradition.

The architects employed the finest of materials—a veneer of Tennessee pink marble, door and window frames of stainless steel, and fountain steps of Minnesota pearl pink granite—for an effect that is serene and symmetrical but sterile and starved to the point of anorexia. The designer strove for compatibility with the columned porticoes of the Federal Triangle neighbors across Constitution Avenue and created a facade stressing the verticality of alternating recessed bays. Cornice strips spanning the bays are supported by outriggers that cast revealing shadow patterns in the afternoon sun; except for this hint of modulation, the long facade is devoid of pediments or columns or ornament of any kind. The result is a classicism so stripped that nothing is left but a boxlike "timelessness"—an esthetic like that of Edward Durell Stone's Kennedy Center, which attempts to reconcile classical and modern by suppressing the best features of each.

Boxlike or not, the place works very well as a museum, for museums today—like department stores—have no need for windows except for a few show windows at street level to entice the customer inside. Natural light simply isn't good enough any more; only artificial light can provide the kind of control needed to preserve and protect objects while exposing them at the same time to dramatic display.

There aren't many museums of national history, not organized that way as a discipline. History is an aspect of cultural self-regard manifest in the NMAH as a collection of objects—the collection and display of artifacts of social custom, military and political events, as well as simple housekeeping and applied technology, objects acquired by a combination of happenstance, default, and curatorial ingenuity. Within the Smithsonian it started as what was called the U.S. National Museum, which included natural history, and took in every leftover to become the nation's attic; in 1858 it received as a transfer the model collections of the U.S. Patent Office; in 1876 Congress added the deposit of the relics from the Philadelphia Centennial Exposition. It grew into an amassment of things, chattels, trivia, paraphernalia, and bags and baggage beyond the limits of any rational program.

Here under one roof are: George Washington's false teeth, the 17-foot-long beard of Hans Longseth, the largest lump of anthracite coal, a 280-ton Southern Railroad steam engine and tender, a painting on cobwebs, Gabrielle Chanel's "plain black dress," Muhammad Ali's boxing gloves, Frank Robinson's baseball mitt, and Judge Sirica's robe from the Watergate trial.

More than any museum in town, the NMAH is a place that has something for everyone. Anyone bored here is jaded indeed. From the Mall level one enters the central hall with the Foucault pendulum and the Star-Spangled Banner that flew over Fort McHenry. It is just a few paces to the most popular display in the museum, the First Ladies Hall, where the most recent addition is a replica of the White House's Red Room as restored by Jacqueline Kennedy in 1961—the walls are of cerise silk with gold borders. Here the inaugural gowns of all the first ladies are displayed, but do not look for likenesses, as the faces of all the mannequins are the same. My favorite display is not the doll house or the soda fountain of 1910 or the classic automobiles, but the trolley cars: a chart shows how street cars peaked in the United States in 1906, a year when you could go by trolley from Cleveland all the way to Chicago. (Some exhibits are almost too dramatic. The Maritime Hall is so evocative of a seafood restaurant that you half expect a hostess to seat you. To me, those ship models were more romantic in the old plain glass cases in which they were displayed before being tarted up with blocks and tackle and cargo nets.)

The curators at NMAH concentrate on *things* rather than patterns and abstractions; they study the development and practical application of artifacts. The NMAH library concentrates on history written in objects, and you will find little on the history of ideas and nothing on literature, but it holds the largest collection in the country of trade association periodicals, manufacturers' product specifications, and technical journals. For instance there are all issues of the journal of the funeral trade—called *Casket and Sunnyside*—going back to 1924, while the serials of *Dental Cosmos* (filed next to *Delaware History*) date back to 1879.

The Smithsonian Institution is constantly making philosophical and organizational adjustments to cope with such a miscellaneous range of materials with some kind of curatorial discipline and consistency. Natural History was the senior disciple and the first to break away from the omnibus U.S. National Museum. (And now the Museum of Natural History itself is on the point of spawning a separate Museum of Man.) At the turn of the century the U.S. National Museum established a Department of Engineering and Industries which subsumed the history of technology, the history of invention, and the history of engineering. These disciplines came into their own when, in 1954, the Smithsonian founded the National Museum of History and Technology (NMHT) and authorized its own new building now called the NMAH. The old NMHT concept incorporated a certain convenient ambiguity in which *history* and *technology*, linked together, embraced two not quite commensurable concepts—

history being local and peculiar to a time and place, while *technology* was more universal in general applicability.

When the present NMAH building was in its planning stage in the 1950s, Dr. Eugen Diesel (the son of the inventor of the Diesel engine) called on the secretary of the Smithsonian to present some unsolicited advice: he urged the Smithsonian not to duplicate the mistake of the Deutsches Museum in Munich in its attempt to present the history of technology as a pure state of the art, an abstraction isolated from its national economic and social context in Germany. A sympathy for this point of view had been reflected in the title of NMHT; it was to be a museum of technology, but of technology in the context of the specific historic experience of the American nation.

When the museum changed its name in 1980 to the NMAH, it perhaps achieved some gain in tidiness but at the expense of having technology relegated to a kind of curatorial limbo. The change also compounded the practical problems of organizing and studying the collections of glass, ceramics, postage stamps, and numismatics, of which the major portions are non-American. In the long run no harm will be done, for as Paul Perrot, the Smithsonian assistant secretary for museum programs, has observed, "The object imposes its own discipline."

In the face of all this taxonomic confusion nothing could be more appropriate than the symbolic sculptural emblem chosen to preside over the museum's entrance from the Mall. It is the first piece of abstract sculpture to be commissioned by the federal government,* and it is called *Infinity*, with no parochial national or historical implications. The sculptor Jose de Rivera conceived of it as a kind of Möbius strip incorporating a reclining figure-8 of infinity (in mathematical expression). It is made of thin strips of polished stainless steel designed to turn very slowly at the rate of a full revolution every six minutes. The result is a lyric creation, much more dramatic than the original plans for a Renaissance orrery describing the movement of celestial bodies in a skeletal globe.

The chief piece of sculpture inside the museum is strictly historical. The ridiculous statue of George Washington by Horatio Greenough has finally found a refuge, if not a home, at the west end of the main hall. It was originally commissioned by Congress in 1832 to be placed under the Rotunda of the Capitol; the resolution stipulated that it should be a standing figure and that the head should be a copy of Houdon's statue of Washington in the State Capitol at Richmond, with "the accessories left to the judgment of the artist." Greenough paid no attention to that kind of official meddling, but what he did pay attention to was the totally nude statue of Napoleon by Antonio Canova and to the seven

---

* Not counting, of course, the Washington Monument.

times life-size statue of Zeus by Phidias. After eight years of labor Greenough finished the statue in his studio in Florence, and the navy had to dispatch a man-of-war to fetch it from Italy in 1841. Then, when the statue arrived at the Capitol, the door had to be partially cut away to bring it into the Rotunda. And when it was finally installed the floor began to sink. The seated, half-naked figure of Washington with a toga draped over his knees and right shoulder provoked only derision and embarrassment. A Virginia statesman said, "The man does not live, and never did live, who saw Washington without his shirt." Greenough was not amused and complained of the public's hypocrisy. "The same purblind squea-

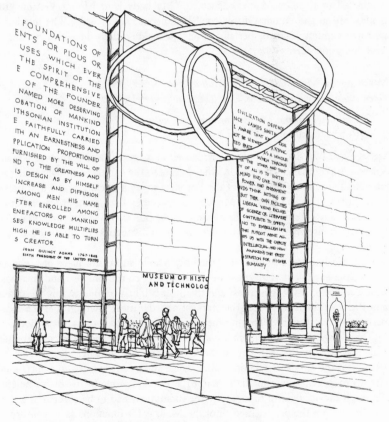

National Museum of American History: *Infinity* by Jose de Rivera

mishness which gazed without alarm at the lascivious Fandango," said Green-ough, "awoke with a roar at the colossal nakedness of Washington's manly breast."

The statue was promptly removed from the Rotunda and banished to the east grounds of the Capitol. In 1908 it was given to the Smithsonian in a gesture more desperate than generous. Here at the NMAH it is preserved as an historic rather than an artistic treasure—perhaps as a suggestion that an American presi-dent is too important a political figure to serve as an imperial symbol. Though the 14-foot ceiling of the hall is too low for Washington to stand up, he is at least out of the rain and the toga in his lap no longer catches water to serve as a bird bath. Some of the guides have various versions of what the seated Washington would tell us if he could speak, such as "My body is at Mount Vernon, my clothes are in the Patent Office," or "I said soap, not sword." The left hand gestures vaguely upward, perhaps toward a hickory limb on which he might have hung his shirt.

Washington Monument   *The Mall at 15th Street, NW*
Open daily 9–5, April–Labor Day 8 A.M. to midnight, free.

Obelisks are markers of beginnings and endings.
—Robert Harbison, *Eccentric Spaces*

George and Martha Washington are buried in a simple family tomb at Mount Vernon; foreign heads of state on official visits to the capital habitually repair to that family crypt on the banks of the Potomac to lay a wreath on the first presi-dent's tomb. The Washington Monument, the city's focal point at the center of the Mall, is not a mausoleum or a sarcophagus but a *cenotaph:* a memorial to a hero buried elsewhere, and a reminder of the indebtedness of the living to the dead.

The Washington Monument is the only wholly successful piece of architec-ture in the capital. It achieves majesty. It is at once the simplest and the most subtly complex; it is the heaviest and the most brightly luminous; it is the tallest and the least forbidding; it is the starkest and the most inviting; it is the most permanent and the most familiar memorial ever devised for a national hero.

The Washington Monument accords to the capital the same kind of symbolic scale and identity that Big Ben does for London and the Eiffel Tower does for Paris. It is the only vertical note lending scale and a central focus to a horizontal city whose skyline is limited by fiat to a fraction—one-fifth—of its height. Through the accident of topography the monument had to be erected at a spot off-center from the proper median of the Mall, yet it functions as a cynosure at the terminus of every main avenue of approach to the city. Though it rises starkly on a grassy knoll, without any landscaping or any monumental street-scape setting, it is nevertheless dramatic in its involvement of the approaching visitor. At a height of 555 feet 5⅛ inches, it is the world's tallest solid masonry structure, and at the time that its capstone was set in a howling gale in 1884 it was the tallest structure on earth.

The monument is visible for many miles beyond the District limits. At night it reveals an impressive display of the floodlighter's art: it was found that un-modulated lighting tended to make the corners of the obelisk disappear, so one axis has brighter light beams than the other to bring the corner edges into sharp relief. The windy spaces of the Mall and passing clouds produce a pattern of constantly shifting intensity, of flickering gossamer shadows on immovable stone. Insects attracted by the brilliance fall prey to whirling nighthawks.

The site for the monument was originally selected by Pierre Charles L'Enfant as the centerpiece of his plan for the Mall: it was to be an equestrian statue of George Washington on the crossing of the western axis of the Capitol with the southern axis of the White House. It is a curious fact of history that while Washington objected to the expenditure of federal funds for his statue, he was a man who knew his own destiny and approved the site at which it should be recorded for posterity. The true intersection of those axes is marked today by a simple stone marker placed there in 1804 by Thomas Jefferson, and replaced in 1889. That particular spot was marshy, and the site of the monument had to be relocated to higher and more solid ground some 360 feet east and 120 feet south of the ideal center position.

The unadorned monument we see today was never the conception of a single artistic genius; it results from a marriage of architectural and engineering skills brought about by force majeure and default. The original design for the monument and many variations later proposed were, without exception, atrocious, and they all failed from delays, from lack of public support, from the intervention of the Civil War, and above all from that last resort which rescued so much Washington architecture from excess—lack of funds. There was of course no Commission of Fine Arts in existence at the time, but we may wonder whether it would have had the courage of Congressman Robert C. Winthrop, who induced the building committee to omit the pantheon at the base with the argument that "I fall back on the simple shaft as . . . free from anything tinsel or tawdry." The design evolved through compromise and pragmatism so that only the essential survived: a simple obelisk.

Even before Washington's death in 1799 Congress had talked of a memorial to the first president, but was always to drag its feet about appropriating funds and even committing itself to the agreed-upon site on the Mall. A National Monument Society was organized (largely by Washington's fellow Freemasons) in 1833 to sponsor a design and a direct appeal to the public. Subscriptions of one dollar were solicited from Americans in every state. The trustees held a design competition prescribing a "harmonious blend . . . of durability, simplicity and grandeur," and notwithstanding those criteria, the award was given to Robert Mills for his design of a decorated obelisk 600 feet high rising from a circular colonnade 100 feet high sheltering a pantheon of tombs for George Washington and other heroes of the Revolution; the entrance portico was to be capped by a Neoclassic statuary group with Washington driving a *quadriga*—a four-horse chariot. It was like a single candle in a birthday cake, and we are fortunate that only the candle survives because all that cake and icing was more than the citizens wanted to pay for.

In its early days the American nation had a poverty of symbolism. The royal sovereign was replaced by a president whose value as a symbol was negligible. George Washington became the symbolic culture hero, but efforts to personify him in classical Roman trappings were clumsy and ineffective. Horatio Greenough's statue of the seated Washington partially draped in a Roman toga was erected on the Capitol grounds in 1841, and it was quickly recognized as an embarrassing failure, a kind of travesty that only helped spur the popular support for some other kind of monument on the Mall. The ideal Washington was to become not personified but abstracted in the Washington Monument as a totally symbolic form: there was a fusion of both romantic and classical impulses that generated the tallest of all 19th-century obelisks.

An *obelisk* is a four-sided pillar, usually monolithic, that gradually tapers as it rises and terminates in a pyramid, or a *pyramidion* as it is called when at the apex of an obelisk. This monument is obviously not a monolith, but the stone blocks that make up its walls taper from a thickness of 15 feet at the base to 18 inches at the top of the shaft. From the days of antiquity obelisks occur as memorials to solar deities. The beveled facets of the pyramidion were designed to be sheathed in electrum, a precious alloy of silver and gold to catch and reflect the sun's rays like a heliograph. Obelisks were employed in Egypt and the ancient world to celebrate royal jubilees, as sepulchers and as sacrificial altars. Imperial Rome greatly admired obelisks and transported a dozen of them from Egypt, including the largest extant. Sometimes they stood in pairs to dignify temple entrances like that at Alexandria, from which two of them, known as Cleopatra's Needles, were moved as trophies, one to London's Thames Embankment and the other to New York's Central Park. Their appeal has a large iconological range from the atavistic and mythical to the Freudian and phallic.

In 1848 funds for the monument had run out and the shaft had reached a height of only 160 feet, prompting Mark Twain to mock it as "a factory chimney with the top broken off." Finally in the centennial year of 1876 Congress voted funds—insufficient funds—to finish the monument, and the task was assigned to Lt. Col. Thomas L. Casey of the U.S. Army Corps of Engineers, the perennial salvagers of the city's waylaid architectural schemes. Casey had great experience in building Civil War fortifications; his first determination was that the base of the shaft was slightly tilted on an inadequate foundation, so he undermined the base and increased its bearing surface with extended concrete skirts. His second initiative was to consult with the American minister in Rome, George Perkins Marsh, for information about the traditional proportions of the classical obelisk. On the basis of the abundant archeological evidence available to him in Rome, Marsh advised that the proper obelisk should have a height 10 times the size of its base and that the pyramidion facets should be at angles of 60 degrees—much steeper than the squat bald cap envisioned by Robert Mills. America has many memorial obelisks from Bennington to Baltimore, but none have the exquisite ratio of proportions exhibited in this epitome of the form.

The monument is maintained by the National Park Service of the Department of the Interior. For many years it charged 10 cents for the elevator ride to the top, but in 1979 it dropped the fee as a nuisance which barely equaled the cost of its collection. More than a million visitors a year now ride the elevator free to enjoy the resplendent views from the small paired windows at the top of each of the four pyramidal faces. Many of them then walk down the 897 steps of the hollow shaft of the monument to be entertained and instructed by the 200-odd tributes in the form of memorial stones expressing the longings and joys of 19th-century America. Here are some of the inscriptions:

CALIFORNIA . . . YOUNGEST SISTER OF THE UNION.
THE CHEROKEE NATION, 1850
THE CITIZENS OF THE U.S. RESIDING IN FOO CHOW FOO, CHINA
THE ISLAND OF PAROS AND NAXOS, GRECIAN ARCHIPELAGO
THE ALEXANDRIAN LIBRARY IN EGYPT
THE MORMON STATE OF DESERET
OTTER'S SUMMIT, VIRGINIA'S LOFTIEST PEAK
A TRIBUTE OF RESPECT FROM THE LADIES AND GENTLEMEN OF THE
    DRAMATIC PROFESSION IN AMERICA
INDIANA KNOWS NO NORTH, NO SOUTH, NOTHING BUT THE UNION
THE SUREST SAFEGUARD OF THE LIBERTIES OF OUR COUNTRY IS TOTAL
    ABSTINENCE FROM ALL THAT INTOXICATES

Since 1959 the base of the monument has been surrounded by a circle of American flags streaming from 50 flagpoles. The office of the National Capital Parks says it has no record of how the circle of flags came to be authorized. Meanwhile the Commission of Fine Arts has never passed judgment on this artless display. Perhaps some day it should.

Constitution Gardens *The Mall along Constitution Avenue between* 17th *Street*
and Bacon Drive, NW
In accordance with the McMillan Commission Plan of 1901, the Mall was extended westward to the Potomac River, whose swampy banks were covered with landfill, and rows of elms were planted along both flanks of the Lincoln Memorial reflecting pool. But more than half a century would elapse before this part of the Mall—designated West Potomac Park—would realize its full potential as an urban park. The site was preempted for temporary office buildings urgently required when the capital was put on a wartime footing. The eight-wing Munitions Building of World War I (also known as "Main Navy") was a factory-like building with a facade of concrete. President Franklin D. Roosevelt prescribed that the barracks-like "Tempos" of World War II should be built of wood in the hope that after the war they would collapse of their own weight.

Like so many of Washington's temporary projects these eyesores survived until their demolition was finally authorized in 1966. When President Nixon saw that all the rubble was finally being cleared away, he said he wanted the Park Service to draw up plans to redevelop the area as an American version of Copenhagen's Tivoli Gardens amusement park—"Something like Walt Disney would do," as he put it. Purists were dismayed and called for a formally landscaped garden. The design of Skidmore, Owings & Merrill for Constitution Gardens—completed in 1976 but still too young for a final appraisal—combines elements of both purist and carnival approaches in a naturalistic picnic ground surrounding an irregular artificial lake.

Vietnam Veterans Memorial. By a joint resolution of 1 July 1980, Congress designated two acres in the western half of Constitution Gardens as a site for a Vietnam Veterans Memorial—a memorial for a war which left such a legacy of bitterness that most of the nation seemed just to want to forget it. The project was initiated by a Vietnam infantry veteran named Jan Scruggs, after he saw a movie about that war called *The Deer Hunter.* What he sought to record was something at once transcendent of and more modest than a patriotic cause: a simple memorial to the memory of comrades lost in the most ambiguous venture in America's military history. He was promptly joined in the project by sponsors ranging from Pearl Bailey and Carl T. Rowan to General Westmoreland.

The fund that Scruggs organized sponsored an open design competition that—in the space of three short months—attracted 1,421 entries, an American record and an international record for competitions of its type. Competitors were asked to submit designs for a reflective and contemplative memorial with room for inscribing the names of the 57,692 Americans who died in the war. There is to be no other inscription. The jury was specifically instructed to select a design that is "without political or military content, one that makes no comment or statement regarding the righteousness, wrongness, or motivation of U.S. policy in entering, conducting, or withdrawing from the war."

The winning entry—to be constructed as funds are raised from private contributors—is that of Maya Ying Lin, a 21-year-old Yale senior, whose parents emigrated to the United States from mainland China. Lin describes her design as appearing "like a rift in the earth—a long, polished black stone wall, emerging from and receding into the earth." The jury regards its wall of names as becoming a place of "quiet reflection . . . a place of healing. . . . It is uniquely horizontal, entering the earth rather than piercing the sky." It promises to be very much a memorial of our times.

Lincoln Memorial *West end of the Mall, at the foot of 23rd Street, NW Open 24 hours a day, every day of the year, free.*

The Lincoln Memorial is Washington's most revered monument and its most widely advertised throughout the land: it is emblazoned on the back of every copper penny and engraved in shadowy detail on the back of every five dollar bill. It enshrines within, the seated figure of Lincoln by Daniel Chester French, the city's most familiar statue; only New York's Statue of Liberty is more famous.

It was Lincoln's fate to "Save the Union" and it was his lasting achievement to make the average American feel that dignity as a citizen of the republic is bound up with the fate of the Union. That is the sentiment commemorated and celebrated in this temple that anchors the west end of the Mall as the Capitol terminates it to the east.

In his *History of the American People* Samuel Eliot Morison provides us with this appraisal of what distinguishes Lincoln as a national hero:

> Lincoln emerged humble before God, but the master of men. He seemed to have captured all the greater qualities of the great Americans who preceded him, without their defects: the poise of Washington without his aloofness, the mental audacity of Hamilton without his insolence, the astuteness of Jefferson without his indirection, the conscience of John Quincy Adams without his harshness, the courage of Jackson without his irascibility, the magnetism of Clay without his vanity, the lucidity of Webster without his ponderousness; and fused them with a sincerity and magnanimity that were peculiarly his.

The Lincoln Memorial in Washington is an expression of gratitude—as well as of continuing hope—that some of our politicians can some of the time achieve some of the attributes of sainthood.

The first commission to erect a monument to the memory of the 16th President was established by Congress two years after Lincoln's death, but 50 years were to elapse before the memorial we see today was completed. The eventual site in West Potomac Park was then a remote and swampy marsh and there were strong objections to it. (The speaker of the House, "Uncle Joe" Cannon, told Elihu Root, "So long as I live I'll never let a memorial to Abraham Lincoln be erected in that God damned swamp.") Some critics wanted an obelisk like Washington's, others argued for sites where Union Station now is or atop Meridian Hill on 16th Street. John Russell Pope sketched a huge pyramid with Doric porticoes emerging from triangular faces. Some automobile and real estate interests lobbied for a 72-mile-long, 200-foot-wide highway from the capital to Gettysburg.

After all these false starts, it was well worth waiting for the present marble temple, which rises from a site that is nothing less than majestic. The memorial sits on an artificially graded rise, overlooking the long Reflecting Pool of the axis of the Mall, rising from the Watergate steps down to the Potomac River, and providing a symbolic link on the direct line of Memorial Bridge to the columned portico of Robert E. Lee's boyhood home in Arlington Cemetery. There is no other possible site in Washington that could provide what the commission had prescribed: "undisputed domination over a large area, together with a certain dignified isolation from competing structures." The site is unparalleled, both figuratively and literally: the search for a firm bedrock foundation for the Washington Monument meant that it had to be placed a little to the south of the true east-west axis of the Capitol front and the Mall, and so the Lincoln Memorial is on the arbitrary visual line of that false axis, providing the whole Mall complex with a subtle and redeeming note of asymmetry.*

The Lincoln Memorial was designed by Henry Bacon as a Neoclassic American version of a Greek Doric temple with a Roman style attic—a Parthenon with the entrance and main facade on the side instead of at the end. The central block of the edifice is surrounded by a peristyle porch of 36 columns representing the 36 states existing at the time of Lincoln's death. The attic parapet is a clear visual extension of the central block within the colonnade, and it is capped with a frieze of 48 bas-relief festoons each representing one of the 48 states, with its name inscribed beneath it, as they existed at the time the monument was completed in 1922. As in the classical Greek manner, and in order to look straight, the walls and columns are slightly tilted in, the line of columns is slightly bowed outward, and the columns themselves have a slight bulge (called *entasis*).

The Park Service provides visitors with a free leaflet supplying a history of

* To compensate for the off-center location of the Washington Monument, the axis of the Mall from the Capitol to the Lincoln Memorial was reoriented one degree south of its true east-west direction.

the memorial, the exact weight and dimensions of its various elements, and the texts of the Gettysburg and Second Inaugural Addresses, which may be easier to read in the hand than they are to decipher as inscribed on the north and south walls of the interior. These two inscriptions are a remarkable marriage of literature and architecture, compelling every visitor to evoke his first memories of those words of Abraham Lincoln in all their familiar cadence.

Daniel Chester French spent 13 years on the colossal seated figure of Abraham Lincoln facing out through the colonnade toward the Washington Monument and the Capitol. French was the premier public sculptor of his day. Though he had no formal training, he worked in the academic vein and with concern, in the Beaux Arts tradition, for the adaptation of sculpture to an architectural setting. He specialized in patriotic subjects and didactic themes (e.g., *Labor Sustaining Art and the Family* in Boston), and his figures are always in correct proportion to the human anatomy. He was partial to sedentary figures, as his statues of Emerson, Gallaudet, Alma Mater, and John Harvard attest. A hundred of his statues may be found today in 35 American cities, but this Lincoln is the nation's favorite marble sculpture.

The chair in which Lincoln sits is a symbolic throne with armrests supported by Roman fasces. (Frank Lloyd Wright deplored the "falsely traditional" Olympian character of this Bacon and French memorial.) The drama of the pose is heightened by the combination of tension and repose; Lincoln's right hand is clenched and charged with energy while the left is relaxed; his gaze expresses not power, but gentleness, compassion, and loneliness.

The figure is designed to be lighted from above, and in natural lighting the

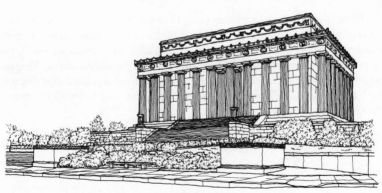

Lincoln Memorial

face almost disappears. Even on the brightest days insufficient natural light comes through the beeswaxed translucent ceiling panels of Alabama marble. Shortly after the memorial was opened the General Electric Company was called upon to design the floodlighting and artificial spotlights required—on even the sunniest days—to produce the requisite shadows for the shock of hair, eyebrows, high cheekbones, and bearded chin.

The Lincoln Memorial was dedicated on Memorial Day in 1922 in the presence of President Harding, Chief Justice Taft, the former president's son Robert Todd Lincoln, and Dr. Robert Moton, the president of Tuskegee Institute. These distinguished guests were all attired in striped trousers and cutaway morning coats. A Marine Corps colonel acting as chief usher greeted the chief justice with the observation that he had expected him to arrive in a blaze of glory; Mr. Taft said, no, he had come in a Dodge. The same chief usher turned to the soft-spoken Dr. Moton (who with Taft was to give a dedicatory address) and ushered him away from the speaker's platform to an all-Negro section across the road from the rest of the audience. It was an ugly reflection of the temper of the times, an indication of the long unreconstructed road yet ahead toward a still unrealized Emancipation.

The inscription carved in the marble wall behind French's solemn figure of Lincoln was composed by Royal Cortissoz, the art editor of the *New York Herald Tribune:*

IN THIS TEMPLE
AS IN THE HEARTS OF THE PEOPLE
FOR WHOM HE SAVED THE UNION
THE MEMORY OF ABRAHAM LINCOLN
IS ENSHRINED FOREVER

The high-speed, eight-lane Inner Loop Freeway (a segment of which survives under the nearby junction of New Hampshire and Virginia Avenues at the Watergate) was originally scheduled to be tunneled under the Lincoln Memorial, which would have isolated it even further from pedestrian access. This outrage was happily averted, as was the effect of a congressional resolution directing the Park Service to add two columns to the peristyle to provide recognition of the new states of Alaska and Hawaii.

Downtown

United States Tax Court   *2nd Street between D and E Streets, NW*
Open by arrangement; see below.

> Tax law is concerned only with the legal aspects of taxation, not with its financial, economic or other aspects.
> —Jean van Houtte, 1977

The United States Tax Court is a huge and complex architectural box, a geometrical caprice of a dark bronze glass core framed by blocks of flame-treated, pink-pearl Georgia granite. The balanced contrast of glass and stone produces an effect of serenity and repose. Would you believe a solid 220-foot-long oblong cantilevered 53 feet over a monumental flight of entrance steps without any visible means of support? All the tax lawyers in Washington could climb the broad stairs abreast with room to spare for their briefcases.

The architect of the court was Victor A. Lundy of New York, and like Edward Durell Stone, he describes his work as "timeless," but with more justification, as his work avoids Stone's traditional decorative elements, stylized as tapered columns, thin eaves, or plaster trellises.

The building is a tour de force of invisible engineering in the service of architecture as a dramatic disposition of masses. The "floating" prestressed concrete boxes are suspended by more than 100 tensioned steel cables three inches in diameter—the largest commercially available. The integrity of the structure is completely camouflaged; the three central courtrooms hang as if by magic. The Dulles Airport Terminal is also a complex cantilevered structure, but you can see how its tension and compression are balanced from a mile away. In the Tax Court all that engineering remains a mystery even when you are close enough to touch it.

In this respect Lundy's courthouse is precious, verging on the overrefined. It has nothing to do with the spirit of Bauhaus; Lundy had no more interest than did Lutyens in his British Embassy on Massachusetts Avenue in expressing the structure of the building in its exterior appearance.

Congress determines tax policy, the executive branch administers and enforces it, and the Tax Court adjudicates controversies over interpretation of the law. There are 16 principal judges augmented by retired judges who may be recalled, and together they constitute the most itinerant court in the land. Trials are conducted by a single judge at places convenient to the petitioning taxpayer; thus the judges actually sit on cases in this nice Washington building on an average of about six weeks a year. Most of their time is spent in New York, Chicago, and San Francisco, where they hold forth like magpies in the courts of other federal judges. Thus the U.S. Tax Court here in the District serves as little more than a homebase for traveling judges.

For all its mundane role in the judicial system, the Tax Court is the most dramatic federal office building erected to date under the authority of the Public Buildings Service of the General Services Administration (GSA). It belies the charge that successful architecture demands an indulgent client indifferent to cost. Building a satisfactory government building is a tough assignment: it has to be big; it usually needs endless rows of windows; and its institutional function is seldom clearly defined. In the past the GSA bureaucracy has all too often sponsored misbegotten esthetic solutions groping timorously for "a tasteful blend of the old and the new." Lundy's radical design utterly rejects that strategy; it is unremittingly and uncompromisingly new—you may search in vain for a pediment, a column, or even an eagle. In plan and scale it is superhuman. The interior affords contrasting textures of bush-hammered concrete and teak strips. The 32 judges and their clerks for whom it was built attest that it is a happy place to work.

"Inside this building," Mr. Lundy explains, "you will always have a sense of where you are, and of the sky outside." And the sky is a much more agreeable view than the undeveloped streets of the neighborhood. The chief defect of the Tax Court is its orientation. It suffered a change in site *after* the working drawings were completed and approved by GSA, the National Capital Planning Commission, and the Commission of Fine Arts. The architect said he liked the new site, since he was able to modify the design to expand that capacious tier of stairs at the entrance plaza facing what he was assured would one day be a tree-lined park. But what those stairs overlook today is the doleful prospect of a below-grade expressway, a putative leg of Interstate 395, which has since been terminated arbitrarily at just that stretch of 2nd Street between D and E Streets, NW. So if you approach the Tax Court from the unlikely direction of this impassable highway barrier, the entrance is overwhelmingly dramatic.

But since that route is not a practical option, the usual visitor approaches the building from its rear—which faces 3rd Street. All the back doors are closed except to certified employees. If you walk around the block along the sidewalk above the freeway you will find a public entrance; but the building cannot be described as Open to Visitors without considerable reservation.

The easy days are long since past when all government buildings were wide open to the public that owns them. In these harsh times of demonstrations, pilferage, vagrancy, and vandalism, buildings have to be closed off for reasons of simple housekeeping, even when, as in the case of the Tax Court, there are no conceivable threats to sensitive documents or information affecting the national security. So if you go to the uniformed guard at the door and ask to enter just to see the pretty teak and granite—as a matter of right or of curiosity—you will be told politely to go packing. But *if* you do a little research, if you call the office of the clerk of the court (376-2754) and find out the exact hours when one of the courts will next be in session, and if you tell the guard that you want to attend that specific session then in progress, *then* he will escort you into a sumptuous courtroom with its rows of empty seats for the public. And then you can listen briefly to what will undoubtedly prove the most tedious kind of litigation—at least to those uninitiated into the splendors and miseries of the Internal Revenue Code.

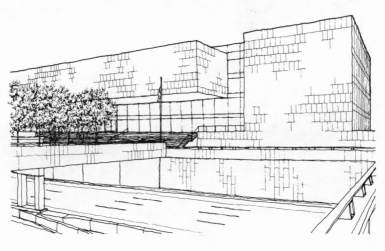

United States Tax Court

Old Pension Building *F Street between 4th and 5th Streets, NW*
National Building Museum, Open Monday–Saturday 10–4, Sunday 12–4.

Washington's own version of the Palazzo Farnese—but naturally, being American, twice as large—may be found tucked away among side streets in a now abandoned but once focal site of the L'Enfant Plan. It is the Pension Building erected in 1883 as a memorial to the veterans of the Civil War. To the north the view is obscured and dominated by the banal hulk of the General Accounting Office, which manages to be even more prosaic than its name. To the east and west are concealing brackets of gingko trees. Only the approach from the south affords enough distance to do this vast building—200 by 400 feet—justice. To come up the escalator of the north exit of the Judiciary Square Metro station and be assailed by the red face brick and orange terra-cotta facade of the Old Pension Building in the glare of a bright morning sun is, so far, the most dramatic prospect that the subway exits have to offer.

From roughly 1930 to 1960 it was fashionable for architects to deplore this monument for its idiosyncrasy and its Victorian excess of style; they regarded it as an embarrassment that might have been better avoided. In 1932 the vice-president of the Washington Chapter of the American Institute of Architects characterized the Pension Building as an "incongruous absurdity," taking it as a principle that "a general harmony of effect between all government buildings, taken as a whole, is more desirable than any discordant originality." In fact, most of the major buildings erected between the end of the Civil War and the turn of the century—the State, War, and Navy Building, the Library of Con-

Old Pension Building

gress, and the Old Post Office—were regarded as blights on the landscape, ineradicable monuments to a lapse in taste.

The most striking feature of the Pension Building on the outside is a three-foot-high frieze, a narrow ribbon of military figures in relief, in endless circular procession a quarter of a mile long around the entire building between the first and second floors. Here the Greek gladiators of the Parthenon are reincarnated as outfitted in government issue by the quartermaster of the Union Army; and here the bas-reliefs are low enough to be easily "read" at the pedestrian level, without any of that neckbreaking inaccessibility of the figures under the eaves of a Greek temple. The sculptor of this grand parade was Casper Buberl, a Bohemian who later did the Muses for the old Metropolitan Opera House in New York. His aim was to portray all aspects of the Union Army in action: mounted generals with tasseled swords, boy buglers on foot, infantry marching with fixed bayonets, sailors pulling their oars in a surf under a palm tree, the wounded returning from battle, supply wagon teams, cavalry, artillery, and hospital corpsmen all with the tools of their trade. Allegorical figures are identified by helpful plaques at the main entrance, the Gate of the Infantry (to the south at the subway entrance), the Gate of the Quartermaster to the west, the Gate of the Invalids to the north, and the Naval Gate to the east.

The greatest Roman columns are not to be found in Rome or even in Italy; Rome's largest buildings and tallest columns were built in its colony of Baalbek

Detail of Frieze on Old Pension Building

in what was then Syria. Enter the Pension Building and witness the eight largest columns ever built in the Roman style; they are 15 feet taller than the six unfluted Corinthian columns still standing at Baalbek. They are 25 feet in circumference at the base and surmounted by colossal Corinthian capitals about 80 feet from the floor; they are constructed of some 85,000 bricks each, with their surfaces smoothly plastered and painted to simulate marble. They span what is quite the largest room in the city and the site of eight inaugural balls. Photographs of President Cleveland's inaugural ball, the first held there, show the massive pillars wound with white muslin and the columns and balconies festooned with swags and wreaths of evergreen.

The architect of the building was Gen. Montgomery C. Meigs, a West Point trained engineer, a former quartermaster general of the Union Army, and the genius who finally succeeded in raising the dome of the Capitol. In an era before efficient artificial lighting or air conditioning he managed to provide a maximum usable working area at minimum cost.

Meigs copied the facade rather literally from engravings of the Palazzo Farnese, but it was clearly the interior that captured his imagination. All the offices are entered from balconies giving on to the central court rather than down the long dark corridors that are still the bane and cliché of government buildings. In total disregard of architectural convention, Meigs added a disproportionately large penthouse or clerestory with little organic relation to the rest of the design; more than anything else this is what made the building "look funny." The clerestory justifies and requires the double colonnade of the interior: what Meigs wanted to do was to admit light and air without the heat of a flat skylight; so all that penthouse glass is awkwardly vertical. But the result is thoroughly justified by the enhanced light and comfort of the interior. Meigs introduced double-hung glazed windows as an insulating strategy now familiar but then untried. Fifty percent of the cost of a modern building goes into mechanicals—the invisible but energy intensive heating, ventilating, and air conditioning. In the Pension Building the designer has achieved the same results by the natural circulation of air augmented only by cast-iron radiators for heating in the winter and by green and white striped awnings sported at every window for shade in the summer. The building was also the first large structure in the capital to be furnished with elevators. The original elevators have not survived, though those in use now tend to give the impression that they have.

The paradox of the building is that it is quite efficient despite the great open courtyard that creates a building essentially hollow. One architect said, "Nothing short of an inaugural ball or a thunderstorm could possibly fill that immense void." But actually over 80 percent of the total floor area is available for useful office space—an exceedingly high ratio even by the meanest of today's standards as found in the law office ghettoes along lower Connecticut Avenue. People reflexively characterize space as wasteful: but what General Meigs has done demonstrates the use and not the waste of space.

During the 40 years that the Pension Bureau had its offices in the building it dispensed more than $8 billion to veterans and widows of the nation's wars from the Revolution through the Civil War. It is sad to reflect that following World War I even this building was not large enough for the task; in 1926 the Pension Bureau was moved to the new building of the Interior Department (to which it was curiously attached) at C Street between 18th and 19th Streets, NW.

In the 1960s there was a congressional initiative—that happily failed—to establish the Air and Space Museum in the Old Pension Building. Currently plans are well under way to devote the building to a permanent national museum of the building arts—to be known as the Building Museum.

National Portrait Gallery, Smithsonian Institution/Old Patent Office Building   *F Street between 7th and 9th Streets, NW   Open daily 10–5:30, free.*

> What wouldn't one give to have a recording of the voice of George
> Washington . . .
> —Dr. Roy Strong, director of the National Portrait Gallery,
>   London, 1970

The National Portrait Gallery (NPG) now occupies the south wings of the Old Patent Office Building, while the National Museum of American Art (formerly the National Collection of Fine Arts) is sheltered in the wings to the north along G Street; they are both bureaus of the Smithsonian Institution. In the original L'Enfant Plan this site was reserved for a national church or mausoleum, the focal point of a spacious setting anchoring 8th Street as a cross-axis to the Mall. The setting now is a little crowded: the broad flight of stairs leading up from F Street to the south portico has been sheared off, while F Street itself has been closed to traffic in a faddish impulse to create "Streets for People" replete with unsightly kindergarten jungle gyms for grown-ups.

The Old Patent Office is the fourth oldest building in the city; as in the case of the second and third oldest—the Capitol and the Treasury—Robert Mills has to share the honors with other architectural collaborators. Over a period of 30 years, William Elliot, Ithiel Town, Thomas U. Walter, and Edward Clark also worked on the design of the Patent Office.

Mills was an engineer before he was an architect, designing locks, canals, and bridges. As a student of Thomas Jefferson he was partial to the Greek Revival style in which he conceived the Patent Office, adopting the portico of the Parthenon—with the same fluted Doric columns and a greatly simplified entablature, but in remarkably faithful proportions—to a building with sober institutional purposes. He placed a high premium on construction that would be both economical and fireproof. The simple marble and granite facing conceals solid load-bearing masonry walls for an effect that is austere and utilitarian. Mills's south wings with their masonry piers largely survived a fire of 1877, while the iron framing of the north wings did not. The building included large exhibition areas for the display of patent models, including the whole western tier of the main floor, with its shallow arched ceilings springing from short dungeony pillars, called the "Rejected Cases Department."

The building with its great vaulted halls was drafted by the Union Army quartermaster during the Civil War to serve first as a barracks for troops, then as a hospital, and finally as a morgue. During those eventful years Clara Barton, the founder of the American Red Cross, and Walt Whitman worked in the building. Clara Barton had worked there first as a clerk in the Patent Office and later as head of a welfare agency and clearing house to tend wounded soldiers that she set up at the request of President Lincoln. And Walt Whitman brought his love affair with America into the wards there as a kind of poetical hospital corpsman.

In 1932 the Patent Office was moved to the new Department of Commerce Building in the Federal Triangle, and the building was assigned to the Civil Service Commission. In those days before air conditioning, every window to the south and west sported green and white striped awnings. By the early 1960s the Civil Service Commission was scheduled to move into its new Foggy Bottom headquarters at 1900 E Street, NW. It seemed perfectly logical to the General Services Administration to schedule the demolition of the Old Patent Office Building in order to provide space for a parking lot. These crazy priorities were reversed only when the chairman of the Commission of Fine Arts—which had only the most tenuous kind of jurisdiction in the case—appealed the issue to President Dwight D. Eisenhower. As a result, the building was rescued and assigned to the Smithsonian Institution, for which its hallowed exhibition areas were adapted, after considerable modification, for the display of works of art.

The National Portrait Gallery is primarily a museum of history rather than of art. When it first opened, Hilton Kramer of the *New York Times* inquired whether that distinction is a valid one: "To what degree," he asked, "can bad art ever be relied on as good history?" He has continued to observe fastidiously that an institution seeking to preserve our national heritage in the form of magazine covers* is "essentially an exercise in vulgarity." John Canaday of the same

---

* *Time* has given the gallery (while retaining control of the copyright) many of the original portraits it commissioned for use as covers.

newspaper is more charitable; he acknowledges that the gallery is for pictures that are of interest more for their subject matter than as paintings: "Some are of course both, but a portrait gallery has more esthetic latitude."

Many portraits in the permanent collection are unquestionably of the first rank by anyone's standards, and some of these are, not surprisingly, self-portraits by artists—by Eastman Johnson, Mary Cassatt, and a superb one by John Singleton Copley. There are even self-portraits by George Gershwin and e.e. cummings. In recent years the gallery tends to compensate—perhaps over-compensate—for the narrowness of its programmatic theme by a certain opulence in display.

The museum maintains a Catalog of American Portraits (CAP) in national and other collections, both foreign and private. For figures from the past—and it accepts into its permanent collection only portraits of subjects who have been dead for at least 10 years—it concentrates on people recorded in the *Dictionary of American Biography,* but even that allows for a pretty large cast of characters ranging from Pocahontas to Sitting Bull to Gertrude Stein to Jean Harlow. The collection was established in the 1960s in the middle of an era when oil portrait painting appeared to be a dying art. In 1976, Congress belatedly included photographic portraits within the gallery's charter.

The Great Hall. A splendid double "floating" staircase with brass railings leads the visitor up from the second floor of the NPG to the Great Hall on the third. This eclectic block-long fantasy is a reconstruction of a later period, by Adolph Cluss, in a style that has been termed "Victorian Psychedelic"—totally unrestrained by the austere mood of Robert Mills's exterior.

Through tall doors of etched glass one enters a large cube of a room designed for the display of patent models, but the setting itself offers severe competition for the attention of the observer. Corridors and balconies extend off the hall on the east-west axis, all united by a dado of green marble with purple marble panels and a tiled floor in which lozenges of blue are embedded in shades of muddy brown that admit of no further polite description.

The ceiling is sugar coated in the palest pink and palest green plaster with carved wood gilt medallions in each of the 14 coffered recesses. The pastel walls are punctuated by fluted pilasters, sponge painted the color of peanut brittle; their capitals feature rosettes surmounted by leafy brackets in an ensemble that is composite, to say the least. An octagonal skylight sports a yellow star in a field of red and blue mosaic contrasting with the restrained pastel geometries of the stained glass windows. Cast iron balcony railings and mahogany doors and window frames provide accents of stark black. Well-concealed indirect lighting installed during restoration in the late 1960s enhances the way the spaces and colors work together.

There are six bas-relief panels of buxom matrons in bisque presiding over troops of chubby cupids and cherubs who are toiling and hammering on anvils in a frenzy of busy invention—a sort of Santa's workshop reborn as an Arcadian kindergarten run by liberated women. There are four solemn medallion profiles of Fulton, Franklin, Whitney, and Jefferson. The total effect is a meringue pastiche of didactic emblems trapped in a Viennese café.

National Museum of American Art, Smithsonian Institution/Old Patent Office Building   G Street between 7th and 9th Streets, NW
Open daily 10–5:30, free.

In a reversal of the European experience, America became a state
before it became a nation or culture.
—Peter Marzio, director of the Corcoran Gallery of Art,
    10 December 1980

The National Museum of American Art (NMAA),* is at last the healthy survivor of an inauspicious history of aborted legacies and disinheritance. From 1938 until 1980 it was known as the National Collection of Fine Arts (NCFA), a serviceable name discarded in favor of NMAA because the old name was supposed to be hard for taxi drivers to master, and perhaps because the concept of *fine arts* has succumbed to the charge of elitism. (It could have been worse; at least it is not the American Museum of "Visual Arts.") The new name allows it a more comprehensive charter that includes photography and arts and crafts—not previously admitted under the rubric of fine arts. The NMAA operates as a bureau of the Smithsonian Institution, and it is now reestablished as the principal official repository of traditional and contemporary art belonging to the federal government.

America grew up without any established tradition of royal, aristocratic, or religious institutions as patrons of art and artists. Most painters were supported—if at all—by private clients and collectors, and enough of these collectors ended up giving their pictures to the government to put Uncle Sam in the art business more by default than by design. The course of government in the arts has been a rocky one, and only in the latter part of the 20th century has the federal establishment finally seemed comfortable in the role.

As the National Institute, the predecessor of the NMAA even antedates the Smithsonian itself, having been designated the custodian of the government's art holdings in 1841 and provided with quarters in the U.S. Patent Office Building.

* Befitting its role as a capital, Washington's institutions tend to be called *National,* while those in New York are termed *American,* as in the American Museum of Natural History, the American Geographical Society, and so on.

The collection was absorbed administratively by the Smithsonian upon its establishment in 1846. In 1858 the works were reinstalled in Renwick's Castle building on the Mall; in 1865 they were largely destroyed in a disastrous fire; in 1874 the surviving art objects were placed on loan to the Corcoran Gallery of Art; in 1896 they were returned to the Smithsonian; and in 1906 a court order bestowed the title of "National Gallery of Art" on the collection to make it elegible for a large bequest from Harriet Lane Johnson. The cachet of that name attracted further gifts, such as the Evans and Gellatly collections. By 1920 it was an administrative entity only, with no gallery space of its own except a temporary installation in a balcony of the National Museum of Natural History, among all the mummies and minerals. As the years went by, its holdings of china and porcelain were transferred to the National Museum of History and Technology, and its portraits to the National Portrait Gallery, and in 1938 it even lost its good name to the new gallery being built for the Mellon bequest on the Mall. Not until 1968 did it find a permanent home in the Old Patent Office Building, where its first objects had been exhibited 127 years earlier.

Thus the NMAA grew up in an environment in which America was as slow to establish its artistic identity as the government was to bring some order to the custodianship of its artistic possessions. Except for patrons like Corcoran and Gellatly, who collected both American and European art, many Americans were timid about the homegrown product as long as they could afford the Old Master painters from abroad. Only in this century are our problems with a national artistic identity being resolved. A recent director of the NMAA, Joshua C. Taylor, has reminded us that "the American colonies represented not a new but a transplanted culture,"* and that American universities did not grant graduate degrees in the history of art until well into the 20th century. Through the National Endowments for the Arts and for the Humanities, and in museological affairs, the government has begun to supplement private patronage, and one of its instruments for this purpose is the NMAA.

At the pleasure of successive administrations the NMAA serves as occasional executive agency for the federal government in international artistic activities, such as arranging for American participation in the Venice and São Paulo biennial exhibitions. The NMAA is also the administrator of the documentary collection and research program of the Archives of American Art (AAA). (The AAA is a national program that began in Detroit in 1954, and now conserves the papers of artists, exhibition catalogs, and records of commercial galleries, and such items as the proposals in Picasso's handwriting for artists to be included in the New York Armory Show of 1913.) These quasi-official functions give the

* *The Fine Arts in America.* (Chicago: University of Chicago Press, 1979), p. 3.

NMAA a special responsibility in the field of American art in a city where it cannot compete with the Corcoran in the breadth of its historical collection, with the Hirshhorn in the sheer range of contemporary artists, nor with the National Gallery (a latecomer in the field) for the cream of the crop. But with its now exclusive concentration on the art of this country, the NMAA seems well on the way to fulfilling a role as a research center and repository of national art, comparable to that of the Luxembourg Museum in Paris or the Tate Gallery in London.

Under the directorship of Joshua Taylor the museum has distinguished itself in the scholarship and documentation of modern American art, in the quality of its special exhibitions, and in the technical standards of its conservation laboratory. It has been conscientious in the management of artists' estates that have come its way, and though it is by no means a small pond, it is attractive to prospective donors as a place where bequests have a better chance of being treated as big fish.

As its apparently permanent home, the NMAA shares with the National Portrait Gallery the Old Patent Office Building which at the time it was completed in 1836 was the largest building in the country. Its colonnaded porticoes and great masonry galleries are of a kind that will never be built again; and although almost destroyed for a parking lot, they survive as part of the nation's heritage of 19th-century Greek Revival architecture. The building is full of wide corridors and vast spaces that were pressed into service as an improvised hospital when the floods of wounded were brought into the city after the bloody Civil War battles at Antietam and Bull Run. The third-floor Lincoln Gallery, 264 feet long by 63 feet wide, and with 64 white marble pillars and pilasters, was a splendid setting for the ball and banquet for Lincoln's second inaugural. But the Old Patent Office Building resists easy conversion to an art gallery and must be considered adequate rather than ideal. The directors of NMAA have made imaginative efforts to repair some of the ravages caused by the General Services Administration in its heavy-handed approach to restoration of the site in 1964.

Among the highlights of the NMAA collection are the largest single group of paintings by Albert Pinkham Ryder (18) and 445 paintings of George Catlin's Indian Gallery, originally acquired by the Smithsonian for their ethnographic interest. The gallery shows to great advantage the haunting and scintillating metal foil and paper collage by the Washington sculptor James Hampton, the artist's only known work and probably uncompleted when he died in 1964; it has the uninhibited title of *Throne of the Third Heaven of the Nations Millennium General Assembly*. The NMAA possesses few important American works of art from the period before the Civil War or from the early decades of the 20th century. In the 102 paintings of the S. C. Johnson collection—each by a prominent

American artist, and all of the pictures painted within the span of about three years, mostly in 1966—the museum possesses a dramatic gestalt slice of instant American art history.

Martin Luther King Memorial Library *G Street at 9th Street, NW   Open Monday and Thursday 9–9, Tuesday, Wednesday, Friday and Saturday 9–5:30.*
Washington has a lot of glass box office buildings, largely because it is a cheap way to build; but none of them has even a hint of the elegance of the Martin Luther King Memorial Library by Ludwig Mies van der Rohe (familiarly known as Mies), the creator and master of the genre. Together with Frank Lloyd Wright and Le Corbusier, Mies is one of the great masters of 20th-century architecture. The city is fortunate that the three district commissioners (who then ran the city) had the imagination to award the library commission to Mies as one of the last projects of his career before his death in 1969 at the age of 83. The library was also the first major building in the modern style to be approved by the usually conservative Commission of Fine Arts.

Mies's great esthetic dictum was one of classic frugality: "less is more." Elegance resides in what you take away, not in what you add on. The austerity of Mies's strategy is well suited to the low-rise rectangular grid site plan of downtown Washington. His design is unmistakably Miesian: a simple block of painted black steel rising on stilts with a recessed entrance lobby in the center. (This

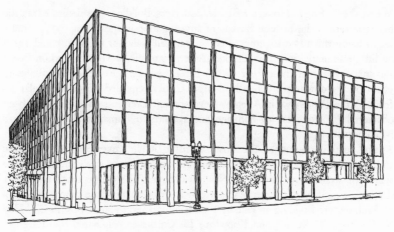

Martin Luther King Memorial Library

same hallmark formula has been copied—to good effect—in a number of the city's recent neighborhood District Police headquarters.)

The library is pristine in the unadorned purity of its composition. Lean, skeletal panels of steel and glass are employed to exquisite effect. It is free of any effort at originality. Though it is somewhat cold in feeling, it is not uninviting and benefits from a dramatic contrast with the conventional buildings that surround it.

Washington has a wealth of specialized libraries from the Library of Congress on down, but they are none of them geared to community use. The Martin Luther King Memorial Library, with its late hours and open-stack system, fills a unique civic role as a central circulating library. There are also about 100 public parking spaces—all underground, as Mies ruled out original plans to have open parking adjacent to the building.

Martin Luther King was assassinated just a few months before the library was scheduled to open in 1972. In an open meeting of the D.C. library board, the board members acceded to the wishes of a predominantly black audience who in effect named the building for King by acclamation.

FBI Building   *Pennsylvania Avenue between 9th and 10th Streets, NW*
Tours (1 hour) weekdays 8:45–4:15, free.

It would make a perfect stage set for a dramatization of George Orwell's *1984*.
—Wolf Von Eckhardt, *Washington Post,* 12 July 1975

When the J. Edgar Hoover FBI Headquarters Building was dedicated as the headquarters of the Federal Bureau of Investigation in the fall of 1975, it did a lot to bring this town together. People from all walks of life who could agree on little else united in cordial dislike of the great hulk newly stranded on Pennsylvania Avenue at the corner of 9th Street, where it exercised a brutalizing effect on the downtown urban landscape. Critics regarded it as a particular affront to the Pennsylvania Avenue Development Commission, which had been chartered by Congress to enhance and restore to human scale the nation's Main Street.

This costly monument—the most expensive building ever constructed by the Public Buildings Service—is the maximum realization on this continent of the school of architecture known as New Brutalism. (The country had two other dramatic examples of the genre under construction at this same time: the School of Architecture Building at Yale by Paul Rudolph and the new Boston City Hall by Kallman, McKinnell and Knowles.) Le Corbusier originated the design in France with the first public buildings of deliberately exposed concrete aggregate—*beton brut* in French and hence *brutalism* in England, where the style next flourished.

The naming of public buildings for people runs the risk not only of offense to euphony but of the perpetuation of incongruity. Two blocks to the north of the J. Edgar Hoover Building is the Martin Luther King Memorial Library designed by the master Chicago architect Ludwig Mies van der Rohe. Le Corbusier and Mies were the two most influential architects of the 20th century, and in these two neighboring buildings they have left their only legacy in the nation's capital—not counting the District Police headquarters buildings in various wards of the city which are derivations of Mies's famous model. The Hoover Building was named by congressional acclaim and bureaucratic fiat. The King Library was named by a spontaneous delegation of fervent citizens who did not suggest or even propose but simply announced to the library board that they were going to call the new building the Martin Luther King Memorial Library—a remarkable testament and a dramatic way to name a building. Martin Luther King got the better building, and J. Edgar Hoover got what some may feel is the monument he deserves.

On one of my first trips to Washington, at the age of 13, I remember taking the ritual FBI tour in the basement of the Department of Justice south of Pennsylvania Avenue at 9th Street, NW. In the summer the waiting lines would stretch for blocks. With the exhibits transferred to a specially designed tour area

FBI Building

in the new building, the number of annual visitors still runs to over half a million, but the FBI has been overtaken by the National Air and Space Museum as the capital's chief attraction for young visitors. On my first FBI tour I learned that *G–Man* stands for "Government Man," and that *F* stands for Fidelity, *B* for Bravery, and *I* for Integrity. The tour ended then—as now—with a wall of staring posters of the Ten Most Wanted Men. Then the guide would tear off the last poster and throw it in the waste basket, explaining that the bum had just been caught that morning.

In a recent tour of the new building (at the same intersection but across the street), our guide was a bright young woman whose enthusiasm transcended the familiarity of the rehearsed routine. She told us that over a third of the 20,000 people in the Federal Bureau of Investigation work in the new headquarters building. When asked, she said she hoped to become an agent someday and to that end was taking a master's degree in criminal justice at night school. All FBI agents have to have a law degree or a certificate in public accounting or the equivalent, such as a degree in criminal justice. Of the bureau's 8,000 agents, 170 are women.

There is a quaint act of Congress still on the books in this permissive age that makes it a felony to portray an FBI agent in any movie or radio or television drama without prior submission of the script to the bureau for approval. Congress also keeps passing laws extending the bureau's jurisdiction. The initial mission of the FBI focused on "interstate flight," but it now deals with such obscure fields as stolen cattle, obscene telephone calls, transportation of fireworks, bond default, "wagering paraphernalia," fraud by wire, impersonation, harboring fugitives, enticing to desert, and train wrecks. In its annual reports the bureau exhibits a morbid flair for statistics, claiming for 1977 a credit for 63,849 man-years, seven man-months, and two man-days of "actual, suspended, and probationary sentences," broken down in over 80 categories according to the statute or offense involved.

It took 12 years to construct the FBI Building. In its early design stage the main facade was not parallel to Pennsylvania Avenue and did not conform to the then-prescribed 75-foot setback for all future avenue construction. The chairman of the Pennsylvania Avenue Development Commission, the architect Nathaniel Owings, broached the problem to Mr. Hoover directly and he graciously acquiesced to the redesign of the front. But the resulting trade-offs were substantial and radical. To compensate for the lost space in front, there was an additional third-level sub-basement (whose construction caused 9th and 10th Streets to sink several feet), and the addition of two hatlike floors crowding the building height restriction limit at the back along E Street with a projecting overhang dominating the building's profile from all aspects. The final result suggests one of Claes Oldenburg's colossal urban monuments—except this time not a lipstick or clothespin or Good Humor bar but a huge breakfast toaster with two great slices of fenestrated toast sitting on the top. Oldenburg would have added only an inflated rubber lever over the 9th Street sidewalk to permit graduated settings from Light to Dark.

Without exception, all of my friends are intolerant of my confessing a certain fondness for the FBI Building. The building is aggressive and conspicuous, but altogether a robust intrusion on the boring streetscape of ordinary office buildings that surround it. The architect in charge of the project was Stanley Gladych of the C.F. Murphy firm of Chicago, and he has given us an architectural boldness that is not an accident and that is not pseudoclassical. It may be ugly, but it is unbanal, and may someday earn the kind of indulgence accorded to the oversize Old Post Office Building across the street. One of the FBI Building's saving graces is the warm buff color of its concrete aggregate.

Franklin School   *13th Street at K Street, NW*

Franklin School today strikes us as an ornate castle stranded among the monotonous facades of K Street office buildings, but when it was dedicated in 1869 it was a model of advanced school design and became the archetype of the many red brick elementary schools that were later to be scattered throughout the District of Columbia. The city was so proud of it that it commissioned an exact scale model of the school in detachable sections for display at the Vienna Exposition of 1873 and the Philadelphia Centennial of 1876, and in both of those places it won a prize for its architect, Adolph W. Cluss.

At a time when public schools were regarded as a system of mediocre charity schools for the poor, Franklin School created a new image of a prestigious institution attractive to all social ranks. The children of Presidents Andrew Johnson and Chester A. Arthur went to school there. It accommodated 900 pupils, and boys and girls were separated, with entrances on either side of the building. A bronze plaque on the front of the building records that it was the scene of the first "wireless" telephone call in history when Dr. Alexander Graham Bell on 3 June 1880 sent a message over a beam of light to a receiver located at 1325 L Street, NW.

The school is an epitome of the Romanesque Revival style: hard-burnt, molded, and pressed bricks, semicircular arches over windows and doors, windowsills connected by string courses, a cornice of corbeled brick arches, and a facade flanked by polygonal towers. The mansard roof of green and blue slate is a Second Empire embellishment. The roof originally had a broken pediment with a colossal bust of Benjamin Franklin, and the central pavilion shafts were originally crowned with bell towers. The original entrance stairs were lost when 13th Street was widened. Despite these minor exterior ravages, the structural and interior decorative elements are still in place; these factors and its central location argue that the city should find an appropriate tenant to justify its restoration and continued use.

Sherman Monument
Hamilton Place between 15th Street and East Executive Avenue, NW

This site was chosen for William Tecumseh Sherman's statue because it is the hillock on which he is supposed to have stood as he reviewed the victorious Union troops when they returned from their march through Georgia and paraded up Pennsylvania Avenue in 1865.

Sherman's campaign brought a new dimension of terror to warfare, and this monument, designed chiefly by the sculptor Carl Rohl-Smith (who died before it was completed), documents the atrocities of the new age. On the west side of the

Franklin School

statue's pedestal is a bronze group, War, with a woman survivor, her hands bound and cuffed, standing with a fallen warrior on whom the vultures have already begun to gnaw. At the four corners of the podium stand life-size sentinels at rest arms, representing the four service branches of Infantry, Artillery, Cavalry, and Engineers. The names of all Sherman's battles and the chronology of his military assignments are inscribed on the pedestal base in bronze letters.

At Sherman's funeral in 1891 his old adversary Gen. Joseph E. Johnston served as an honorary pallbearer, standing bareheaded on that rainy February day. A friend urged the 83-year-old Johnston to put on his hat. "If I were in his place and he were standing here in mine, he would not put on his hat," answered Johnston. And 10 days later he died of pneumonia.

Southwest

Hubert H. Humphrey Building: Department of Health and Human Services *Independence Avenue at 3rd Street, SW*

Compared to its nameless, chronologically numbered federal office building neighbors to the west along Independence Avenue—FOB No. 5 and FOB No. 10—the Humphrey Building is an idiosyncrasy, unlikely to become a model for future buildings for the government or for anyone else. In contrast to the bland and effete character of those other buildings, which look as if they had been extruded uniformly by processing marble veneer through computers, this building by Marcel Breuer is a gutsy structure conveying a sense of power and energy. As Paul Goldberger has said, all Breuer buildings "give a sense of being objects before they are buildings."

The walls are distinguished by those convex trapezoid windows that have become a Breuer hallmark, as in his Housing and Urban Development Building a few blocks to the southwest. Behind all that textured fenestration, its curious and expensive cantilevered skeleton articulates at the corners and at the roof line. The rationale for all this heavy engineering is that the structure also serves to harbor exhaust shafts from the freeway tunnel over which it is sited—the same is true of the ungainly Department of Labor on the opposite side of the Mall to the north.

Unlike all those government departments in the Federal Triangle, there is no attempt here to tie in a design esthetic with the departmental program of the tenant. The arbitrary bureaucratic process of the Public Buildings Service seems to have assigned the place to the next fledgling department in line—the Department of Health, Education, and Welfare before it was renamed the Department of Health and Human Services. *Health* is clear enough, but what is a *human service*? The word *human* has only recently become an adjective and benefits little from all the associations of the word *service*.

Arena Stage *6th Street at M Street, SW*

When they opened this 800-seat theater-in-the-round in 1960, they had to call it a stage because the District's building code required a theater proper to have a proscenium arch and a fire curtain. Like most Washington institutions, Arena Stage has its own unique priority: its founder, Zelda Fichandler, claims it to be "the first theater to be built in America on the basis of the collective experience of a company." This 30-year-old resident company was a pioneer of theater-in-the-round and one of the first of the nation's regional repertory companies. It was founded in 1950 at a time when the National Theater was reduced to showing movies because the Actors Guild refused to perform in a segregated theater. Its first home was the old Hippodrome movie theater at 9th Street and New York Avenue, NW. It held only 240 people and had a top ticket price of $2.50; to make a stage right entrance after a stage left exit, the actors had to go around outdoors through a side alley. For five years the company performed in a converted arena in the Heurich Brewery (where the Kennedy Center now stands), and earned themselves the name Old Vat.

In 1960 the company engaged the Chicago architect Harry Weese to design its first permanent home, an inexpensive but handsome structure, elegant in its effect though made of simple materials: exposed concrete, gray-buff face brick, and sheet metal roofing painted dark gray. Weese also designed the matching Kreeger Theater addition of 1971. The whole complex is very functional with no superfluous decoration. Arena Stage has flourished for two decades in the

Hubert H. Humphrey Building

impossible to look out of them without standing up. The wide pavement areas under the building provide an elegant but not very inviting geometry screened by a perimeter of pyramidal bollards that keep automobiles out but allow pedestrians through. The building suffers from an ungainly relationship to its neighbors; it is surrounded to the south by a freeway—no help for any structure—and on the other three sides by monolithic office buildings that provide little contrast in texture or scale.

Auditor's Building/Old Bureau of Engraving and Printing
14th Street at Independence Avenue, SW   Not open to the public.

The slender red brick tower of the Auditor's Building dominates the landscape of the Mall looking south down 14th Street or west along Independence Avenue from the latitude of the Smithsonian. It was the first facility designed and constructed by the federal government to accommodate the Bureau of Engraving and Printing of the Treasury Department, erected in 1879 at a time when the government decided it could no longer allow its currency to be manufactured by private contractors. From 1880 to 1914 all of the government's money, and most of its postage stamps, bonds, presidential commissions, patent certificates, White House invitations, and tax and alcohol stamps were engraved or printed in this building.

President Andrew Jackson didn't like banks and he didn't like what he called "folding money." But Lincoln's secretary of the treasury, Salmon P. Chase, loved paper money and he printed enough of it to finance the Civil War. In Chase's day the private contractors delivered their engraved notes to the attic of the old Treasury Building on Pennsylvania Avenue, where they were signed, sealed, and numbered before being issued. The procedure was too makeshift to dignify a dollar which was destined to supplant sterling and serve, for the better part of a century, as the monetary standard of the world.

The building was designed by James G. Hill, the supervising architect of the treasury. As a composite of Romantic Revival styles, it is one of the last to exhibit elements of the Italianate Revival which peaked in the 1860s, and it anticipates features of the Queen Anne mood which flourished till the turn of the century. The industrial character of the structure is revealed in the extreme regularity of its fenestration. The front facing the Mall has rows of tall windows to provide clear north lighting for the engravers. The podium at the basement level was to support the bearing walls and to provide security. The fourth floor has 18-foot ceilings to accommodate the huge old rotary presses.

After World War I the printing and engraving operations were reinstalled in a new plant immediately to the south. The old structure was then inexplicably renamed the Auditor's Building and referred to as a complex because of the number of outbuildings it had acquired over the years to the rear and to the west; together they provide a unique legacy of industrial archeology.

In a building where you print money you don't want a lot of doors, and this one has only a single main entrance—under the clock tower and up a pair of double stairs to the second floor—through which all employees passed and visitors were screened before admission to any of the manufacturing operations, which were further shielded behind wire screens. Each press printing money or other valuable papers was equipped with a register recording the number of impressions, and for every impression there had to be a record of a sheet of finished work, a spoiled sheet, or a proof. No free samples.

The main tower of the building features a prominent inscription of the date of its construction—1879—and four round window openings, called *occuli*, which

Auditor's Building

In the depths of the Civil War, Lincoln was criticized for continuing the construction of the Capitol, but his response was resolute: "If the people see the Capitol going on," he said, "it is a sign we intend the Union shall go on." So Walter and Meigs worked on their dome without stint, employing cast iron because it was fireproof and because it was stronger, lighter, and more versatile than stone. They took as their models Paris's Pantheon and Invalides, and also St. Isaac's Cathedral in Leningrad, completed in 1842 with one of the first great cast iron domes in Europe. Their accomplishment at the Capitol was a considerable technical tour de force, for they applied the only real innovation in dome engineering between the coffered masonry domes of Rome and the Renaissance and the prestressed concrete and the geodesic domes of today. (The period when architects employed cast iron so imaginatively was a brief one; when structural steel supplanted cast iron, all the designers seem to have gone back to the box.)

The Capitol dome is Baroque in silhouette and scale. The cast iron structural elements of the outer shell are not concealed behind a veneer, although they are partially disguised as molded arches and columns with Corinthian capitals. It is Baroque in its huge mass, and in its complex and expansive composition that dominates the sweeping vistas of the Mall; its self-confidence derives from an exuberance restrained with dignity. Some guides will tell you that the 36 columns around the base are for the 36 states of the Union at the time it was built and that the 13 columns of the lantern atop the dome stand for the original colonies—which are nice thoughts, but in fact there were only 32 states when the dome was completed and the lantern has only 12 columns.

The lantern and dome are surmounted by Thomas Crawford's 19-foot bronze statue of Freedom, sometimes called "Armed Freedom" as the female figure clad in flowing draperies clasps in her right hand a sheathed sword and in her left a shield. Crawford had originally given the lady a headdress in the form of a Phrygian cap of the freed Roman slaves and emblematic of the liberty cap or *bonnet rouge* worn by extremists in the French Revolution. When Jefferson Davis, who was then secretary of war in Lincoln's first cabinet, inspected the model for the casting he regarded that cap as an exercise in Yankee subversion, inciting the slaves to rebel; he insisted that it had to go. Crawford then improvised a crested helmet with feathers; the resulting plumage is often mistaken for that of an Indian warrior.

Freedom's perch is a precarious one. She has been struck by lightning many times but is grounded by 10 platinum-tipped lightning rods on her shoulders and headdress. Even without lightning, her platform is not all that secure; in an experiment in 1865 Professor Joseph Henry of the Smithsonian determined that as a result of the heat of the sun during the day and the cooling off at night, the dome regularly oscillates in an orbit of three to four inches. When the statue was finally hoisted into place on 2 December 1863, a field battery on Capitol Hill fired a national salute of 35 guns answered by a similar salute from the line of 12 forts then surrounding the city.

About half of the State Capitols have domes patterned after the Capitol in Washington. Twenty-five years after Freedom was dedicated, the state of Texas was to complete its domed Capitol in Austin, capped with a Goddess of Liberty, a reassuring seven feet higher than the statue on top of the dome in Washington.

Under the Rotunda is a crypt with 40 Doric columns designed by Bulfinch as a showcase of natural sandstone construction. The former House of Representatives Chamber, just south of the Rotunda, was refurbished for the 1976 Bicentennial as a Statuary Hall displaying some of the best and many of the worst sculptural portraits in the city. This assembly of past notables—two from every state—is presided over by a splendid sculptured timepiece showing Clio, the Muse of History, astride her winged car (or chariot) precariously taking notes of significant historical events as they transpire.

By far the handsomest public room in the Capitol—at once sumptuous and intimate, though patterned after a Greek amphitheater—is the Old Senate Chamber, the scene of the great speeches of Calhoun, Clay, and Webster. From 1860 to 1935 it was the home of the Supreme Court, which enjoyed then a finer architectural setting than it has since.

The early architects of the Capitol showed great ingenuity and self-confidence in their modification of the classic Corinthian column capitals to incorporate designs of the three indigenous plants most important to the American economy—tobacco, corn, and cotton. The North Small Senate Rotunda outside the Old Senate Chamber has columns capped by tobacco leaf and corn cob capitals designed by Benjamin H. Latrobe with the encouragement of Thomas Jefferson. Latrobe also did the cotton plants in bloom atop the columns of the gallery entrance to the Old Senate Chamber.

Probably no building in Washington receives more constant use during the day than the Capitol. On a typical day—particularly when it is raining—about 25,000 tourists visit the Capitol, and when Congress is in session it is used by about the same number of members of the legislative branch—senators, representatives, and their staff and committee employees. About half of the visitors are members of group tours; the other half are individuals or family groups. The Capitol Guide Force maintains a free guided tour service which lasts a little less than an hour and departs from the Rotunda every 15 minutes. Visitors who are not in groups and who wish to visit the House or Senate galleries must obtain passes—good for the whole two-year session of a current Congress—from the congressman (for the House) and senator (for the Senate) who represent them. Visitors with a serious interest in observing the legislative process will not waste

man car reserved for presidential use. On Christmas Day 1945 the station shepherded 175,000 travelers through its gates for the first peacetime holiday in five years. The funeral trains of Presidents Franklin D. Roosevelt and Dwight D. Eisenhower and of Senator Robert F. Kennedy arrived or departed from Union Station.

In those days state visitors arrived in the capital by train and were received on the red carpet of the oval Presidential Waiting Room (furnished with tapestries and chandeliers) before proceeding to the front arcade with its dramatic framed view of the Capitol dome. Among the kings, prime ministers, and celebrities who had their first glimpse of the Capitol in this manner were Charles Lindbergh, Mary Pickford, King George VI, Georges Clemenceau, Nikita Khrushchev, Winston Churchill, and Queen Elizabeth II.

At the peak of its operations, over 200 trains a day pulled in and out of the 38 tracks. It took more than 4,000 employees to serve its various facilities, including a mortuary, a bowling alley, a YMCA hotel, turkish baths, a restaurant, a pharmacy, and a soda fountain—and peepholes for police to scan the concourse for fugitives.

The architect of the station was Daniel H. Burnham. He had been director of works for the Columbian Exposition—the Chicago World's Fair of 1893—which revived an interest in the Beaux Arts style of architecture and stimulated an impulse toward urban planning which called itself the City Beautiful movement. Burnham was also a member of Washington's McMillan Commission of 1901, which revived and extended L'Enfant's plan for the Mall and sought to refurnish the capital with classical federal buildings in the image of Rome. The McMillan Plan was issued on the centennial of the founding of the District of Columbia, and Union Station was the first building to be constructed under its esthetic and planning criteria. Railway terminals were the chief objects of attention of the City Beautiful movement, and new stations were spawned in Detroit, Kansas City, New Orleans, Chattanooga, and Toronto—but Washington's Union Station is the prototype and handsomest survivor of the breed.

The westernmost panel in the frieze above the station's entrance colonnade contains the following inscription:

HE THAT WOULD BRING HOME THE WEALTH OF THE INDIES
MUST CARRY THE WEALTH OF THE INDIES WITH HIM.
SO IT IS IN TRAVELING. A MAN MUST CARRY KNOWLEDGE
WITH HIM IF HE WOULD BRING HOME KNOWLEDGE.

The passage is from Boswell quoting Samuel Johnson quoting a Spanish proverb. It is apt for the ephemeral population of a city like Washington, whose temporary inhabitants can find in the place little more of the American spirit than they have managed to bring with them: the capital is a repository and an arena but not a net exporter of whatever there is in the American genius.

In recent years—since 1973—Congress, specifically the Public Works Committee of the House of Representatives, has presided over an inane desecration of the interior of the station in a costly and ugly attempt to transmogrify—what they couldn't mogrify they transmogrified—a classic and useful civic ornament into an unappealing, sprawling, and idle National Visitor Center conceived as a celebration of the nation's Bicentennial. The appalling result is that passengers now have to walk one-third of a mile from the front of the station to the train platforms through a labyrinth of makeshift passages and a mean borax lobby that would disgrace a small-town motel. The rows of fine old mahogany benches in the main waiting room have been replaced by an unseemly pit with escalators to nowhere but with a large screen for an automated slide show called PAVE (for Primary Audio Visual Experience) to orient the visitor to sights he can see better by simply walking out to the sidewalk in front of the building. PAVE now doesn't work and neither do the escalators. Construction was halted on a structure for 4,000 parking spaces when cost overruns reached a level of $40,000 per space for each car. The several hundred parking spaces around the station have been reassigned for Senate use, and only 23 metered parking spaces in front of the station are available for railroad patrons.

The *New Yorker*'s late resident train correspondent E. M. Frimbo declared, "Everything about it is ugly. . . . What kind of idiocy is this?" It is hard to believe that such wanton and savage disfigurement could have been acccomplished without some kind of evil talent—but it is all totally artless. It has eaten up four times as much federal funding as the Kennedy Center, while all these years the roof is still in dire need of repairs. All we now have is a berserk memorial to the ineptitude of congressional committees as clients for architectural projects.

Supreme Court   *1st Street at East Capitol Street, NE*
Open weekdays 9–4:30   Tours (30 minutes) when Court is not in session, free
Court sessions Monday–Wednesday (10–12 and 1–3).

> Oyez! Oyez! Oyez! All persons having business before the Honorable, the Supreme Court of the United States, are admonished to draw near and give their attention, for the Court is now sitting. God save the United States and this Honorable Court!
> —The Court crier

The Supreme Court Building by architect Cass Gilbert is probably the largest marble building in the world. Its massive scale and unrelieved symmetry epitomize the academic classicism that reached its peak in the federal architecture of

Washington in the 1930s. The passing years—so far—have not dimmed the dazzling effect of the building's polished marble surface; the effect is blinding even on an overcast day.

The building housing the Supreme Court is dignified by legislative fiat; *dignity* was prescribed in the act that authorized its construction. The result is a Roman temple whose final effect comes perilously close to being pompous— which is an exaggeration of dignity. A design aiming at grandeur verges on the grandiose. The pediment is crowded with sculpture. The frieze has the carved legend EQUAL JUSTICE UNDER LAW* bracketed by festoons of fruit and flower garlands hanging from urns in high relief. The leafy capitals of the Corinthian† columns—the most elaborate of the classic orders—supply a note of exuberance in an otherwise static facade. The great bronze doors open every weekday for business, a front door and porch signifying that the work done in this place is solemn indeed.

As an icon of Justice one misses the simple austerity of America's finest colonial and federal architecture. But the effect of solemnity is nevertheless achieved, and solemnity is the precise requirement for a building housing an institution whose invisible power is based solely on the authority of written opinion.

At the head of the judiciary system, the Supreme Court is the least familiar of the government's three branches. Its chief function is to ensure—through the machinery of the courts—that the president and the Congress abide by the Constitution; it is thus the one institution that confers legitimacy on the others. It has no independent power to enforce its decisions on the other two branches. For two centuries the Court has remained Supreme only because its authority has been voluntarily observed. Its authority has been widely decried but never successfully challenged. Its decisions can be reversed only by the Court itself, as it modifies its views in the light of experience.

The Supreme Court has its own independent police force to guard its precincts, receive writs at midnight, and keep public visitors in order. But its jurisdiction is limited to that single trapezoidal city block—a judicial Vatican City— on which the Court building stands, and its authority stops at the line of the curbstone. Seldom is right so recklessly indifferent to might.

---

* The phrase "Equal Justice under Law" was adopted by the architect without apparent benefit of advice from legal scholars or constitutional historians. The simple word "Justice" would have been less complicated. The urge to qualify and explain is carried to even greater lengths in the legend over the Hamilton County Court House in Cincinnati: EQUAL AND EXACT JUSTICE FOR ALL MEN OF WHATEVER STATE OR PERSUASION, RELIGIOUS OR POLITICAL. The contest is closed with no further entries invited.

† A modified version of the Corinthian order in which cornstalks have been substituted for acanthus leaves—in what one scholar has called "Iowanian."

The reason the Court is the least well known aspect of government is that most of us are not sued and are not parties to suits, most of us are not jurors, and fewest of all of us go into court as spectators to observe the dramatic proceedings they so often provide. The obscurity in which the judicial branch functions is furthered by the absolute barrier against coverage by radio, television, or even still photography.

In a surprising concession to the age of technology the Supreme Court is one of the few in the capital to dispense with a shorthand court reporter. When the justices sit, the marshal turns on the tape recorder and that is usually the end of it. The proceedings are not even transcribed as a matter of routine. Lower courts have to prepare transcripts as the basis for higher court review; but in this court there are no appeals except to god or history, and so transcriptions are made only in response to special petitions.

The location of the Supreme Court—in a sort of armpit between the Capitol and Maryland Avenue, NE—is not a felicitous one. It has no avenue of approach. It is on the axis of no street. It does not even command a clear vista of the Capitol it faces. Considering that the legislature is symbolized by the Capitol, and the executive by the White House, it seems regrettable that another one of L'Enfant's schemes never materialized: he had planned to reserve a conspicuous site for the court near what is now Judiciary Square. It may be an irony or a default or a complicity, but the site and construction of the Court building was negotiated by, and some of its current maintenance is administered by, the

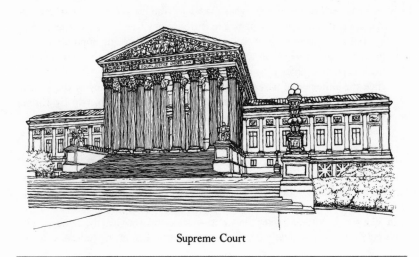

Supreme Court

Architect of the Capitol—an agency, even an imperial agency, of the legislative branch.

This building is the Court's first permanent home. It was constructed chiefly on the initiative of William Howard Taft (the only person to serve as both president and chief justice), and it resulted in part as an overcompensation for past indignities. When the Court was young it had met in Manhattan's Royal Exchange over a market, in the Philadelphia City Hall, in a spare room in the Capitol basement, in a tavern off Pennsylvania Avenue, and from 1860 to 1935 in the Old Senate Chamber of the Capitol. The justices had no assigned offices for their personal use and they were accustomed to doing their work in their homes except when actually sitting. When the great new edifice was finally open and ready for them in 1935, Mr. Justice Stone suggested, "We ought to ride over on elephants," and another justice feared that "we will look like nine black beetles in the Temple of Karnak." Justice Black was a junior justice but he got his pick of the chambers—a nice corner suite; he had the place almost to himself—because only two of the others bothered to move in. The chambers filled up later as new justices were appointed.

The Constitution provides only for the independence of the Court, but does not specify the exact powers and prerogatives or even the number of justices, which remained to be set by the Congress. Its powers have been reinforced principally by tradition through the tenure of 15 chief justices since 1790. (Lifetime tenure is a legal privilege and a tradition. In the same period there have been more than twice as many presidents—Ronald Reagan being the 40th.)

There has been a record that every president who has served at least one full term has appointed at least one justice to the Supreme Court; Jimmy Carter was the first full-term president not to have a chance to make any appointment. A new justice is appointed on an average of once every 22 months. Franklin D. Roosevelt appointed eight justices during his presidency. Long after they have left office the influence of past presidents lingers on in the legacy of the Court. Of the present Court, four were appointed by Richard Nixon, two by Eisenhower, and one each by Kennedy, Johnson, and Ford.

When a vacancy occurs in the office of chief justice, the president may elevate a sitting associate justice to the post, but that rarely happens, as he usually appoints a new member to the Court as its chief. There is no law that says members of the Court have to be lawyers. No laymen have ever been nominated, perhaps because presidents perceive that the Senate might be reluctant to confirm them.

In addition to presiding over the Court—where his vote has the same weight as his colleagues'—the chief justice is by statute chairman of the Judicial Conference, a body that administers the 500 federal judges in the 92 U.S. District Courts and the 11 U.S. Courts of Appeals throughout the nation. He is also a trustee of the National Gallery of Art and chancellor of the Smithsonian Institution. These assignments are far from ceremonial, and Chief Justice Warren E. Burger performs them with an obvious relish.

Some of the most distinguished justices in the Court's history—Oliver Wendell Holmes, Louis D. Brandeis, Benjamin N. Cardozo, and Hugo L. Black— were never chief justices.

The Court's term begins on the first Monday in October and generally alternates between two weeks of sittings and two weeks of recesses. The Court deals only in cases, specific cases of law that come before it for review—where the abstractions of the Constitution become manifest as concrete questions to be resolved—and schedules from 25 to 30 of them for oral argument at each sitting, at the rate of an hour for each case, four cases a day, every Monday, Tuesday, and Wednesday for two weeks out of every month. All sittings are in public session from 10 in the morning till 3 in the afternoon. The schedule is arduous and inexorable—with a minimum of five justices present for oral arguments to be heard. They now recess for precisely one hour at noon for lunch. (In earlier days the lunch recess was 45 minutes, and before that just a half hour.) The rest of the week they review cases, consider writs and petitions, and draft opinions. On Fridays they convene in private conference to deliberate on cases argued with no outsider present, with no recording or transcript, and with the junior justice acting as doorkeeper. It does not require much indulgence to accept Chief Justice Burger's claim that he averages a 77-hour work week.

The Supreme Court is an American invention and no other country has anything like it. The unwritten English Constitution assigns no equivalent powers to Parliament or Privy Council or attorney general. No English judge can say that a law passed by Parliament is void. Here in the American invention grafted on to the heritage of the Anglo-Saxon common law system, it was the Court that could tell President Franklin D. Roosevelt that his New Deal legislation was unconstitutional. It was the Court that forbade President Truman to seize the U.S. Steel Company. It was the Court that told President Nixon to hand over the White House tapes to the Watergate prosecutor. And it was the Court that upheld Louisiana's Jim Crow segregation law in 1896 (*Plessy v. Ferguson*) only to reverse itself nearly 60 years later in rejecting the doctrine of "separate but equal" (*Brown v. Board of Education,* 1954).

Only once have the other branches of government failed to accept the voluntary observance of the Supreme Court's decisions. In 1857 (*Dred Scott v. Sandford*) the Court ruled that Congress lacked the power to limit the expansion of slavery by law; it ruled the Missouri Compromise of 1820 null and void. The result was more than the abolitionists of the North could stomach; the result was the tragic resort to force as an alternative to the rule of law; the result was the Civil War.

Americans may have a healthy contempt for much of the federal apparatus, but their intuition tells them that there is something sacrosanct about the Supreme Court. At the height of his popularity in 1937 President Franklin D. Roosevelt attempted to "reorganize" the Court, demanding authorization to pack it with one additional justice for each over the age of 70. He failed utterly. Though no president ever had a better grasp of popular sentiment, he greatly underestimated the profound resistance of people everywhere to any notion of tampering with the Court.

Meanwhile the nine justices on the Court appear to be the optimum number; any fewer could barely cope with the rising work load; any more might lead to assignment of cases to panels and impair the consideration of every case by every justice.

Cass Gilbert was appointed to the original Commission of Fine Arts when it was established in 1910; thus he was a charter member of the group of architects spearheading the building splurge that transformed Washington in the Imperial Neoclassic style—culminating in the completion of the Federal Triangle and the Supreme Court in the mid–1930s. Gilbert believed it was one of the functions of public buildings "to educate oncoming generations." He was a versatile designer and his early work was his best: the U.S. Custom House (1901–07), Bowling Green, New York City, a Beaux Arts masterpiece; the Woolworth Building (1911–13), a 60-story eclectic Gothic skyscraper; and the Allen Memorial Art Museum (1915–17) at Oberlin College, Ohio, a Renaissance palace. His later buildings are less successful as he became committed to a rigid Neoclassicism as in the U.S. Court House (1936), Foley Square, New York City, and Washington's Supreme Court—completed after his death.

The court chamber is unfortunately not one of the city's great rooms (see p. 312). The beautiful Old Supreme Court chamber in the Capitol shows how a courtroom can be both intimate and solemn. The Scottish Rite Temple on 16th Street, NW (1910) shows how a classical revival room can be grandly ceremonial and flooded with natural light. But these examples were lost on Cass Gilbert, who accorded slight architectural justice to a courtroom of certain historic destiny. It was an irrevocably missed opportunity.

When the building first opened, the public was admitted to the chamber by a silent Negro usher dressed in cutaway coat and striped trousers, holding open the bronze and leather center door with a tasseled velvet cord; nowadays the public files through an airport type electronic security screen managed by uniformed police. The room itself is 64 feet square but only 30 feet high. The high windows along the north and south sides were designed to ensure that light would not shine directly into the eyes of the justices on the bench or the counsel facing them. But in practice the light from the white marble courtyards is so dazzling that the windows have to be covered in heavy velvet curtains; even on the sunniest of days the court's proceedings are conducted by artificial light. There are four friezes of allegorical bas-relief sculpture, but they are placed much too high for any of their details to register.

On the west side of the building is a formal dining room where the justices have lunch every day when the court is in session. It is entered off the main hall through an anteroom containing, to the right, a desk for the clerk who ensures their mealtime privacy, and to the left, a large carved mahogany sideboard in the Sheraton style. Resting on top of the sideboard is an inscribed label designating it as a gift to the court from Covington and Burling, Washington's largest law firm, in a gesture that raises a question of taste, if not propriety.

Tour guides at the Court brag about two cantilevered marble staircases, claiming that the only two others like them are in the Vatican and the Paris Opera. That may well be. They are a caprice of the architect's, curiously not only closed off to the public but seldom used by the staff; they are simply expensive fire escapes.

The sculptured pediment over the main entrance (west front) is an artistic and iconographic puzzlement—an anachronistic group of character actors playing charades at an improbable house party. The three central figures are allegorical with an unrelenting gravity of demeanor. They are flanked by three oblivious chief justices (Marshall, Taft, and Hughes) chatting with Wall Street lawyer Elihu Root, the architect Gilbert, and Robert Aitken, the pediment's sculptor—all decked out in togas but assuming casual postures. For Gilbert to have placed a caricature of himself in bas-relief in the lobby of the Woolworth Building (which he did in a crazy Gothic tradition) is one thing, but to flirt with posterity so casually in a temple pediment achieves bathos—a ludicrous descent from lofty symbol to low comedy. Are we witness here to a sense of humor, or the lack of it?

On the back of the building (east front) may be found a much finer sculptured pediment, by Herman A. MacNeil, displayed to its great disadvantage high up over a narrow street of nondescript row houses. Here is Imperial architecture gone adrift, worse than the British Museum stranded in Bloomsbury.

Reprise. The Supreme Court building was officially designated a National Landmark in 1977, only 42 years after it first opened for business. Congress is the court's landlord and the holder of its purse strings, as administered by the architect of the Capitol and his 72 assistants. The Office of the Architect has issued a Master Plan for the Capitol: Phase II, which notes that Congress must bear part of the onus for failing to locate the court in Judiciary Square as L'Enfant had proposed; the plan also notes that the Court's staff seems to increase every year and will thus eventually outgrow its present building. Thus the plan contemplates a second move of the Court "to create a major new center somewhere in Monumental Washington to symbolically represent the separation of the Judiciary" from the other branches.

In some of the bleakest dreams a planner ever spun, the Phase II report continues to speculate whether there will be additional courts "either to screen cases, or as a referral court . . . as the Federal Court System expands and responds to the increasingly litigious nature of American society. . . . In the event of a move the present Supreme Court Building could become a museum of the Court's history and/or an adjunct to . . . the Library of Congress as a location of symposia and seminars."

Folger Shakespeare Library
East Capitol Street between 2nd and 3rd Streets, SE
Open Monday–Saturday, 10–4, free.

> Genius is the consoler of our mortal condition, and Shakespeare taught
> us that the little world of the heart is vaster, deeper and richer than the
> spaces of astronomy.
> —Ralph Waldo Emerson, 1864

This is one of America's great "treasure-house" libraries, which are mostly the fruit of collections begun not by scholars and academics but by industrialists— men like John Carter Brown, James Lenox, Henry E. Huntington, J. P. Morgan, and Henry Clay Folger. Folger had a law degree from Columbia, but he became a businessman, starting as a part-time clerk in the office of Charles Pratt, a partner of John D. Rockefeller. In time Folger was to become president and then chairman of the board of the Standard Oil Company of New York, the company which later became Socony-Vacuum (with the sign of the winged flying horse) and which now survives as the Mobil Oil Corporation. As the company prospered, so did Folger's personal fortune, providing him with the means to become the foremost collector of Shakespeariana of his time. During the working day he was a marketer of oil and gas products, but he spent his evenings and weekends in the single-minded pursuit of buying rare books.

Folger first showed an interest in English literature as an undergraduate at Amherst in the class of 1879, where his papers on Dickens and Tennyson both won prizes. In his senior year at college he went to a sparsely attended lecture by the aging Ralph Waldo Emerson on the very Emersonian topic of "Mental Temperance." A few days later he came upon an essay on Shakespeare that

Emerson had written in 1864 to commemorate the Tercentenary of the poet's birth.

Never underestimate the power of an essay: those four short pages of Emerson's tribute were to kindle in young Folger a lifelong devotion to the life and work of that singular poetic genius. Emerson's glowing eulogy described Shakespeare as "our metre of culture":

> He fulfilled the famous prophecy of Socrates, that the poet most excellent in tragedy would be most excellent in comedy. . . . At the short distance of 300 years he is mythical, like Orpheus and Homer. . . . Yet we pause expectant before the genius of Shakespeare—as if his biography were not yet written; until the problem of the whole English race is solved. . . . Shakespeare, by his transcendant reach of thought . . . unites the extremes. . . . He is yet to all wise men the companion of the closet. The student finds the solitariest place not solitary enough to read him.

Those words so fired Folger's imagination that he bought a cheap 13-volume edition of all the plays and began to read them straight through late into the night. He mastered the works of Shakespeare with the same kind of determination that he later devoted to collecting them as a lasting avocation.

Henry Folger was not at all rich when he bought his first copy of the Fourth Folio at Bang's auction rooms in New York; his winning bid of $107.50 was more than the funds he had at hand and he had to get credit for payment 30 days later. With the growth of his fortune his purchases gradually increased, and his efforts were not without competition from other millionaires, particularly from Henry E. Huntington and J. P. Morgan, who were amassing their own libraries; but their appetite for unique objects covered the whole range from Mesopotamian seals to the scores of Gilbert and Sullivan. Folger had the advantage of concentrating on a single field, and book dealers on both sides of the Atlantic began to accord him the first offer of new properties to come on the market, and they were even known to interrupt board meetings of the Standard Oil Company to do so. The famous New York dealer in rare books, A. S. W. Rosenbach, called Folger "the most consistent collector I have ever known. . . . he had a plan and he never deviated from it."

Folger was a shy and reticent man, almost reclusive in his hours away from the office. He had no particular interest in sports and his creative energies were consumed in the joy of acquisition—poring over the catalogs of book dealers, scanning the notices of antiquarians, and traveling by freighter to England to take in the auction sales. This was a matter of intense concentration, the single-minded pursuit of his few hours of leisure. These were interests that he shared only with his talented wife, Emily Jordan Folger, a scholar and teacher of

Church directly across East Capitol Street. The library also gained instant historic fame; in less than three decades after it was completed it was officially listed in the *National Register of Historic Places*—quite possibly the first example of "modern" architecture to be so recognized. Cret in fact saw no contradiction between traditional Beaux Arts symmetry and modernist restraint in ornamentation; his Folger Library reconciles the two tendencies in a new style of peaceful coexistence which the critics—with their penchant for labels—termed *starved classicism.*

The American Institute of Architects has conducted annual polls asking its

FOR WISEDOMES SAKE, A WORD THAT ALL MEN LOVE
LOVES LABOURS LOST

Folger Shakespeare Library: Statue of Puck

member architects to list their rating of the "proudest achievements" of their profession; in 1949 Paul Cret's Folger Library was accorded the No. 1 spot, but since 1976 it has disappeared completely from the annual list of "top 20." To my eye, it is just the kind of modern building that ages well: the exterior is free of any taint of the misguided historicism that burdens the theatrical replica within.

When the Folger was built in the early 1930s it was given deep basement vaults for rare books because in those days it was thought reasonable to provide such measures of protection from the threat of bomb damage in the event of war. But the library's expanding collection has outgrown even the space in those deep vaults, and a new wing to the rear of the building is being built with additional stack areas for rare books, according to the designs of the Washington architectural firm of Hartman-Cox.

Library of Congress *1st Street between East Capitol Street and Independence Avenue, SE   Open weekdays 8:30–9:30, Saturday 8:30–5, Sunday 1–5   Exhibit areas open weekends til 6   Tours (1 hour) weekdays 9–4 on the hour, free. Recorded information 287–6400.*

> The Library is the best public building in Washington. . . . I am proud of it. My constituents are proud of it. . . . It is a great show building. It is our building and worth the money.
> —Rep. Joseph G. ("Uncle Joe") Cannon, later Speaker of the House, November 1897

The Library of Congress is the most ultra of the ne plus ultra examples of those extravagant, eclectic late Victorian government buildings in Washington that enjoyed such huge disfavor for the greater part of this century. So fickle and unsympathetic is the taste of one age for that of another that buildings such as the library, the Old Post Office Building on Pennsylvania Avenue at 12th Street, NW, and the Old State, War, and Navy Building, even the Smithsonian Castle on the Mall, have all only recently regained a measure of esthetic respectability. Of those four 19th-century relics, only the library has not—so far—been threatened with demolition.

Shortly after the library opened, a critic named Russell Sturgis deplored its "false idea of grandeur which consists mainly in hoisting a building up from a reasonable level off the ground, mainly in order to secure for it a monstrous flight of steps which must be surmounted before the main door can be reached." In a survey of American architecture in 1934, Charles H. Whittaker dismissed the library as "a dreadful medley of waste and maudlin virtuosity." And in the same year no less an expert than President Franklin D. Roosevelt sounded out the Architect of the Capitol on the practicality of refacing the library building and removing its dome; the president felt that the dome was "out of tune" and that the exterior decoration was just so much "gingerbread." Even the official WPA Guide Book of 1942 describes the library as a period piece, "a masterpiece of architecture in its day, . . . over-lavish in ornamental detail."

For most of the 19th century Congress's library had occupied a single large chamber in the middle of the Capitol's west front overlooking the Mall. Members in either house could send a page down the hall to get any book that might be needed in the course of a floor debate. After a disastrous fire in 1851, a triple tier of cast iron balconies and alcoves was installed. As the collections grew and piles of atlases and maps were jammed under every table, Congress authorized an expansion, but occupants of the neighboring offices refused to vacate them. Eventually the need for a new and separate building was recognized.

Though no precise site had been determined, a congressional commission sponsored an open architectural competition in which 27 architects submitted a variety of designs. The winning award was a scheme in the Italian Renaissance style (some say "Victorian Rococo") submitted by John L. Smithmeyer and Paul J. Pelz. Smithmeyer was born in Vienna and Pelz in Silesia; they had recently completed the Healy Building for Georgetown University, and their collaboration on the joint library project was to consume the balance of their professional careers, without providing either lasting recognition or fair compensation for their efforts. After the running start of the initial competition, the project staggered into a swamp of feckless congressional committees and commissions. Good architecture is supposed to require a good client, and seldom was that dictum put to a severer test. Twenty-four years were to elapse between the competition of 1873 and the completed library of 1897.

One of the members of the commission, a Senator Howe, on his return from a vacation in Europe in 1874, declared that the Smithmeyer and Pelz design—remarkably similar to the building that survives today—was "too small and plain." At this instigation the two partners submitted new designs in the French Renaissance, "Modern" Renaissance, Romanesque, German Renaissance, and 13th-century Gothic styles. And a dozen other architects submitted new designs—for which they were never paid. While the architects involved had their patience tested and their reputations injured, political support for the project remained strong. The chairman of the Joint Committee on the Library, Senator Daniel W. Voorhees of Indiana (he was to become a legend as "The Tall Sycamore of the Wabash"), championed the library's cause on the floor of the Senate on 5 May 1880, with the sentiment that "the crystal fountain of accumulated knowledge . . . will continue its growth . . . to a sphere of endless and unlimited development."

In 1882 the joint committee asked Gen. Montgomery C. Meigs of the U.S. Army Corps of Engineers if it would be feasible to raise the dome of the Capitol by 50 feet to obtain additional space around the rotunda for the growing hoard of books. This kind of amateurism and procrastination continued until finally in 1886 a modified version of the original Italian Renaissance design was reapproved and purchase of the site between Independence Avenue and East Capitol Street authorized. The final orientation of the library on that site totally blocked the L'Enfant Plan vista of the Capitol from Pennsylvania Avenue, SE. (A similar political decision had blocked the line of sight between the Capitol and the White House with the siting of the Treasury Building at Pennsylvania Avenue, NW.)

In 1888 Smithmeyer was abruptly fired and Gen. Thomas L. Casey of the U.S. Army Corps of Engineers was put in charge of the project. Shortly thereafter Smithmeyer died with his fees still due him, and Pelz had to borrow money to bury him. Casey was shrewd enough to retain Pelz as a consultant, but it would not be long before he was to install his own son, Edward P. Casey, as Pelz's successor with particular responsibility for the library's interior. Behind all the Renaissance marble and mosaic the engineers left their mark on the functional details of the building: they designed the pneumatic tubes and dumbwaiters to move the books around, the fireproof bookstacks of iron and marble or glass, and the electric illumination from the building's own power plant.

General Casey insisted on employing only American artists to work on the decoration of the building; it was seen as a great showcase for native talent in the absence of imported sculptors and mural painters from Europe. The Columbian Exposition in Chicago in 1893 had dramatized a belief in the unity of art and knowledge, the capacity of the visual arts of the present to express the great ideas of past civilization. This was a bookish notion, the allegory of word and picture, for which the decoration of a library was particularly suited. At the outset James A. McNeill Whistler was invited to superintend the program of murals, but he sent word from London that he "had once worked for Uncle Sam—as a draftsman in the Coast Survey—and he didn't want any more of it." So General Casey ended up commissioning—at nominal fees—19 artists to paint a total of 112 murals, and 22 sculptors to complete uncounted numbers of statues, tympanum friezes, spandrel reliefs, and cartouches. In his study of *The Fine Arts of America*, Joshua C. Taylor, the former director of the National Museum of American Art, describes the library as "the first federally commissioned building in which all the arts were included in the initial planning."

The Main Entrance Hall of the library is nothing less than gorgeous. From its stained glass skylight to the zodiac inlays of its polished floor it is resplendent with disparate decorative elements executed in an opulence of materials and with a quality of workmanship that can never again be duplicated. To visit the Main Hall for the first time is to have one's visual faculties taxed to the limit of their capacity: it is like a visit to the inside of a square Easter egg that Fabergé might have made for a Romanov or to an opera setting of an Old Testament palace by Gustave Doré or to the interior of a Baked Alaska with pistachio and gold meringue executed in marble and bronze.

As part of the legislative branch of the government, the Library of Congress is an anomaly, consuming 15 percent of the billion dollars a year that Congress and its appurtenances cost. Actually, the library has three constituencies: the Congress, the library world, and the nation's scholars. Its first priority is to serve Congress—the committees, the members, and the staff (in that order). To this end it maintains the Congressional Research Service (CRS), currently headed by a former member of Congress, with a sophisticated and versatile staff of full-time researchers. It prepares studies on request in the fields of law, history, economics, and political science, and it digests bills, prepares maps and charts, writes speeches, and answers letters on technical subjects. It gets 2,000 questions a day on such topics as: "How many people are on food stamps?" or "What is the origin of the term *silent majority?*" (The first instance of the use of that term was found in an article on funeral practices in an 1874 issue of *Harper's* magazine.) The CRS is the second largest division of the library with a budget of $20 million, exceeded only by the division serving the blind and handicapped, which provides talking books to half a million people through local branch libraries throughout the country.

The close association of the library with the Congress is not without its parochial consequences. For instance, the architect of the Capitol, who serves in effect as the library's landlord, states in his Master Plan, Phase II (1977) that "Congress's power to investigate cannot have any bounds put upon it. The Library is its principal source of information and must be a national library to carry out its Congressional function." This remarkable notion was reinforced in a task force report chaired by Gerard Piel in the same year, but nothing could be more absurd. Congressional control of the library has only the most tenuous relationship to congressional power to investigate, and if the library and its books are Congress's principal source of information, that will be news indeed to most of its members.

When the library's third building, the James Madison Memorial Building (designated by the official initials LM), was opened in 1980, the dubious program of naming the Capitol buildings for heroes of the past continued to advance. Not content with the Russell, Dirksen, and Hart Office Buildings on the Senate side, and the Rayburn, Longworth, and Cannon Buildings on the House side, the architect of the Capitol and the librarian of Congress have rechristened the Library of Congress as "The Library of Congress Thomas Jefferson Build-ing" (LJ), and the annex, long known as the Thomas Jefferson Building, has been renamed as "The Library of Congress John Adams Building" (LA). This annex building in Art Moderne style was a fitting tribute to Jefferson, with a splendid reading room and murals celebrating his name; it has chiseled in marble his finest quotation ("The earth belongs always to the living generation"*)—all now to be called by the name of John Adams, while the association of Jefferson with the florid old Library of Congress is particularly uncongenial in the light of his taste for the classical.

The Library of Congress got its start in 1800 when $5,000 was appropriated for the purchase of books to be selected by (guess who?) the secretary of the Senate and the clerk of the House. It got its second boost with the purchase of over 6,000 volumes of the private library of Thomas Jefferson—only a third of which were to survive a disastrous fire of 1851. Jefferson, characteristically, had developed his own system of classification for the books in his collection; it was a system derived in part from the abstract philosophical categories—Memory, Reason, and Imagination—laid down by Sir Francis Bacon. The library got a third boost when it fell heir to the extensive book collection of the Smithsonian Institution, which had already developed an active program of exchange of pub-lications with scientific societies abroad. Joseph Henry, the secretary of the Smithsonian, relinquished the books in 1866, not because he did not believe in a national library but because he thought it just didn't belong as a part of the Smithsonian; he wanted his institution to concentrate on basic research in sci-ence. The Smithsonian Deposit, as it was called, made the Library of Congress a major library overnight; the deposit was held as a separate collection and not until 1950 was it integrated and intershelved with the other holdings of the Li-brary of Congress.

It is likely that the history of these varied collections has had some bearing on the library in developing its own *A* through *Z* system of classification, a prag-matic and rather arbitrary reflection of the way the books found themselves on its shelves, now being adopted for convenience by most university libraries, free of any pretensions to a philosophical system or any thesaural hierarchy—as ex-isted in the old Dewey Decimal System or the compendium of Peter Mark Roget.

The Smithmeyer and Pelz design is based on the floor plan of a Greek Cross; it derives in principle from the European library system of the Bibliotheque Na-

---

* This was before the age of concern with the conservation of natural resources; surely Jefferson's intention was to free the living from the dead hand of the past, not to flout the needs of future generations.

tionale and the British Museum, providing a central reading room surrounded by enormous stack areas for the storage of books, maps, and manuscripts. But the American version was designed for a broader clientele than just academic researchers; it had to be hospitable to the omnivorous reading and browsing habits of the general public, even to people unfamiliar with the use of a card catalog. The great Circular Reading Room of the British Museum (now being replaced by the new British Library near Euston Station) was largely the resort of scholars; it was—and remains—inhospitable to readers without formal academic credentials. The American policy is much more lenient. Listen to this generous statement of the Library's policy regarding its use by the public:

> Although this is the Library of Congress, it is also a general reference library for public use. The aim of the Library is to offer the widest possible use of its collections consistent with their preservation and with its primary obligation of service to Congress and other governmental agencies.
>
> Admission to the reading room is free. No introduction or credentials are required for persons over high school age who wish to read in the general reading rooms. . . . Visitors who wish merely to see the Main Reading Room may do so from the Visitor's Gallery.
>
> Every reader is entitled to prompt and efficient service—that is the aim of the Library of Congress. The user should feel free to ask the library personnel for help and report to the assistant in charge if the requested material is not received.*

It was not ever thus. In the beginning the use of the library was restricted to congressmen, and then shared grudgingly with members of the Supreme Court, agencies of the executive branch, members of the diplomatic corps—and finally the public. High school students have had to be restricted because they were overwhelming the facilities in search of the kind of materials available in their school or public libraries. The unfailingly polite staff hates to disappoint young people; they explain that if they have a special project in mind and can bring a letter from their principal, they can return for material not otherwise available. More of a trial to the staff is the fringe element of street people and the mentally disturbed who are attracted to the library—open seven days a week—as a friendly haven for eccentrics and loners.

The Visitor's Gallery offers a splendid view of the octagonal Main Reading Room with its mahogany reading desks arranged in concentric circles around a central distributing desk. This is the heart of the library's service to the public, and it is surrounded by alcoves and tiers of balconies presenting easy access to an

---

* Information for Readers, 1975.

abundance of open-shelved reference books. This is the idea of a panopticon: a round room embodying an encyclopedia of learning.

Clusters of richly veined marble columns support the 125-foot-high dome; brown marble from Tennessee, dark red from Numidia, and shades ranging from light cream to topaz from Siena. In the collar of the dome is Edwin Blashfield's great mural of *The Progress of Civilization,* 100 feet in diameter, and, even above that in the dome of the lantern, the depiction of Human Understanding in the figure of a woman lifting her veil to look beyond finite knowledge as a cherub holds a book at her feet. The statues arrayed on two levels represent excellence in the chief aspects of civilized life and thought. Barely legible in the triangular pendentives between the eight arched, stained glass windows are gilded literary or biblical quotations selected by the ever-willing President Charles W. Eliot of Harvard—who was later to perform the same services for the city's Union Station and Post Office.

Through all the maze of this rich iconography, the lighting concentrates on the myriad shelves of old books in their various bindings; through all the ornament, one can sense the intangibility of knowledge, as Virginia Woolf wrote in *Jacob's Room* of a sister institution: "There is in the British Museum an enormous mind . . . hoarded beyond the power of any single individual to possess it."

For all the architectural symbolism of its setting, the Library of Congress has never been established formally as a national library like the Bibliothèque Nationale or the British Library, and it is a national library only de facto and by default. The American Library Association in its statement of federal legislative policy (January 1979) recommends yet again that Congress designate the library as *the* National Library, but all these years Congress has chosen not to do so.

In addition to the Library of Congress, the federal government maintains two other libraries that are considered *national* in scope, in the specialized fields of medicine and agriculture. The National Library of Medicine, housed in two huge buildings on the campuslike grounds of the National Institutes of Health in Bethesda, Maryland, is operated as part of the Public Health Service, an agency in the Department of Health and Human Services. The governnment's second largest library is the National Agricultural Library of the Department of Agriculture, housed in a striking 20-story brown brick skyscraper in the Washington suburb of Beltsville, Maryland, adjacent to the agricultural schools of the University of Maryland. The Library of Congress attempts to collect definitively all aspects of science and technology other than clinical medicine and technical agriculture, as concentrated in the specialized collections at Bethesda and Beltsville. (A fourth federal institution similar to a national library is the National Archives, the custodian of *official* government documents and reports. But note that the extensive papers of Thomas Jefferson, George Mason, and James Madison were considered to be private and personal rather than official, and are thus held by the Library of Congress.)

Among the comprehensive national libraries of the world, most tend to concentrate on the language and literature of their nation of origin. But this is not true at all of the Library of Congress; it is unique in that, of its 75 million items on 350 miles of bookshelves, two-thirds are in languages other than English. And they continue to be accessioned in the same ratio—at a rate of 100 new items a minute—two-thirds in foreign languages. The current librarian of Congress, Daniel J. Boorstin, was once accosted by the director of a European library who asked him why the Americans were not content to stick to American history and to works in English—as if it were presumptuous to venture so deeply into the vast areas of Hispanic, Slavic, Oriental, and other cultures. The answer is, of course, that our origins as a nation are so various that our national identity demands the paradox of an *international* library to reflect the whole range of a society of immigrants.

The 120 linguists on the library staff have command of 168 literary languages. The most tangible expression of the library's commitment to the universality of culture are the 33 keystones on the second-story windows of the building's central and corner pavilions. They are 18 inches high and were carefully sculptured on the basis of scientific data accumulated by Professor Otis T. Mason, who was then the curator of the department of ethnology at the Smithsonian. The sculptors, William Boyd and Henry J. Ellicott, had to enlarge them to a uniform size to agree with the architectural scale. Thus even the outside fabric of the library was to have a didactic role in depicting not only the civilized but the "savage and barbarous" races of mankind. Beginning at the north end of the entrance pavilion, heading south, and then circling the building, the heads represent the racial groups described as follows: Russian Slav, Blonde European, Brunette European, Modern Greek, Persian, Circassian, Hindu, Hungarian, Semite, Arabian, Turkish, Modern Egyptian, Abyssinian, Malayan, Polynesian, Australian, Negrito, Zulu, Papuan, Sudan Negro, Akka, Fuegian, Botocudo, Pueblo Indian, Eskimo, Plains Indian, Samoyede, Korean, Japanese, Aino, Burmese, Tibetan, and Chinese. (The Akka are hill tribesmen of northern Thailand and the Botocudo are from the Minas Gerais state of Brazil.)

Fountain of the Court of Neptune. At the extreme west front of the library at pavement level, fitting into three niches of the retaining wall between the two staircases of the main plaza leading to the library's grand entrance, is a 50-foot semicircular pool containing the Fountain of the Court of Neptune. This sculptural showpiece, completed by Roland Hinton Perry at the age of 27, can be easily missed by visitors who customarily enter the library at the ground entrance on the road through the porte cochere.

The bronze mythological figures of the fountain seem much at home in their grottolike setting. The colossal figure of Neptune in the central niche is twice life-size; if he were to stand up, he would be 12 feet tall. Two Nereids (that is, two of the 50 daughters of Nereus, "the Old Man of the Sea") are mounted on galloping sea horses in the niches on either side; the exaggerated poses of these two figures charge the fountain with a sense of energy. Neptune's throne is flanked by Tritons—fish with human heads—blowing conch shells from which jets of water spurt crisscrossing other jets issuing from a writhing sea serpent and frogs and turtles. The whole composition vibrates with a kind of frenzied exuberance suggesting that Rome's Trevi Fountain might have been its inspiration.

National Union Catalog. In 1901 the Library of Congress reached an informal exchange agreement with the New York Public Library by which each library would have a card list of the important books held by the other. By 1909 nine other libraries had joined the exchange system, which has since grown to include over 1,100 libraries in the United States and Canada. The resulting National Union Catalog now has over 13 million entries, comprising a unified record—with locations—of all the cooperating major research libraries. The retrospec-

Library of Congress: Fountain of the Court of Neptune

tive publication of pre-1956 imprints was completed in 1981. It has been described as the greatest single instrument of bibliographic control in existence, and will probably remain so until eventually superseded by an automated system.

The Library of Congress did not have the funds or the technological capacity to convert the central card file catalog into printed books for benefit of other libraries. It remained for the British firm of Mansell Publishing, Ltd., who put out the British Museum Catalog, to provide the daring and the financial resources to underwrite a series of 700 volumes of 700 pages each (running over 100 feet of shelving in the familiar green bindings with gold letters), issued to over 1,300 subscribing libraries in 46 countries, with new volumes being issued at the rate of one a week. Every week 19,000 cut-and-paste card files would leave the Library of Congress for London where they were reduced by Mansell's automatic cameras for facsimile offset printing at Wisbech and eventual distribution to research libraries around the world.

Museum of African Art, Smithsonian Institution   *316 A Street, NE*
Re-established at 950 Independence Avenue, SW.   Open daily 10-5:30.

> We're using the instrument of an art museum for purposes of social education.
> —Warren Robbins, director of the Museum of African Art,
>   September 1980

The Museum of African Art was established in 1964 as an experiment in communication between cultures. It is very much the personal creation of its founder and director Warren Robbins, who says, "I've always been fascinated by the moment when divergent peoples come together and suddenly understand each other." That impulse to explain the workings of cultural reciprocity—not clinical but moral—has become the museum's abiding theme.

It is the first museum of its kind in the country, and its aim is nothing less than to attempt the portrayal of an entire antecedent civilization of 20 million Americans of African extraction. Like other art museums it is concerned with conservation and art education, but its unique curatorial program stresses the social implications of the objects on display. In its brief period of existence it has acquired 7,000 masks, tools, sculptures, textiles, musical instruments, weapons, and artifacts representing 35 tribes and 18 nations of present-day Africa. They are presented in exhibits that stress their symbolic and ceremonial functions in settings where religious forms and agricultural or domestic or military forms are often inseparable. The museum dramatizes for all Americans a creative tradition going back over a 1,000 years, the art of a whole people with handsome and exciting icons full of emotional content—for some visitors reinforcing a sense of identity, for all visitors providing an essay in the ambivalent effects of one culture upon another. The museum is an exercise in applied social anthropology with a sense of mission that verges on the polemical.

The museum has adopted as its logo one of its prize possessions, an antelope headdress carved from wood by the Bambara tribe of Mali. It is a mythical creature half man and half antelope, with an attenuated nose and horns whose beautiful patina suggests years of use in telling Bambara ancestors how to plant

Museum of African Art

successful crops. The museum has a Comparative Gallery illustrating the influence of African scultpure on many of the pioneers of 20th-century art; it uses reproductions of works by Picasso, Braque, Modigliani, and Matisse to show the strong interrelationship with African exemplars. Other rooms range from bold geometric murals from the N'debele tribe of Southeast Africa to a painstaking reproduction of Frederick Douglass's study. The gallery has been host to such temporary exhibitions as "The Image of Blacks in Western Art," showing photographs of blacks in roles created by whites but free of stereotypes and bigotry. One of the great resources of the collection is the bequest of 100,000 photographs, slides, and films made by Eliot Elisofon, the late *Life* photographer. It is a unique archive of Africana.

In 1979 the Museum of African Art, with congressional approval, was incorporated as an integral bureau of the Smithsonian Institution, ensuring its permanent survival and relieving its pioneer founder of the relentless burden of almost day-to-day fund raising. The collection continues to find its home in the row of restored town houses from 316 to 332 A Street NE, a preservation showpiece of residential conversion to institutional purposes. The gem of the row houses is No. 316, the first residence of Frederick Douglass, the former slave who became one of the greatest abolitionists and most brilliant orators of his day—a distinction he shared with Abraham Lincoln.

Rayburn House Office Building
Independence Avenue between 1st and South Capitol Streets, SW

> Authoritarian architecture must be clear and regular on the outside, and let the passing eye deduce nothing of what goes on inside.
> —Robert Hughes, *The Shock of the New*

The worst thing to be said about the Rayburn Building is that the congressmen whose home it is don't seem sufficiently embarrassed by it. It is the most impractical, most unlovely, most expensive building in town, tactlessly symbolizing the power system that created it. The offices and hearing rooms for which it was designed occupy only 15 percent of its space; the rest is halls, public areas, and parking spaces. Congress is the only branch of the government that authorizes its own buildings, appropriates for them an open-ended budget, and executes their design without any professional review, except that of the architect of the Capitol, who has functioned more as a building superintendent than an arbiter of taste. The ultimate clients are the elder members of the building committees whose seniority permits them to operate behind closed doors, and who have given us as well the desecration of Union Station, the pomposity of the Library of Congress's Madison Building, and the not yet completely perpetrated

Hart Senate Office Building. It is not a very good system of constructing buildings, as it excludes both competence and common sense. One wonders if they order these matters any better in Moscow.

The Rayburn Building has nine hearing rooms, the most important areas of the building. Here most of the work is done and history often made; the rooms are uniformly cavernous and poorly lit, with poor acoustics and bad sight lines, and no vestibules to filter the frequent coming and going of spectators and members. Their decor is one of four different shades: green, blue, gold, or red. A congressman who has served 10 or 12 terms in the House will have enough seniority to get one of the 169 office suites, but he will not be able to choose the color of his walls; suites to the north and west are tan, those to the south and east, a soft, robin's egg blue.

The east and west facades of the building are each graced with four colossal sculptured Greek vases nine feet high. They are called *rhytons*—wine cups in the shape of a ram's head joined to a cornucopia sitting on a wave crest of carved leaves—and provide both a hint of comic relief and a note of energy or movement to an otherwise static exterior. When Ada Louise Huxtable reviewed the final product for the *New York Times* she described it as "profligate, elephantine . . . the apotheosis of humdrum," and concluded that "to be both dull and vulgar may be an achievement of sorts." She also complained that the statue of Speaker Rayburn in the main entrance had his back to the front door; shortly after that they turned the statue around and he has been facing out ever since.

Marine Barracks and Commandant's House   *8th and I Streets, SE*
Throughout the corps they are known as "the Eighth and Eye Marines"—those on largely ceremonial duty in the Marine Barracks in Southeast Washington at a site chosen by Thomas Jefferson during a survey of the area on horseback a few days after his inauguration. This military enclave is midway between the Navy Yard and the Capitol, just a short march to either place if the need for armed guards arises. Today, the most important place guarded by the Eighth and Eye Marines is the president's retreat at Camp David, 60 miles away in the Catoctin Mountains.

This is the oldest Marine Corps post in the nation. The Commandant's House at the north end of the parade ground has been the home of every commandant of the corps since the capital was moved from Philadelphia to Washington. Since the white bay-fronted house was built to the plans of George Hadfield, it has been much altered, and it is placed on the National Register of Historic Places for historical rather than esthetic reasons.

Until 1901 the barracks compound served as Marine Corps headquarters; it is now the home of the Marine Band (which was once headed by John Philip

Sousa, who lived only a few blocks away at 636 G Street, SE), the Drum and Bugle Corps, the Marine Corps Institute (a correspondence school), and special security and ceremonial details for the president and official visitors. The entire quadrangle with its row of duplex houses for officers on the west and barracks for enlisted men on the east was rebuilt (1902–06) by Hornblower and Marshall in a restrained Romanesque Revival style. The complex gives an effect of stunning austerity: severe, narrow Roman face brick in a rich shade of brown, partially relieved by a belt course of white stone.

The east range is dominated by a tower with a machicolated parapet: here we have whimsy combined with military sentiment to recreate *machicolations*— stepped-out brick openings (*corbelings*) designed to allow the defenders at the top to pour boiling oil or molten lead on any who might dare to attack the tower at its base. Such architecture lends itself to the marines' flair for pageantry and self-celebration, essential traits for a minority service that habitually fields five to ten times the ratio of combat troops than the other three services in terms of its share (3½ percent) of the total defense budget. It is not easy to be an elite corps in a liberal democracy.

Peacetime allows for ceremonial, and every Friday night at 8:20 from May to

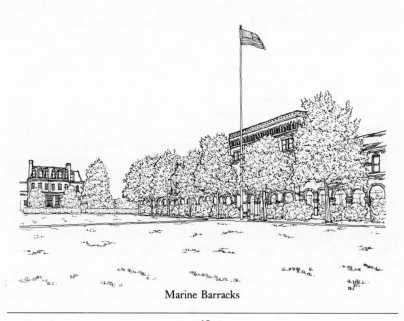

Marine Barracks

September (for reservations in advance call 433–4073) the Band, the Drum and Bugle Corps, and the silent drill team assemble on the quadrangle for Evening Parade, the ceremonial standard of the corps. First the band marches in wearing red coats and white trousers. A woman marine sounds two bells. The mascot bulldog precedes officers' call. In dress blues the silent drill team marches without command to front and center. The band plays "Semper Fidelis" and the "Marines' Hymn." The marines retire the colors with its 47 battle streamers with palms, oak leaf clusters, and stars representing over 400 awards, campaigns, and expeditions. A solitary spotlit figure sounds "Taps" from the parapet of the main tower. It is easy to believe that Gunnery Sergeant Dan Daly at Belleau Wood in World War I, who called the advance with the charge "Who wants to live forever!" had his first training as an Eighth and Eye Marine.

Navy Memorial Museum
Washington Navy Yard, M Street between 1st and 11th Streets, SE
Open weekdays 9–4, weekends, 10–5, free   Enter at 9th Street gate.
Housed in a cavernous factory shed with its overhead crane still intact, this is a sort of low-budget naval version of the National Air and Space Museum. The name *Memorial* in its title should prepare the visitor for a sentimental journey through naval history from the Revolutionary War to the age of space exploration. There are dioramas illustrating the penchant of naval heroes for laconic bluster: "I have not yet begun to fight!" and "I intend to go in harm's way" and "Damn the torpedoes! Full speed ahead!" Models of fighting ships range from crude and amateur efforts in fancy period cases to exquisitely accurate large-scale models of almost every naval ship type and auxiliary. There are Do Touch exhibits, like the gun turrets where you can sit behind the range finders and level a salvo at any target that suits your fancy. There are three periscopes where you can tune the hairlines to launch imaginary torpedoes on imaginary targets across the river in Anacostia.

Technological exhibits range from unlovely atomic bombs to elegant inertial guidance systems. Four mannequins model World War II WAVE uniforms designed by the Parisian couturier Captain Molyneux. There are cans of powdered eggs, ham loaf, pickles, and tripe—still edible, according to the label—recovered from Captain Scott's Antarctic Expedition of 1910.

The museum is the chief showpiece of the Washington Navy Yard, which functioned for a century as the Naval Gun Factory, and is now in the process of slow rejuvenation as a Historic Precinct with a self-guided walking tour. The Navy Yard Gate (at M and 8th Streets, SE) and some of the officers quarters were originally designed by Benjamin H. Latrobe, but whatever distinction they may have had has been pretty well obscured by later Victorian accretions.

Adjacent to the museum is a new Combat Art Gallery and the Willard Park outdoor collection of naval weapons. Now that the last presidential yacht has vanished from its accustomed berth in the yard, the navy hopes to install the U.S.S. *Nautilus,* the first nuclear-powered submarine, as a permanent exhibit in this area of history and ceremony.

On Wednesday nights at 8:45 from June through August, the U.S. Navy Band, the Sea Chanters, and a ceremonial guard present a military drill and pageant called "Summer Ceremonies." (For information and reservations call 433-2218.)

Marine Corps Museum
Washington Navy Yard, M Street between 1st and 11th Streets, SE   Open weekdays and Saturday 8-4:30, Sunday 12-5, May-Labor Day 8:30-4 but Friday evenings 6-11, free   Enter at 9th Street gate.

The object of Marine Corps indoctrination is to instill in its members a keen sense that they must always be prepared—*semper paratus*—for circumstances in which there may be no honorable alternative to valor. This destiny is the source of their fierce pride, and in the curriculum of the service it is a kind of indoctrination that never ends. Certainly it is manifest in this museum of over two centuries of Marine Corps history. Among all the flags and trophies to be seen here are well-lit displays of military miniatures and personal relics of some of the corps' most colorful characters. There are galleries of Marine Corps art, uniforms, weapons, and technology, and military music featuring memorabilia of John Philip Sousa. Here the Halls of Montezuma and the Shores of Tripoli are reproduced in graphic tableaux: the occasions for each of the 47 battle streamers recorded for all to see.

Despite this richness of thematic material, the displays and exhibits are taut, low-key, and straightforward; in the captions the headline slogans are muted, and there is background martial music on the public address system, but the volume is very low.

The museum occupies the first floor of Building No. 58, a well-preserved example of 19th-century industrial architecture. Upper floors house the Marine Corps Historical Center and a substantial library of military history.

Foggy Bottom

Watergate
Rock Creek Parkway between Virginia Avenue, NW, and Memorial Bridge
The name Watergate derives from the sweeping arc of monumental steps between Rock Creek Parkway and Arlington Memorial Bridge leading from the banks of the Potomac up to the circle surrounding the Lincoln Memorial. This was conceived of as a vast architectural conceit, partly reconciling the conflict between the east-west axis of the Mall and the skewed line of Memorial Bridge anchored on the porch of the Lee Mansion on the ridge of Arlington Cemetery.

When the bridge and steps were completed in 1932 there was already some concern that the four pylons at each end of the bridge (rather than tall columns to commemorate the North and the South) should be low enough not to interfere with aircraft approaching nearby Hoover Airport. The notion that the Watergate Steps would serve as a ceremonial area of reception to welcome distinguished visitors to the city must have been a rather slender pretext. There might have been a time when a ceremonial barge with uniformed watermen might have rowed a visiting prince to the shallow steps of the Watergate. (England maintains a Royal Barge for ceremonial purposes on the Thames.) But that never happened.

When Pope John Paul II arrived in Washington in 1980 he came by helicopter from Andrews Air Force Base and was formally greeted by the mayor at the other end of the Reflecting Pool by the lily pond at 17th Street.

Kennedy Center   *2700 F Street, NW, between Rock Creek Parkway and New Hampshire Avenue, NW   Open daily 10–9   Tours daily (45 minutes) 10–1:15, free   Regular performance times: American Film Institute Theater 6:30 and*

8:30, * *Concert Hall 8:30, Eisenhower Theater 7:30, Opera House 8, Terrace Theater 7:30   Performing Arts Library open Tuesday, Thursday, Saturday 10–6, Wednesday and Friday 10–8:30.*

> The Kennedy Center is in a peculiar position. In a way it is a government project, but it is being run as a private enterprise. . . . It was built after grudging appropriations . . . the government did not particularly extend itself . . . and refused to go the whole way.
> —Harold Schoenberg, *New York Times* music critic,
>   12 September 1971

The prominent buildings in the Watergate area of Foggy Bottom—Columbia Plaza, the Watergate Apartment complex, the Howard Johnson's motel, Peoples Life Insurance Company, and the Kennedy Center itself—were each conceived by separate interests at separate times and developed and designed as unrelated ad hockeries. Here Washington's familiar rectangular street grid has gone berserk; the grid has been supplanted by the gentle curves of the automobile tunnels and ramps, and the architects were left with site plans determined by highway engineers.

The buildings are left with no rational orientation, not to each other nor to people approaching by highway or at sidewalk level. The headquarters of the insurance company, for instance, is resolutely symmetrical, but crammed into a triangular block on a slanting segment of New Hampshire Avenue and lacking any axis of relationship to its overpowering neighbors. The buildings are all strange bedfellows, and they look as if they had just been plunked down at random—like cardboard models for sale on a shelf in a toy shop or like the crazy juxtapositions of temporary pavilions at some World's Fair. But the end result is very permanent indeed, and all the ivy we could plant till the end of the century is not going to help much; so we might as well get used to it.

On the riverside margin of this area is the oversize, gleaming white Kennedy Center, rising above a spaghettilike tangle of roads and streets, where Rock Creek Parkway goes under the scissors-handle approaches to Theodore Roosevelt Bridge, between the sunken leg of a high-speed Inner Loop Freeway (since aborted) and the splayed ramps leading off Whitehurst Freeway. Most people come to performances at the center by automobile, as the nearest Metro station (Foggy Bottom) is five blocks away, and the bus service is reduced to sporadic departures for vestigial destinations. Here is culture marooned on a traffic island, barely accessible on foot.

The principal approach to the center through New Hampshire Avenue is not an auspicious one; it affords no open prospect of the massive facade. Automo-

* Subject to change, depending on length of film; often three films on weekends.

biles have to thread their way around the Watergate Apartments and up a short rise to an utterly unexpected place for cars to let off their passengers—a marble and bronze portico over 600 feet in length. This is a porch that stretches for three city blocks—and even that is a modification of the architect's original scheme for a curving portico of 900 feet. If E Street had not been converted into a sunken expressway from 20th Street west to the river, it could have provided a fine approach anchored on the dead center of the long facade.

The best view of the Kennedy Center would be from Theodore Roosevelt Island, a forested sanctuary in the middle of the Potomac. If you don't have a helicopter or a canoe, a distant glimpse may be had from the slope of Wisconsin Avenue as it descends from R Street to Q. And conversely, the view of the river from the center itself is spectacular, particularly from the terrace over the parkway—easily reached during intermissions—looking up the Potomac toward Georgetown. (Jacqueline Kennedy had hoped to have stairs leading from the terrace down to the river bank, but this was found to be impracticable.)

So in the end result, the location of the center is a testament to the sophisticated impotence of urban planners. They all wanted it in the middle of downtown to liven up the decaying business district and to serve as what they hoped would be a magnet for bookstores, cafés, and art galleries. They had visions of a carless urbanity, like Vienna or Venice. But the urban planners had nothing to do with it. During all of this period of agonizing negotiation, the center had an extremely canny chairman in the person of Roger L. Stevens of New York, who, before he came to Washington, had already had two careers, first as a Manhattan real estate developer and second as a Broadway producer. He knew that to saddle the project with other objectives of urban policy would be its doom. Stevens argued that cultural centers were no more suitable than highway programs as instruments of urban renewal. He knew from Broadway experience that theaters liven up a neighborhood only for the brief intervals before and after performances. To him, the planners must have seemed as inflexible, as remote from compromise, as the legislators. Roger Stevens was the henchman of *performance,* the whole raison d'être for which the building was erected. Only a single individual acting out of conviction, self-interest, or sheer nerve, can decide which productions should be produced and which shouldn't, the very role for which government—any government, any committee—is unsuited.

The National Capital Planning Commission had created the Watergate complex in the first place by authorizing the demolition of the gas storage tanks and the brick brewery and the wartime temporary buildings occupied by the Central Intelligence Agency that had characterized the whole depressed area between

Georgetown and the rest of the city. But it was the highway engineers who were to win the day, with the construction of road projects under three separate park and highway jurisdictions—all acccelerated by federal subsidies. When the Commission of Fine Arts intervened in October 1959, it was too late; its news release urging a "drastic restudy" of the highway programs and pedestrian access to the center from the Mall and the Lincoln Memorial was as vain then as it would be today. Just as "no-politics is a kind of politics," no-plan is a kind of plan. The results of such an ingenue approach are not particularly commodious, but less boring than, say, Brasília.

The idea for the Kennedy Center had its genesis in the search for a civic auditorium for Washington in the 1930s, with most of the sites proposed involving expensive downtown land or entailing the destruction of historic buildings. Under the Eisenhower administration in 1954, Congress authorized a national cultural center (or, as it called it, a "National Cultural Center"). By 1957 John Russell Pope's successor firm of Eggers and Higgins had been commissioned to design a Roman temple in the Beaux Arts style, looking much like the Supreme Court building, and described as "A National Theater Project for Washington, D.C."* A year later, in 1958, Congress set aside 17 acres of West Potomac Park for the project, but without reference to the Eggers and Higgins, or any other, architectural conception. The scheme was that federal park land would be donated to the project if construction funds could be raised privately within five years.

But public support for the project lagged, perhaps in part because the idea of the capital of a nation-state as a fountainhead of art and culture appears to some citizens as a baroque notion alien to our federal system. (Parallel efforts to establish the National Endowment for the Arts, and for the Humanities, have stressed the regional aspects of their control and participation.) Anyway, it did not seem likely that a cultural center could be created by legislative fiat at a time when the talented youth of the land were not exactly flocking to Washington for a rendezvous with the muse. The town's last great composer was John Philip Sousa. The last novelist then of any note to come to town was Sinclair Lewis in 1920, and Sauk Centre, Minnesota—his birthplace—was not much competition.† The patterns of American cultural expression seem to be disparate and regional, and rather immune to any central or organic principle.

(There is something *retardataire*, even Victorian, about the self-conscious preoccupation with culture per se—as if current history weren't having enough

* *New York Times*, 8 September 1957.
† Today, Washington's most famous resident novelist is Herman Wouk.

trouble without taking on more cheerleaders. When a newspaper like the *New York Times* unabashedly designates cultural correspondents, one wonders just why it stopped there: why not also correspondents for gentility, refinement, breeding, or taste? . . . or laboratory fermentation?)

Be all that as it may, a national cultural center is here to stay, even though experience, particularly American experience, suggests that culture is achieved more as a by-product or side effect than by deliberate cultivation—much less legislative will or corporate sponsorship. The stigma lingers, even though Washington abounds in such non self-concious forms of culture as politics, newspaper reporting, litigation, network newscasting, not to mention its penchant for the most generous of all the arts, conversation.

So it might have been worse: the center's original broad program has become somewhat more focused as "The John F. Kennedy Center for the Performing Arts." This same kind of architectural–performing-arts-complex is happening all over: in London's South Bank, New York's Lincoln Center, Sydney's opera house, the National Arts Centre in Ottawa, the Atlanta Memorial Arts Center, Montreal's Place des Arts, and even Paris's Centre Pompidou-Beaubourg has its superstereo concert chamber annex.

The aftermath of President John F. Kennedy's assassination in 1963 brought a national flood of horror and grief. When his name was then attached to the center it galvanized support from all over the country and sparked a spate of generous contributions from foreign governments. The Kennedy grave in Arlington Cemetery, paid for by his family, is his most poignant memorial. And the Kennedy Library on the shore of Boston's harbor, erected under legislation providing instant and ever-larger shrines for presidential papers, is his most sentimental and personal monument. But the Kennedy Center for the Performing Arts, as the sole official memorial to the president in the capital, is a living institution* with a continuing artistic and educational program that transcends the merits or demerits of its particular architectural setting.

The colossal bronze head of the handsome young president completely dominates the center's foyer, unquestionably the longest, narrowest, and highest room in town. The sculptor was Robert Berks (who also did the sedentary statue of Einstein, in the same plaster chewing-gum style, in front of the National Academy of Sciences on Constitution Avenue); it is an excellent likeness, and few other sculptors would want to cope with the difficulties of the setting.

In 1959 the National Cultural Center chose Edward Durell Stone as the

---

* The only other official "living memorial" to a president is the Woodrow Wilson International Center for Scholars established by Congress in 1968 as an affiliate of the Smithsonian Institution.

project's architect.* (If they were looking for the ghost of a Neoclassicist like John Russell Pope, could Stone be far behind?) Stone was not a newcomer to large federal design projects. In 1939 he was the third-prize winner (behind the team of Eliel and Eero Saarinen, and Paul Cret) for a never-constructed Smithsonian Art Museum complex for the Mall. In 1952 he designed the American Embassy in New Delhi, which was sort of a prototype of the Kennedy Center, but with metal filigree grilles. In 1958 he did the United States pavilion for the Brussels World's Fair, which, in a circular way, also rather anticipates the Kennedy Center.

It would be kind to judge Mr. Stone's achievement at least in part in the light of the technical problems that he was asked to solve, as they were multifarious and they compounded the burden of his commission.

The *first* "given" with which he was faced was that all of the theaters involved in the project were to be under one roof. The legal and philosophical assumptions of the project dictated a single building, and not a complex of separate structures facing a central plaza as at New York's Lincoln Center. This restriction complicated the handling of the crowds and the pattern of audience circulation, and it also placed an absolute premium on the stipulation that the sounds of performances in one hall should be totally insulated from those of its neighbors.

The architect's strategy was to separate the Concert Hall from the Opera House and the Opera House from the Theater by two vast galleries transecting the building from the east portico to the grand foyer along the river bank. These two areas, conceived of as the Hall of the States and the Hall of the Nations, provide a clear and logical pattern of circulation while ensuring the separation of the performance arenas as if they were in different buildings. The high gallery walls of marble veneer would have the effect of a mausoleum were it not for the free-standing gilded columns, so long and thin that they do not appear to articulate any structural function at all; they are artifices whose dramatic effect is heightened by the taffeta flags of the 50 states (to the north) and of every nation recognized by the United States (to the south). The halls provide access not just from the east entrance through to the foyer but to box offices, checkrooms, elevators, and escalators from the underground parking areas.

* The role played by Senator William J. Fulbright in Stone's selection was probably more than coincidental. They were both natives of Arkansas and had for a brief period been business partners in a small furniture manufacturing project. Fulbright was the author of the act establishing the National Cultural Center. When the center was completed, the senator's evaluation of it was recorded in the *Congressional Record* of 10 September 1971: "Without any credentials as an expert, I nevertheless venture the opinion that in time . . . it will be acclaimed as one of the truly great structures of the world, situated on the most beautiful site for such a center that one can imagine."

There are architects who believe that architecture can be too dramatic, but Mr. Stone is not one of them. Nowhere is this trait more evident than in the grand foyer along the river front connecting the entrances to the three theaters. It is 630 feet long and six stories high and its ivory plaster walls alternate four floor-to-ceiling mirrored panels on one side with 10 floor-to-ceiling glass windows on the terrace. The foyer is graced by no fewer than 18 Swedish Orrefors crystal chandeliers, 15 feet long and hung just 12 feet above the plush crimson carpet. Portable plastic gilt bars have been improvised to serve intermission drinkers anything from Coke to brandy and champagne at reasonable prices. The unpredictable harmonics of performance times and schedules can result in theater and opera and concert audiences all debouching at the same interval. Then you can see how the foyer really works, and it seems not an inch too large—and without ceilings of such great height the hum of conversation would be compressed to a roar.

Here is an architectural tour de force exuding a kind of comfort and opulence that verges on high camp, the envy of Morris Lapidus for any of his Miami Beach hotel lobbies. Members of the audience are spared any sense of how the concealed structural elements of the building may work. The deck of the terrace and projecting eaves of the roof are severely cantilevered and held in tension by attenuated bronze columns—all original hallmarks of the work of Edward Durell Stone, and though they are innocent of subtlety, they are not without a certain refinement of proportion. The effect of the terrace and foyer together is to provide a kind of theatrical thrill suggesting that there can be as much drama on one side of the curtain as the other.

Like so much self-conscious modern architecture, the Kennedy Center is very photogenic—at least while it is new. (How well its gilt and shiny complexion will age may be another question.) If the center is inaccessible from the middle range, it photographs well from a distance and close-up. The bronze and marble fountains and weeping willows of the terrace—reeking as they do of solvency—are in great demand as backdrops for glossy advertisements of Cadillacs and Continentals from Detroit.

The architect's *second* constraint was that of combining a theater complex and a building to serve as a national monument. It may seem compatible in spirit to have a place serve both for theatrical and musical performances and as a permanent memorial to a martyred president, but in practice the two functions are often at cross-purposes. When Houston named its Jesse H. Jones Hall for the Performing Arts it was a simple salute to a regional hero; Paris's Pompidou Center is a nominal tribute, not a memorial. But the Kennedy Center is a national shrine attracting pilgrims from all over the land—it now ranks with the Capitol and the National Air and Space Museum as one of Washington's most popular tourist attractions, drawing 10,000 to 12,000 visitors a day. In a fragile compact, the National Park Service polices the public halls and the grounds outside with rangers in broad-brimmed hats, while the center manages the backstage operations with stagehands under union contract. Floods of group tours do not make it easier to manage rehearsal schedules.

For the first two months after the Kennedy Center opened in 1971, tourists—mostly adults, not children—devastated the place. Most of the shallow ceiling chandeliers in the center's elevators were stripped of their glass pendants for souvenirs; sockets were left with dangling wires, marble fixtures were pilfered from the center's restrooms, silver and linen were stolen from the restaurant, and swatches were cut from the red rugs and seats. (In the light of this experience it is easy to understand why, for the first century of its existence, the Paris Opera was off-limits to tourists except during performances and has only just recently admitted the public on tours at restricted hours and for a steep fee.)

Mr. Stone's solution of the problem of the center's dual mission was to design not a quiet temple of culture but a powerful symbolic statement designed to win immediate popular approval. Visitors feel at home here and as exhilarated as they were by the movie palaces of the 1930s. There is no cool refinement of style, none of the high-brow remoteness that might be intimidating to all but the artistically literate. The architect has provided a shrine, but his commitment to the quality of the theatrical or musical experience remains uncompromised. This is what the center's board must have had in mind when it commissioned him, and this is certainly what he produced.

The *third* constraint of architectural design was as unique as the first two: the problem of airplane noise. The first jet planes did not begin to arrive at National Airport until after the center's first plans had come off the drawing board. The roof was to be right under the glide path of the most frequently used runway approach to the airport, with arriving flights slotted in at saturation intervals. (During the days of propeller aircraft, the nuisance had become so great that the National Symphony had long since had to abandon the summer open-air concerts from the nearby Watergate barge.) Mr. Stone was no newcomer to theater design; he had helped to create Radio City Music Hall in 1936, and on the center project his role was augmented by a panel of the best theatrical and acoustic consultants available. The result is that—at a greatly increased cost—the auditorium areas are among the most hermetic ever conceived; they are sealed off, insulated by double walls and by double doors as thick as a bank vault's and closing on each other like lock gates of a canal. This is a claustrophile's delight, just the opposite of the breezy sound-thinning openness of the Filene Center shed at Wolf Trap. Though the location of the Kennedy Center is closer to the flight paths of National Airport than Shea Stadium is to those at LaGuardia, in the hush before the curtain goes up in the Opera House not the least hint of jet vibration intrudes.

Not only has outside noise been excluded, but the acoustics of all four of the performing arenas—under the expert guidance of Cyril Harris—represent an optimum of the state of the art, some say a splendor, ranking with the best-established halls in the country. For the Concert Hall, Harris insisted on a rectangular design and the extensive employment of wood. White-painted wooden panels surround the orchestra stage, the plaster walls of the auditorium are veneered with wood, and he even rationed the amount of red carpet so that the exposure of wooden floors can let you sense the resonance of the music through your feet. The ceiling has a pattern of interlocking hexagons with varying steps and rises to reflect varying harmonics of wavelengths of sound. It's as taut and neatly fitting as a wooden cigar box. Poor sight lines on some of the side tier seats are a small price to pay for excellence of acoustics.

Although the seating in the Opera House is according to the classic horseshoe floor plan, it has the effect of a closed circular room paneled in cylindrical segments of dark red woven fabric. The house has a 1,000 fewer seats and a much lower proscenium arch over the stage than the Metropolitan Opera House at New York's Lincoln Center, with a consequence that the audience gains (at the expense of certain production economies) in comfort and closeness to the stage an effect that, for an opera house, approaches intimacy.

Trucks can unload scenery at ground level directly onto the 64-foot-deep Opera House stage. Huge as it is, it is smaller than the stage at Lincoln Center, and when the Bolshoi and Metropolitan Opera companies come to Washington, they find that their scenery is sometimes a bit cramped and they may have a little trouble crowding their full choruses onto the stage.

Yet architectural critics have not been reticent in their esthetic judgment of Edward Durell Stone's center. They range from the facetious—"the Watergate Apartments are a wedding cake and the Kennedy Center is the box it came in" (apocryphal)—to the precious—"the alternate coarse and mincing frigidity of the Kennedy Center" (*Time,* 5 June 1978). When the center opened, the architecture critic Ada Louise Huxtable greeted it in a bitter indictment in a front page article in the *New York Times:* "The architect opted for something called 'timelessness' and produced meaninglessness. . . . its character is aggrandized posh. . . . this is gemütlich Speer. . . . the building is a national tragedy. It is a cross between a concrete candy box and a marble sarcophagus in which the art of architecture lies buried." This is not just show-off; it is the impassioned appraisal of a critic who cares deeply.

The most obvious defense of the center's design is to invoke its principal raison d'être; its interior—inside the big showy box—is replete with superb facilities for the performance of opera, concerts, chamber music, experimental theater, plays, and movies, with the highest standards of acoustics, generally fine sight lines, and luxurious comfort for the audience. Is all this not mollifying to Mrs. Huxtable? Not at all; she says that "housing the arts is also an act of art, and how they are housed is terribly revealing of the state of the arts, or at least the state of mind of the sponsors." Her point is that architecture is one art in which the United States excels, and what Mr. Stone has given us by default is a crowd-pleaser, substituting theatrical glamour for true elegance. What is distressing is that the center's approach to the performing arts themselves, of all civilized pursuits, is not free of the taint of vulgarity.

Terrace Theater. The Terrace Theater on the center's top floor was completed in 1979 as a gift of the government and people of Japan. It opened with a performance of the Grand Kabuki of Japan, and it is uniquely flexible as a recital hall for chamber music or for a variety of theatrical performances. In one configuration the orchestra pit accommodates an ensemble of 40 members; in another it provides a modified thrust stage.

The steep-thrust theater was designed by Philip Johnson in sumptuous upholstered tones of rose and mauve alternating with flat matte silver. The innovative off-Broadway producer Joseph Papp has raised questions about the Terrace Theater—about whether any stage can well serve both concert and theatrical purposes, and about whether the decor isn't just a little too elegant to accommodate the four-letter-word diction of so much modern playwriting.

Washington's premier music critic, Paul Hume, says that for chamber music performances, the acoustics of the Terrace Theater could equal those of the Coolidge Auditorium of the Library of Congress if only the carpet could be removed from under the seats.

Performing Arts Library. As a joint venture with the Library of Congress this branch library serves to support the center's programs in all areas of the performing arts. It is open to the public visiting the building or attending performances as well as performers, directors, artists, and designers, composers, writers, and musicians. It maintains current files of over 200 periodicals covering theater, dance, opera, music, film, and broadcasting and is a comprehensive source of information on federal and state government programs of grants to the arts, of pending arts legislation, and corporate, museum, and conservatory programs of related interest.

It has a video display terminal offering access to the major holdings at the main Library of Congress, but this is a complex and limited piece of machinery which few visitors have the time to learn how to operate. The audio links to the center's tapes, disks, and recordings are easier to master. It is informal in operation, its open stacks provide easy access, and it is expertly staffed and stays open until 8:30 two nights a week.

St. Mary's Episcopal Church   *730 23rd Street, between H and G Streets, NW*
Washington has ever been slow to fulfill its role as a neutral meeting ground between the cultures of the North and the South; long after the Civil War its customs and values still mirrored those of the Old South. As a matter of Christian obligation Episcopal churches admitted blacks to their services, but as parishioners whose franchise was restricted. At St. John's Church, Lafayette Square, blacks were required to sit in the church balcony; at Epiphany Church on G Street, NW, whites received Holy Communion before blacks. The black population of Washington grew as more and more slaves were freed, earning the city the name "the Poorhouse of Virginia." And if these growing number of Christians were to receive equal treatment in their worship, it seemed they would be compelled to form parishes of their own.

The situation eventually struck some of the white members of St. John's and Epiphany as sufficiently unchristian that they helped the blacks establish their own church in 1886 in Foggy Bottom. The result is St. Mary's Episcopal Church. Part of the land was donated by a parishioner of St. John's. Secretary of War Edwin M. Stanton of the Epiphany congregation arranged to have an abandoned frame wooden chapel building brought down to the site from the Civil War Kalorama Hospital. Randall Hagner among others at St. John's Church raised funds for the project and was instrumental in engaging the services of James Renwick as its architect.

Here on 23rd Street the master architect of St. Patrick's Cathedral in New York and the Smithsonian Castle on the Mall created a replica of an English village church in pure Victorian Gothic. Like the old wooden chapel the new church was sited on the perimeter of the property to provide a cloisterlike courtyard in the center. Funds were very restricted and the original Gothic concept was almost discarded in favor of a more utilitarian substitute. The architect had the ingenuity to meet the client's brief while preserving the integrity of his design by lowering the roof and completing only half of the nave.

The entrance to St. Mary's is at the rear through the courtyard; this arrangement orients the sanctuary conventionally to the east and permits the morning sun to flood the stained glass windows over the altar. The old hospital chapel has been sheathed in a veneer of brick to harmonize in scale and texture with the main church.

Renwick devoted extraordinary care (given his comparatively modest commission) to the decoration and the design of the individual furnishings of the church. The pews are of hand-carved oak. The walls are decorated with polychrome stencil. The floors are patterned in red marble and encaustic tile. The sanctuary rail is of bronze and the gas lamp fixtures are of brass. And the cast iron radiators with quatrefoil molds are particularly handsome. The whole varied business employs the best technology and the most suitable materials available at the time, but with a sustained esthetic spirit—an evocation by the Victorians of their romantic notion of the Gothic. Here there is no attempt to revert to medieval methods of construction. The hammer beam trusses over the nave are reinforced with steel rod braces as a simple necessity since the fabrication of wood trussing was a complex and long-lost art.

Some of the stained glass windows are from Lorin of Chartres and some are from the studio of Louis C. Tiffany. They achieve that exact literal sentimentality that was to become so prevalent in American churches at the turn of the century.

Though it has had to struggle through some lean years, St. Mary's parish has a long record of practical vocational programs for its congregation and its neighbors, as well as leadership in obtaining neighborhood improvements for the Foggy Bottom community. Its congregation has remained predominantly black since its inception; it is surely one of the earliest churches in the city to be untainted by segregation.

As an ecclesiastical, architectural, and social artifact, St. Mary's Church is a relic of urban felicity in the nondescript landscape of Foggy Bottom.

George Washington University Law Library   *718 20th Street, NW*

Something in the unpredictable creativity of a large architectural firm like Mills, Petticord, and Mills permits it at one time (1965) to turn out a product as insensitive as the wings of the National Museum of Natural History, and at another time (1970) to blossom forth with as wholly innovative and elegant a design as the Jacob Burns Law Library of George Washington University. Its dark brick fabric is framed between strips of precast matte red concrete, and it has inviting entrances on two levels under a reverse-ziggurat superstructure supported by two attenuated columns. Here is a real gem affording dramatic relief from the sameness of the other GW buildings and the neighboring World Bank offices, which taken together have been described as the bland leading the bland.

George Washington University   *Foggy Bottom*

We're in the education business in such a high-rent district that we can't afford to be in the education business unless we're also in the real estate business.
—Administrative vice-president of George Washington University, 28 February 1980

George Washington University

The George Washington University (GWU) is the largest single private holder of real estate in the city—exceeded only by the federal government itself.* It began to acquire land just prior to World War I and has since consolidated 20 square blocks of properties west of the World Bank on H Street and south of Washington Circle. In the Depression period, with the utmost economy, it put up factory-type buildings of brick painted white, and much of the original Spartan character survives in the new campus as reconstructed in the 1970s. In this process a formerly residential area has been replaced by a terminal moraine of office buildings that the university rents to commercial tenants for current in

* As an institutional owner of downtown property, the C & P Telephone Company is a close second.

George Washington University Law Library

come to supplement its slender endowment. Economic forces have prevailed over the protests of homeowners and preservationists.

Both L'Enfant and George Washington had envisioned a national university to be established near the junction of 23rd Street and Virginia Avenue, NW. Washington actually left his stock in the Potomac Company to endow such a university, but the government failed to act and his shares reverted to other stockholders. James Madison proposed a national university but Congress turned him down. In 1821 Congress granted a charter to a group of Baptists who selected the District as the site of Columbian College, which was to be the mother college of their denomination and was designed to attract a national constituency. The college's first commencement in 1824 was attended by Lafayette, Henry Clay, John C. Calhoun, and President James Monroe; but after that auspicious start it was to have many lean years before its attainments justified the early high hopes. In 1909 the university absorbed the George Washington Memorial Association, broadened its sectarian character, and assumed the name of the George Washington University. It has become a national university in the nation's capital by default and without federal assistance, as Congress has remained firm in its resolve that it is not the business of the federal government to establish and operate a university.

It is a curious fact of the history of GWU that none of its graduates has ever served as its president in permanent tenure.

Georgetown

Buffalo Bridge over Rock Creek Park   *Q Street at 23rd Street, NW*
This striking bridge designed by Glenn Brown and his son Bedford Brown was completed in 1914, and it is a remarkable example of successful collaboration between architect, engineer, sculptor, and city planner. The site is a difficult one because it crosses a roadway and a creek with uneven banks and it connects two ends of Q Street that are not on the same alignment. In the early design stages the architects employed scale models of the natural setting and their proposals for bridging it. The solution was to build the bridge with a 12-degree curve, a pleasing variation on the city's straight grid and something no present-day highway engineer would tolerate.

As the architects intended, the stone balustrade and solid masonry construction are reminiscent of a Roman aqueduct. The concrete was mixed with pigment and given a course tooled finish to match the trim of the reddish buff stone from West Virginia. Deep-bracketed arches (called *corbels*) support a cantilevered archway. The 28 corbels on each side of the bridge are anchored on rows of sculptured Indian heads in full headdress modeled from the life mask of Chief Kicking Bear. (These heads are attributed to the architect Glenn Brown. Similar heads were employed as keystones on the former J.P. Morgan residence in Princes Gate, Knightsbridge, London—used for many years as the American Embassy residence.)

Four massive buffaloes—the work of A. Phimister Proctor—guard the approaches to the bridge and have survived the years well despite occasions when pranksters have painted their gonads red. Proctor did many statues of animals and cowboys and Indians for the Chicago Columbian Exposition of 1893; he also did the proud lions on the Taft Bridge that carries Connecticut Avenue over Rock Creek Park.

One block south of Buffalo Bridge is P Street Bridge built on the site of an old ford across the creek where Lafayette and Rochambeau led French units to the road north during the Revolution.

Dumbarton Oaks   *R Street at 32nd Street, NW*
Gardens, R Street at 31st Street, NW, open daily 2–5, $1 April–October (season passes available), November–March; collections and museum, 1703 32nd Street, NW, open Tuesday–Sunday, 2–5, $2 contribution
Recorded information 338-8278.

Dumbarton Oaks is a palatial house and garden in the finest setting in Washington, enshrining three disparate cultural pursuits of its benefactors, Mr. and Mrs. Robert Woods Bliss: (1) Byzantine studies, (2) Pre-Columbian art and archeology, and (3) landscape gardening. Under the trusteeship of Harvard University and with endowment funds provided by the Blisses, Dumbarton Oaks supports continuing research in these three completely nonoverlapping areas, maintaining separate but congenial specialized libraries, collections, and fellowship programs. The approach to gardening is particularly broad, including as it does botany, horticulture, and the history of landscape studies.

In the past, visitors were often frustrated by finding the facilities at Dumbarton Oaks so frequently closed, but in recent years the collections have been open year-round and the hours have been extended. The recorded information on 338–8278 is full of useful details, not just hours and bus routes and parking, but dates of special tours and lectures, advice on which flowers are currently in bloom, and the reminder that weddings and picnics are not permitted on the grounds.

This Georgetown estate was bought in 1920 by the Blisses and given to Harvard in 1940. Ambassador Bliss was a career diplomat and, during their two decades of ownership in which he and his wife completely reconstructed the mansion and its gardens, they actually resided under its roof for a total of only seven years, between assignments abroad. Like Anderson House and Hillwood, it was designed primarily as a cultural and institutional legacy to the nation's capital.

Dumbarton Oaks was built about 1800 and since then it has changed hands nine times, and has had almost as many changes in its name and in its architectural style. The first owner of the tract, bordering what is now Rock Creek Park, was Col. Ninian Beall, who had a habit of giving Scottish place names to his various holdings throughout Maryland. He named this tract for the Rock of Dumbarton, a castle high on the bank of the River Clyde near where he was born in Scotland. About 1800 William Hammond Dorsey built the original house of red brick with a curved central bay in the Federal style. In 1805 Robert Beverley bought the house from Dorsey, added an orangery and named the place Acrolophos in recognition of its setting in a grove on a hill. Beverley's son sold the estate to members of the Calhoun family of South Carolina, and John C. Calhoun lived there as senator, secretary of war, and vice-president. The Calhouns called the place Oakly. The next owner, Edward M. Linthicum, rebuilt the house in 1860 in the style of the French Second Empire, adding a mansard roof, an octagonal tower and cupola, and wrought iron decoration. Linthicum rechristened the house Monterey to celebrate a victory in the Mexican War. In 1891 the estate was acquired by Henry Fitch Blount, a farm tool manufacturer

Buffalo Bridge

not everybody's bag. The field embraces the whole millennium between the collapse of the Roman Empire in the 5th century A.D. and the coming of the Renaissance in Italy in the 15th century. It involves the art and architecture, the theology and archeology, the whole intricate cultural complexity of the Holy Roman Empire centered on Byzantium, the ancient name of Constantinople—now Istanbul. For any dedicated Byzantine scholar—and there is no other kind—the rest of Western civilization is an anticlimax, if not an irrelevance.

Byzantine scholars are at once the greatest specialists—ploughing a turf from which all but the most linguistically accomplished historians are excluded—and the greatest generalists, for they are recreating an entire Universe: the world of Byzantium, a half millennium of Christian-Hellenistic complexity in which culture and religion are inseparable. Byzantine studies assume a fluency in Greek, Arabic, Latin, Syriac, Armenian, Turkish, and Russian, not to mention various levels of vaguely Hellenistic languages unintelligible to most of society even at the time they were written. The Byzantine scholar spends most of his day poring over manuscripts which haven't seen the light of day for centuries; to do this requires a kind of zeal and passion that relieves them from any capacity to mind the store or hold the tiller or feed the baby. Scholars who work at Dumbarton Oaks find it a privilege and an obsession. (The library has a rule that a scholar may not sign out more than 50 volumes at any one time.)

The core of the Dumbarton Oaks museum is a gallery and atrium of Byzantine and Hellenistic relics. The Music Room was not only the scene of the Dumbarton Oaks Conference, but a place where Paderewski and Stravinsky had performed for the Blisses in private concert. The chief ornament of what is called the House collection (in the Music Room and its antechambers) is *The Visitation* of El Greco, one of the last pictures he finished before his death in 1614. This painting shows two abstract figures in swirling tension, in a twisted violence of confrontation. It is fitting that for the one great Old Master in their collection, the Blisses were able to acquire an El Greco, an artist whose Mannerist style had Byzantine roots—and the price they paid for it, in 1936, was only £6,500.

A glass-walled passage leads to the separate garden pavilion housing the display of Pre-Columbian art.

Pre-Columbian Art. The very term *Pre-Columbian art* is more revealing of the patronizing bias of our approach to a distant culture than it is of a whole artistic genre created by peoples who probably did not think of these objects as works of art and certainly had no idea that Columbus was going to come to discover them. The first conquerors of the Olmecs and the Incas and the Mayas of South and Central America did not recognize either the historic or the intrinsic esthetic worth of these artifacts of stone and wood and feathers. The Blisses started to collect them in the 1920s, at a time when they had attracted little interest except to ethnographers in museums of natural history. The gorgeous American Indian items on display at Dumbarton Oaks represent, not the first or the largest collection to be amassed in America, but one of the first to be acquired purely on the basis of esthetic considerations.

Curiously, the Byzantine items in the Bliss collection—the Christian icons from another hemisphere—seem less exotic than the heritage of our own continent. Nothing could be psychically more remote than the world of terror and brutality revealed in the Aztec goddess Tlazolteotl agonizing in the labor of childbirth.

Philip Johnson's Pre-Columbian Museum. When John S. Thacher was director of Dumbarton Oaks in 1960, he said that one of the reasons he invited Philip Johnson to design the new wing in the garden to house the Pre-Columbian art was to get away from what he called the "Long Island Georgian" style of the main house. Johnson did so with abandon, and came up with a jewel-like complex of eight Byzantine-Turkish domes surrounding a central circular garden and fountain in a tic-tac-toe pattern affording easy circulation. The low domes are unobtrusive from the street or garden approaches, particularly since they are heavily screened by rhododendrons and other evergreens—something that Mr. Johnson was indulgent to allow, as he is not a man to hide his candle under a bushel. In recent years it has become necessary to plant even denser holly around the pavilions to end the slaughter of birds flying into the window glass. (And Mr. Johnson says he approves.)

But the interior provides a setting of sumptuous materials giving an effect that is rich and lush in the extreme: a juxtaposition of ivory and green marble with bronze, teak, glass, and lucite, amplified by semitropical foliage. This is the kind of architectural frame that competes intensely with the objects on display for the attention of the visitor. But the marvelous masks and shirts and axes of jewels and feathers and jade of the Bliss collection have an extravagant brashness of their own, and they are not about to be upstaged by a mere architect.

When the Pre-Columbian Museum started to emerge on the landscape of north Georgetown, the city of Washington had very little to be seen in the way of modern architecture. The National Geographic Society headquarters of Edward Durell Stone was still on the drawing boards and Eero Saarinen's Dulles Airport Terminal was just beginning to rise above the flat plain of Chantilly. But Johnson's new museum did not create much of a stir—perhaps in part because it is walled off from the street. Stone's National Geographic Building was to attract much more attention.

The Dumbarton Oaks wing is classic in spirit, and in it no attempt was made to introduce any structural or stylistic innovations. Nevertheless, in 1964 in the

Architectural Forum an innocent and curiously prophetic article appeared under the caption: "Pre-Columbian Art in a Post-Modern Museum"—one of the first conspicuous uses of that troublesome term *post-modern* by a headline writer, probably just indulging in the tricks of his trade, just verbal counterpoint, and probably not trying to stake out a new critical and historical category for the pigeonholing of a school of art and architecture. It is possibly a matter of carelessness that the school of art playing such a feature role in this century was called *modern** instead of *contemporary;* and attempts to introduce the term *post-modern* only compound the ambiguity.

In 1977 the Museum of Modern Art in New York held its first exhibition of contemporary architecture in over two decades under the aegis of its curator of

---

* All new art is modern for a while; it might have simplified matters if the ardent New Yorkers who founded the Museum of Modern Art in 1929 could have named it the Museum of Contemporary Art or the Museum of 20th-Century Art.

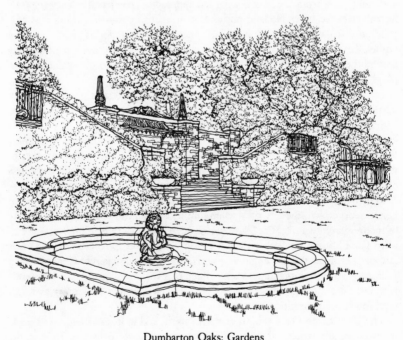

Dumbarton Oaks: Gardens

architecture, Arthur Drexler. The show presented photographs of over 400 buildings by more than 300 architects, and the city of Washington had no buildings represented in the entire show—except for Philip Johnson's Pre-Columbian Museum, an artifact of post-modernism's search for antecedents.

The Gardens. The gardens of the 16 acres of the Dumbarton Oaks estate are a surviving testament to the skill of one of America's great landscape architects, Beatrix Ferrand. Earlier she had done landscape commissions in Bar Harbor, Maine, both for the Blisses and for Abby Aldrich Rockefeller. Her talents were not limited to horticulture and design; she left her impress on the brickwork, the carved lead sculptures, and the garden furniture of oak as well. The crowning distinction of Dumbarton Oaks garden is the way its terraces, alleys, pools, and orchards and formal geometries all interlock in three dimensions to accommodate the steep bank of the site as it slopes down to Rock Creek to the north. It is one of the few gardens in this country whose design and execution permit comparison with those gardens of the first rank in Europe.

The extensive gardens and horticultural library are open for use by application in writing, and the handsome annex housing them designed by the architect Frederick Rhinelander King in 1963, is open to the public for casual inspection on weekends.

Wisconsin Avenue

Wisconsin Avenue is one of the town's few main thoroughfares that predate the rectangular street grid of the city. (Within the District, Columbia Road and Bladensburg Road are two other nonconforming streets that survive from the Colonial era.) For its first mile after rising northward from the banks of the Potomac, the avenue serves as Georgetown's main street, in which capacity it had previously been called High Street and later 32nd Street until Congress renamed it for the State of Wisconsin in 1906.

In Colonial days it served as a principal route of commercial and military traffic from the tobacco port of Georgetown on to Rockville Pike and westward to the Ohio Valley. In 1753 and again in 1754, Col. George Washington led troops along this route to support the British General Braddock in the campaign against Fort Duquesne (later Pittsburgh) in the French and Indian Wars.

Soviet Embassy
2600 Wisconsin Avenue, NW   Entrance at 2601 Tunlaw Road, NW

This new Soviety Embassy complex, which has been under construction since 1974, is an exercise in reciprocity: by a pact signed in 1969 the Russians allotted 12.6 acres for the construction of a new American Embassy in Moscow while the Russians were awarded 12.5 acres in the Mt. Alto area between Wisconsin Avenue and Tunlaw Road—the former site of an obsolete Veterans Hospital. Both our embassy and theirs, sadly, are essentially security compounds where all members of the mission spend most of their days in each other's company isolated from the rest of the community.* Construction on both projects is sup-

---

* Americans in Moscow live in an enclave because there is no other place for them to go; Russians in Washington live in an enclave for reasons of their own as a matter of social policy.

posed to be phased for completion in 1984. At the Mt. Alto site a rambling tower with 160 apartments follows the contour of the hill and around a court-yard containing an elementary school, a cafeteria, a swimming pool, and a picnic area with grills for shishkabob. An indoor gymnasium contains first-class facili-ties for basketball and volleyball. Volleyball is the big thing with the Russians, and in the diplomatic league here they have been champions for nine out of the last ten years. (Soccer is next most popular; for this they have to leave their compound to play against the World Bank and other diplomatic teams in West Potomac Park near the Lincoln Memorial.)

There is a 400-seat theater suitable for movies, concerts, or dramatic per-formances, with a separate entrance on Tunlaw Road. Over the proscenium arch of the stage, the curtain proclaims "Forward the Victory of Communism" in two-foot-high Cyrillic letters.

Construction blueprints for the embassy buildings bear the label "1974–MOSPROEKT–2," otherwise known as the Executive Committee of the Moscow City Soviet Planning Department; more specifically the architects are given as M. Posokhin, S. Egorov, U. Semenov, and V. Eniosov. They have come up with a group of buildings—the chancery, ambassador's apartment, and consular offices are still under construction—well sited on the hilly terrain, of a uniformly buff color and texture that has the insipid feeling of new plaster. Red and blue Pepsi-Cola vending machines in every courtyard add an inadvertent note of color to the otherwise unrelieved buffness of the scene. The whole complex is surrounded by a high steel fence and closed-circuit television monitors. Within the gates the speed limit is five miles per hour.

Washington National Cathedral
Wisconsin Avenue at Massachusetts Avenue, NW
Open daily Memorial Day–Labor Day 10–9, rest of the year 10–4:30
Tours (45 minutes) 10–12, 1–3:15, Sunday at 12:15 and 2:30, free.

My house shall be called a house of prayer for all people.
—Matthew 21:13, and Congressional charter of 1893.

Cathedrals are by their nature obtrusive—the monumental payment of a debt owed to God by Mammon—and few in the world are grander or more obtru-sive than Washington Cathedral on the crown of Mount St. Alban. In this low-profile city, where high-rise buildings are outlawed, there are three structures that dominate the skyline: the Capitol, the Washington Monument, and the cathedral—all of which provide anchoring vistas for some of the radial avenues within the city and many of its distant approaches from miles around.

The site of the cathedral is nothing less than magnificent, high on a wooded

and Rome. Its development was dominated by engineers; they made technical refinements of the pointed arch and the flying buttress to reach greater heights and cover ever more complex ground plans, and to open up wider areas of wall for windows. What they were doing was—to them—wholly modern. In fact the history of architecture was not to produce such an original new style until the advent of the International School in the 20th century. The Gothic style invites asymmetry and improvisation. All of the stones actually *work*—the stone fabric is not applied superficially as the Victorians did in their revivals. There are no keystones in Gothic arches; instead bosses and cross-vaults translate the thrust into clustered and buttressed columns. Since the stress is not borne by the walls, they may be opened up into lacy networks of windows for stained glass. The rib vaults torque into "ploughshare" *voussoirs** twisting the stress into attenuated pillars—the whole complex held together dynamically by gravity.

The nave of the cathedral is a tenth of a mile long, and to complicate the visual perspectives and enhance the view from the altar to the balcony under the rose window—and vice versa—the basic floor plan employs an inherent and essentially Gothic asymmetry. At the crossing, the nave and the north transept are skewed 1.113 degrees from the axis of the choir and the south transept. The extent of this subtle and complex variance means that if the choir axis were extended to the west front it would emerge six feet south of the center of the main door.

The chief decorative elements in medieval churches are sculpture and stained glass, both subordinated to the functions of their architectural setting. Most of the cathedral's sculpture has been carved in situ of the same Indiana limestone as the rest of the fabric. Among the glories of Washington Cathedral are its many great bosses—it has over 600, more than any other cathedral—at the apex of every roof bay. Bosses serve the structural function of absorbing the stresses and articulating the intersection of the arched Gothic rib vaults; as ornaments they are deeply carved, for the nave and aisle heights require that most of them must be read at a distance.

Stained glass is likewise a restricted, almost self-abnegating, medium for the artist. The iconographic message of stained glass windows is conveyed in chromatic prisms designed to give flickering pastel reflections on molded stone, suggesting that the building itself is not substantial and producing an ephemeral effect to dramatize the medieval esthetic in which the church prefigures Heaven itself. The most successful example of this is Rowan LeCompte's rose window in the western front, for which the Cathedral Chapter, for the first time, freed the

---

* *Voussoir* means "wedge." The stone infill wedges between the pointed arches prevent the ribs from twisting.

designer of all liturgical restraints, permitting a completely abstract circular window giving the fullest play to the patterns of sunlight being filtered on and through stone; this unique window is seen most dramatically against a setting sun.

The cathedral's many artistic treasures and programs are conscientiously documented in beautifully illustrated guides available from the bookstore at the crypt level. The guides cover in detail the sculpture and carving, stained glass, brass rubbings, and Rare Book Library, wrought iron grilles and gates, carillon, organ, and peal of bells. The cathedral's musical facilities are unparalleled: it is the only building in the world with both a carillon and a peal of bells. (The *carilloneur* is now called a *carillonist,* presumably easier for Americans to say.) Its 10-bell peal is the largest of 13 sets of bell peals in this country. And the Skinner organ was completely rebuilt in the 1970s to include among other amenities a 64-foot-long wooden "pipe" designed to meet the organist's request for base notes so low that they would sound like a 100-car freight train running off the dock at Norfolk.

Though the building is modern, it has already taken twice the 40 years it took to finish Salisbury Cathedral. It is now one of the dozen or so greatest cathedrals on earth. In the United States, Washington Cathedral is exceeded in size only by New York's unfinished St. John the Divine; in Europe the only larger churches are St. Peter's in Rome, the Duomo in Milan, and the cathedrals of Seville and Liverpool. (The National Shrine of the Immaculate Conception has about the same floor area as Washington Cathedral although it is not as long or as large.)

Many people find it easy game to scoff at the cathedral, and some few irate writers of letters to the editor reject its basic conception. They ask: How can we take seriously the idea of a medieval church in the 20th century? How can a building be called Gothic when it has radiant heating, steel beams, and lighting for television cameras? But do not laugh. The answer is: How can we do other than recognize a deep—almost atavistic—longing to create, as it were, from our European heritage a historical past of our own? Henry Adams took a long look at the growing industrialism of the world around him and decided that the only thing he could recommend was the 13th century. (Much later, Ezra Pound told us that the act of thinking about history alters history.)

The birth of the city of Washington coincided with the birth of the modern era; the capital like the nation itself was devoid of relics of the past, the cultural imprints reflected in the architectural monuments of Europe. The one truly native symbol was the white frame church and steeple of the New England village green. But only part of our culture is new; the other part is transplanted, and the

groom, the donor suggested the inscription "The Mostest Man That Ever Was on the Mostest Hoss That Ever Was." The inscription was dispensed with, but the anachronism of horse and rider survives.

Cleveland Park *Wisconsin Avenue east to Connecticut Avenue, between Woodley Road and Rodman Street, NW*

In the days before air conditioning, the White House was a hot place to spend the summer. John Adams swam in Tiber Creek two blocks away, and Lincoln drove out every evening to spend the nights at the Soldiers' Home. As Van Buren, Tyler, and Buchanan discovered when they stayed at Woodley it was 10 to 15 degrees cooler after you climbed the ridge of the Piedmont Plateau. In 1881 President Grover Cleveland bought a country house (he had hoped anonymously) just a three-mile drive by carriage out on Newark Street. He and his bride Frances Folsom added a cupola and Victorian verandahs to the place and painted its rooftops red. At some expense to their privacy, the neighbors named the area Cleveland Park in a gesture of welcome. The Clevelands lent respectability, but it was the advent of the trolley cars on the first iron truss bridges across Rock Creek Park that brought growth to the area.

When Cleveland Park became a year-round suburban community at the turn of the century it attracted many of the city's best architects like Paul Pelz and Waddy B. Wood, and the unique character of their large frame houses with front and back porches and sometimes turrets and gazebos surrounded by elms and picket fences has remained largely intact as an almost accidental architectural preserve. Its schools, playgrounds, and backyards continue to attract fiercely loyal families of lawyers, bureaucrats, and journalists—the city's three leading professions, now augmented by a sprinkling of academics and television personalities. It remains an enclave with suburban amenities as the city has grown up around it.

Maret School/Woodley *3000 Cathedral Avenue, NW*

This stucco-covered manor house with two levels of cornices with block modillions was built in 1800 by an uncle of Francis Scott Key, who spent much time there before composing "The Star-Spangled Banner." Woodley was a summer home for four presidents from Van Buren through Cleveland. During World War I it was the home of Woodrow Wilson's powerful alter ego, Col. E. M. House. In 1929 Woodley was bought by Col. Henry A. Stimson, who served in the cabinets of Taft and Hoover and was secretary of war for Franklin D. Roosevelt. A picture survives of the Stimsons entertaining—at tea on the lawn—the egregious French premier Pierre Laval wearing his habitual white four-in-hand tie. Maret School bought the estate in 1940, and though it has saved the main house from oblivion, the front lawn is now encumbered with an ugly gimcrack classroom building that hardly improves each shining hour.

Rosedale *3501 Newark Street, NW*
This unpretentious farm house dating from 1740 has a certain rambling, vernacular charm. It was built by Gen. Uriah Forrest, who lost a leg in the battle of Brandywine, and it is one of the oldest surviving houses in the District. George Washington and Major L'Enfant dined here when they were working on plans for the boundaries of the 10-mile-square federal district. In 1920 Rosedale was bought by Avery Coonley of Chicago, and the once vast tract has shrunk to an enclave of houses designed by the Coonleys' son-in-law Waldron Faulkner, and their grandson Winthrop Faulkner.

Waldron Faulkner House *3415 36th Street, NW*
This is the first of seven houses built by the Faulkner family of architects after Mrs. Faulkner inherited Rosedale, the historic centerpiece of Cleveland Park. Waldron Faulkner designed 3415 as his own residence in 1937. In its rigi_ symmetry and integral decoration the house reflects his training in the Beaux Arts tradition; the classic conventions have been recreated in the spirit of Art Moderne. It strikes most of us as a period piece of Art Deco, although the architect himself rejected the term. The front elevation is dominated by a doorframe of brick and tile capped by a modernistic *anthemion* (a conventional design of radiating lotus petals that Mr. Faulkner borrowed from the Greeks who had borrowed it from the Egyptians). Above the second-story windows there is a Greek key string course; and behind a brick parapet is a shallow roof crowned by a square attic cupola with *ante-fixae* (crestlike tiles at the corners). Windows are severely restrained and the landscape is subordinated to the rhythm of the facade. In a custom that now appears to be waning, the architect designed much of the hardware, light fixtures, and furniture including desks and table tops covered in dark blue linoleum. That new composition material was much in vogue, and the floors throughout are of inlaid linoleum.

Winthrop Faulkner Houses *36th and Ordway Streets, NW*
As his family waxed and waned, architect Winthrop Faulkner built for himself a series of houses encircling the Rosedale tract that are uncompromisingly modern in spirit yet blend harmoniously into the streetscape of nondescript Cleveland Park houses of an earlier period. The first, built in 1964, rises modestly behind an artificial terrace berm at 3530 Ordway Street. Four years later he built 3540 to house five children in a handsome shelter with much more room than is apparent from the street. His last house (1978), on the same block but at the cor-

sin Avenues, NW, in his memory. The Highlands is graced with spectacular vines of wisteria which grew from sprigs originally presented by Dr. Caspar Wistar, the man who introduced wisteria (not wistaria) to America from Japan. In 1920 The Highlands was bought by Woodrow Wilson's friend and physician, Adm. Cary T. Grayson. Subsequent tenants were the French minister André de Limur, John Hay Whitney, and Allen Dulles. It is now an administrative building for Sidwell Friends School.

Amalgamated Transit Union
5025 Wisconsin Avenue, NW, at Garrison Street, NW
This international headquarters of the transit workers is a pioneering example of a mixed-use structure providing for both residential and office spaces in the same building. The arrangement takes advantage of recent changes in D.C. zoning regulations that allow a high floor-area ratio for residential applications. The three lower floors are offices; the two upper floors contain 14 duplex apartments with an entrance off the back street. It was designed by Hellmuth, Obata and Kassabaum, and completed in 1981.

Northeast

National Shrine of the Immaculate Conception   *Michigan Avenue at 4th Street, NE   Open daily 7–6, April–Labor Day evenings till 7   Tours (45 minutes) Monday–Friday 9–5, Saturday 9–4, Sunday 1:30–4, free.*
The National Shrine of the Immaculate Conception is the largest Catholic church in the Western hemisphere and the seventh largest church in the world, rivaling—at least in size—the greatest monuments of Christendom. Though its massive cruciform plan incorporates many Byzantine and Romanesque formal elements, the monument itself is a thoroughly contemporary building, 20th-century in its liturgical expression and very modern in its decorative spirit.

It is not a cathedral; it is not a basilica; it is not even a parish church—but it is a place of Christian worship where the sacraments are celebrated daily for pilgrims who come to the shrine of the Virgin Mary as patron saint of the United States.* The project began in 1914 when the rector of Catholic University obtained papal sanction for a large church to be built on the university campus. By the time the crypt church was completed in 1926 the shrine had acquired a national constituency with support from every diocese. Between 1954 and 1959 the superstructure and bell tower were completed with an iconography devoted almost exclusively to the adoration of the Virgin Mary. Since 1973 its administration has been separated from Catholic University, and it now belongs to the National Conference of Catholic Bishops.

Marianism is an aspect of Catholic worship that has flourished in this country and in this century coincident with the rise of women's liberation. For many non-Catholics the concept of the Immaculate Conception may not be familiar. It should not be confused with the Virgin Birth, which refers to the birth of Christ.

---

* In 1847 Pope Pius IX approved a petition from 19 bishops at the Council of Baltimore asking that the Virgin Mary be made "heavenly Patroness of the United States."

What is being celebrated here is the Catholic dogma that Mary, the mother of Jesus Christ, from the moment of conception in *her* mother's womb was preserved from any taint of original sin—conceived in pure virginity. Catholics pray to God through Mary as the most powerful intercessor among the saints and as the mother of mankind. As Christ said on Calvary, "Behold the Mother." The declaration of Vatican II attempted to prevent Marianism from becoming separate from the established pattern of salvation, but worship with emphasis on Mary as intercessor thrives today, and the National Shrine is a living visual catechism embodying all the symbolic profusion of "The Many Faces of Mary."

Columbus discovered America in a flagship named *Santa Maria* and most of his immigrant successors have preserved their cultural and ethnic heritage with some aspect of identity with the Virgin. Of the 32 chapels in the Upper Church, 10 are devoted to various manifestations of Mary in widely differing historical contexts. Here are a series of bright mosaic altars to Our Lady of Guadalupe, Our Mother of Sorrows, Our Lady of Czestochowa, Our Lady of Siluva (Lithuania), Our Mother of Perpetual Help, Mary Queen of All Hearts. At the crypt level are chapels of Our Lady dear to congregations from Croatia, Ruthenia, and Slovenia. And the center altar of the east apse even has a copy of Andrea del Sarto's *Madonna of the Harpies.* The apparent iconographical range is inexhaustible.

At his coronation in 1963 Pope Paul VI was crowned with a magnificent gold and silver tiara of modern design and workmanship. When he removed the tiara from his head, he placed it on the altar in an act of surrender as a gift to the poor of the world. No pope has ever worn a tiara since. Through the offices of Cardinal Spellman the tiara was brought from Rome and installed in the shrine's crypt gallery, where it has occasioned substantial donations to support the work of Mother Theresa in Calcutta.

The shrine has fine stained glass windows in the modern mode and much splendid sculpture—particularly by Lee Lawrie and Ivan Mestrovic—but its chief glory is in the mosaics which illuminate so much of its interior fabric.* The sanctuary dome over the main altar has a colossal mosaic by Millard Sheets on the theme of the Triumph of the Lamb, an interpretation of chapters 4 and 5 of the Book of Revelation done in a very modern idiom that is one of the shrine's most successful artistic achievements. Just think of it: how to portray a lamb in triumph and escape all hint of risibility. Unfortunately, some of the lesser chapels (not that any of them are small) focus on doll-like figures verging on the cloying and mawkish, reminiscent of Hallmark in their pastel sentimentality.

Originally each of the three radiating altars of the Upper Church were to be

---

* The Byzantine style requires vast areas of interior veneer; to cover the walls, the shrine contractors bought—and exhausted—an entire quarry in Italy.

dedicated to the Virgin Mary. Perhaps in anticipation of the direction of Vatican II, the prominent north apse was completed with a mosaic by John de Rosen of Christ in Majesty, putting matters in proper perspective: it is God alone that is to be adored; the honor that is Mary's is that the Lord of the Universe was once her infant.

It is hard to describe the shrine gift shop with Marian charity: from the plastic prettiness of the goods on sale you would never guess that Christian religious art draws on the richest thematic material in Western civilization.

National Shrine of the Immaculate Conception

Beaux Arts Buildings: The Eclectic Tradition

It is not surprising that Washington possesses many fine examples of the Beaux Arts tradition in architecture, as that style embodied the cumulative art of Western civilization adopted for monumental use in public buildings. This was the academic method taught in Paris at the Ecole des Beaux Arts, where generations of American architects were trained.

Beaux Arts classicism is characterized by grandeur of scale, symmetry of design, and the employment of free-standing columns, pronounced roof cornices, and decorative sculpture in an eclectic tradition borrowing from diverse classical sources. The Beaux Arts style made its greatest impact in America with the Columbian Exposition in Chicago in 1893, which inspired the City Beautiful movement, manifest in Washington in the McMillan Plan of 1901 as well as the later Federal Triangle proposals of 1926.

Although the movement survived until the advent of World War II, it fell into decline under the increasing influence of the Bauhaus and International School. A renewed interest in the Beaux Arts and a revived respectability of its values were expressed in a show of 1975 held by New York's Museum of Modern Art.

The dean of the Harvard University School of Architecture, H. Langford Warren, writing in 1899, provides us with a good description of the value of Beaux Arts training:

The strength of French training and practice was its insistence on composition, its excellence of proportion and mass, and, above all, its splendid mastery of monumental planning. . . . It insisted that a building must tell its story; that it must be expressive of its purpose, and that the exterior must be expressive of the interior arrangement of the plan, which is the key to the whole composition. Interior and exterior, plan and elevation, must work together to produce one organic and rhythmically connected whole. In insisting upon these things, it was teaching that architectural design depends, not upon caprice, but upon principle.

The best examples of buildings in the Beaux Arts style in Washington are listed here chronologically:

1897   *Corcoran Gallery of Art   Ernest Flagg*

1902   *Old District of Columbia Central Library   Ackerman and Ross*

1903   *Army War College   Stanford White*

1906   *Canadian Embassy Chancery/Moore House, 1746 Massachusetts Avenue, NW   J. H. de Sibour*

1908   *Union Station   Daniel H. Burnham*

1908   *District Building, 14th and E Streets, NW   Cope and Stewardson*

1909   *Eastern Star Temple/Belmont House, 1618 New Hampshire Avenue, NW   Ernest Sanson, with Horace Trumbauer*

1910   *OAS Building: Organization of American States   Paul Cret with Albert Kelsey*

1920   *Meridian House: Washington International Center, 1630 Crescent Place, NW   John Russell Pope*

1935   *Departmental Auditorium, Interstate Commerce Commission Arthur Brown, Jr.*

1935   *National Archives   John Russell Pope*

1941   *National Gallery of Art, West Building   John Russell Pope*

1943   *Jefferson Memorial   John Russell Pope*

Great Public Rooms

1836 Great Hall, National Portrait Gallery, Smithsonian Institution/Old
-67   Patent Office Building   Robert Mills et al.

1859 Grand Salon, Renwick Gallery/Old Corcoran Gallery of Art
       James Renwick

1883 Interior Court, Old Pension Building   Gen. Montgomery C. Meigs

1897 Main Entrance Hall, Library of Congress Thomas Jefferson Building
       Smithmeyer and Pelz

1899 Main Banking Floor, American Security Bank
       York and Sawyer

1910 Council Chamber, House of the Temple: Scottish Rite
       John Russell Pope

1910 Hall of the Americas, OAS Building   Cret and Kelsey

1910 Library, Memorial Continental Hall, Daughters of the American
       Revolution   Edward Pearce Casey

1935 Departmental Auditorium, Interstate Commerce Commission
       Arthur Brown, Jr.

1978 Main Courtyard, National Gallery of Art, East Building
       I. M. Pei

Art Deco and Art Moderne Buildings

Buildings in the Art Deco and Art Moderne style in both residential and commercial applications flourished sporadically in Washington during the period 1925–45 as a legacy of Art Nouveau and as carom shots from the impact of the International School and other modernist forces in their assault on traditional forms. The terms derive from a movement emanating in Paris in the Exposition Internationale des Arts Décoratifs et Industriels Modernes of 1925. There is no clear distinction in the character of the two modes, but Art Deco emphasizes angular geometric decoration while Art Moderne expresses rounded streamlined surfaces.

They were something of a fad that came to the Washington scene and went quickly; many of the best examples of the genre were capital losses in the haste to replace buildings that have overnight come to look dated. But some of the best examples, listed here by building types, happily survive.

Apartment Houses and Hotels

The Bader Apartments, 2515 K Street, NW

Dorchester House, 2480 16th Street, NW   1940

General Scott Apartments, 1 Scott Circle, NW   Robert O. Scholz   1939

Hightowers Apartments, 1530 16th Street, NW

Kennedy-Warren Apartments, 3133 Connecticut Avenue, NW
Joseph Yunger   1931

Langston Dwellings, off Benning Road between 21st and 24th Streets, NE
Hilyard R. Robinson   1935

Macomb Gardens Apartments, 3725 Macomb Street, NW   1940

Shoreham Hotel, 2500 Calvert Street, NW   Joseph Abel   1930

2100 Connecticut Avenue Apartments, at Wyoming Avenue, NW

Yorkshire Apartments, 3355 16th Street, NW

Churches
Nineteenth Street Baptist Church/Old B'nai Israel Congregation, 4606 16th Street, NW

Reorganized Church of Jesus Christ of Latter Day Saints, 3526 Massachusetts
  Avenue, NW   Eimar Capplemann

St. Stephen's Catholic Church, Pennsylvania Avenue at 24th Street, NW
  Johnson and Boutin

St. Thomas Apostle Catholic Church, 2665 Woodley Road, NW
  Johnson and Boutin

Houses
Alexander Hawes House, 3210 Reservoir Road, NW
  Theodore Dominick   1937

3718 Calvert Street, NW

2915 University Terrace, NW

2933 University Terrace, NW

Waldron Faulkner House, 3415 36th Street, NW   Waldron Faulkner   1937

Public Structures
Apostolic Delegation, 3339 Massachusetts Avenue, NW
  Frederick V. Murphy   1938

Central Heating Plant, 13th Street between C and D Streets, SW
  Paul Cret   1933

Connecticut Avenue Bridge over Klingle Valley, Connecticut Avenue between Devonshire
  Place and Macomb Street, NW   Paul Cret   1931

Department of Justice, 9th Street and Constitution Avenue, NW
  Zantzinger, Borie, and Medary   1934

Folger Shakespeare Library, East Capitol Street between 2nd and 3rd Streets, SE
  Cret and Trowbridge   1932

Government Printing Office Warehouse, North Capitol Street at G Place, NE
  Victor D. Abel   1938

Hecht Company Warehouse, 1401 New York Avenue, NE   1936

Art Deco and Art Moderne Buildings

*Library of Congress John Adams Building, 2nd Street at Independence Avenue, SE
Pierson and Wilson   1938*

Manhattan Laundry, 1326 Florida Avenue, NW   1935

Municipal Center, 300 Indiana Avenue, NW   Nathan C. Wyeth   1941

*National Naval Medical Center, Wisconsin Avenue, Bethesda, Maryland
Paul Cret with Frederick Southwick   1940*

Washington National Airport, Alexandria, Virginia   Howard Cheney   1940

Theaters
Penn Theater, 650 Pennsylvania Avenue, SE

Uptown Theater, 3426 Connecticut Avenue, NW

Senator Theater, 3950 Minnesota Avenue, NE

Sculpture
Marconi Memorial, 16th and Lamont Streets, NW   Attilio Piccirilli   1941

Hitt Memorial, Rock Creek Park   Laura G. Fraser   1938

Architects
and Their Buildings

This list provides representative examples of the work of architects in current practice. Listings of the work of architects of the past are more exhaustive, but include only those buildings which survive as of 1981.

Abel, Joseph
> *Shoreham Hotel, 2500 Calvert Street, NW 1930*

Abel, Victor D.
> *Government Printing Office Warehouse, North Capitol Street at G Place, NE 1938*

Ackerman and Ross
> *Old District of Columbia Central Library, Mt. Vernon Place, Massachusetts Avenue at 8th and K Streets, NW 1902*

Andersen, Henry
> *Indonesian Embassy/Walsh-McLean House, 2020 Massachusetts Avenue, NW 1903*

Architect of the Treasury
> *Department of Health and Human Services, Independence Avenue between 3rd and 4th Streets, SW 1941*

Architects Collaborative, The (Cambridge)
> *American Institute of Architects, 1735 New York Avenue, NW 1973*

Bacon, Henry
> *Lincoln Memorial, West end of the Mall at the foot of 23rd Street, NW 1922*

Bates, Smart and McCutcheon (Melbourne)
> *Australian Embassy Chancery, 1601 Massachusetts Avenue, NW 1965*

Bedford, Eric (London)
> *British Embassy Chancery Annex, Massachusetts Avenue at Observatory Circle, NW with the British Ministry of Works 1960*

Bennett, Parsons, Frost
> *Botanic Gardens, 1st Street and Maryland Avenue, SW 1902*
> *Federal Trade Commission, Constitution Avenue at 6th Street, NW 1937*

Bergstrom, George E.
> *The Pentagon, Arlington, Virginia with the U.S. Army Corps of Engineers 1942*

Bodley, George F. (London)
> *Washington National Cathedral, Wisconsin Avenue at Massachusetts Avenue, NW with Henry Vaughan 1907-16*

Breuer, Marcel, & Associates
> *HUD Building: Department of Housing and Urban Development, 7th Street at D Street, SW with Nolen, Swinburne & Associates 1968*
> *Hubert H. Humphrey Building: Department of Health and Human Services, Independence Avenue at 3rd Street, SW 1978*

Brooke, Frederick H.
> *Dumbarton Oaks reconstruction, R Street at 31st Street, NW 1921*

Brown, Arthur, Jr.
> *Customs Service, Constitution Avenue at 14th Street, NW 1935*
> *Departmental Auditorium, Constitution Avenue between 12th and 14th Streets, NW 1935*
> *Interstate Commerce Commission, Constitution Avenue at 12th Street, NW 1935*

Brown, Glenn
> *Chilean Embassy Chancery, 1732 Massachusetts Avenue, NW 1890*
> *Beale House, 2012 Massachusetts Avenue, NW 1898*
> *Egyptian Embassy, 2301 Massachusetts Avenue, NW 1909*
> *Buffalo Bridge over Rock Creek Park, Q Street at 23rd Street, NW with Bedford Brown 1914*

Browne, Herbert W. C. *See* **Little & Browne**

Bulfinch, Charles
> *Capitol Gatehouses, 15th Street and Constitution Avenue, NW 1818*
> *The Capitol, Capitol Hill with others 1819-29*

Bunshaft, Gordon. *See* **Skidmore, Owings & Merrill**

Burnham, Daniel H.
> *Union Station and Plaza, Massachusetts Avenue at Delaware Avenue, NE 1908*

Southern Building, 1425 H Street, NW   1912
City Post Office, Massachusetts Avenue at North Capitol Street, NE   with
*   Graham   1914*

Cain, Walker O. *See* Steinmann, Cain and White

Campos, Olavo de
Brazilian Embassy Chancery, 3000 Massachusetts Avenue, NW   1973

Carrere and Hastings
Cosmos Club/Townsend House, 2121 Massachusetts Avenue, NW   1900
Cannon House Office Building, Capitol Hill   1908
Russell Senate Office Building, Capitol Hill   1909
Carnegie Institution of Washington, 16th and P Streets, NW   1910
Arlington Memorial Amphitheater, Arlington Cemetery, Arlington,
*   Virginia   1915–20*
Tomb of the Unknown Soldier, Arlington Cemetery, Arlington, Virginia   1920
Washington Hotel, 15th Street at Pennsylvania Avenue, NW

Carson, Charles (Baltimore)
Church of the Ascension and St. Agnes, Massachusetts Avenue at 12th Street, NW
*   with Thomas Dixon   1875*

Casey, Edward Pearce
Library of Congress, Thomas Jefferson Building interior, 1st Street between East
*   Capitol Street and Independence Avenue, SE   1897*
Daughters of the American Revolution, Memorial Continental Hall, 17th Street
*   at C Street, NW   1910*
Grant Memorial, east end of the Mall, at 1st Street, NW   1922

Chatelain, Leon, Jr. *See also* Porter, Lockie and Chatelain
National City Christian Church addition, Thomas Circle, NW   1952
Federal National Mortgage Association, 3900 Wisconsin Avenue, NW   1960
Westmoreland Congregational Church, Westmoreland Circle, NW   1969
Kiplinger Building, 1729 H Street, NW
Suffridge Building, 1775 K Street, NW
Washington Gas Light Company, 100 H Street, NW

Chatelain and Gauger
Sixth Church of Christ, Scientist, first stage, 4601 Massachusetts Avenue, NW
*   1962*

Chatelain, Gauger and Nolan
National Broadcasting Company, WRC–TV, 4001 Nebraska Avenue, NW
*   1957*
Federal Deposit Insurance Corporation, 550 17th Street, NW   with Perkins &
*   Will   1963*

Cheney, Howard L.
> *Fourth Church of Christ, Scientist, 16th Street at Meridian Place, NW   1929*
> *Washington National Airport, Alexandria Virginia   1940*

Childs, David
> *Granite Fountains, Constitution Avenue at the Ellipse, NW   with Nathaniel*
> *Owings   1967*

Clark, Appleton P.
> *Foundry United Methodist Church, 1500 16th Street, NW   1904*
> *Jewish Community Center, 16th and Q Streets, NW   1910*

Clarke, St. Clair
> *St. John's Parish Building/Old British Legation, 1525 H Street, NW   1824*

Clas, Riggs, Owens and Ramos
> *National Rifle Association remodeling, 1600 Rhode Island Avenue, at Scott*
> *Circle, NW   1965*
> *International Monetary Fund, 19th and G Streets, NW   with Charles*
> *Kling   1973*
> *Quality Inn Motel, 30th and M Streets, NW   1981*

Cluss, Adolph W.
> *Smithsonian Castle reconstruction, The Mall, SW   1865*
> *Franklin School, 13th Street at K Street, NW   1868*
> *Calvary Baptist Church, 8th and H Streets, NW   1868*
> *Sumner School, M Street at 17th Street, NW   1872*
> *National Museum of American Art and National Portrait Gallery, Smithsonian*
> *Institution/Old Patent Office Building reconstruction, 8th and G*
> *Streets between 7th and 9th Streets, NW   1880*
> *Seaton Elementary School, 10th Street and Rhode Island Avenue, NW*

Cluss and Schulze
> *Arts and Industries Building, Smithsonian Institution, The Mall, Jefferson Drive*
> *at 9th Street, SW   1881   with Gen. M. C. Meigs*

Codman, Ogden
> *Codman House, 2145 Decatur Place, NW   1907*

Cook, Robert E.
> *Decatur Terrace Steps and Fountain, 22nd Street between Decatur Place and*
> *S Street, NW   1911*

Coolidge and Shattuck (Boston)
> *All Souls Church, 16th Street at Harvard Street, NW   1924*

Coolidge, Shepley, Bulfinch and Abbott (Boston)
> *Rochambeau Bridge over the Potomac River   1950*
> *George Mason Bridge over the Potomac River   1962*

Cope and Stewardson
> *District Building, 14th Street and Pennsylvania Avenue, NW   1908*

Corning, Moore, Elmore and Fisher
> *B'nai B'rith International, Rhode Island Avenue at 17th Street, NW   1957*
> *The Watergate, apartments and office buildings, Virginia and New Hampshire*
>   *Avenues, NW   with Luigi Moretti   1964–72*
> *B'nai B'rith headquarters addition   1976*

Cret, Paul
> *OAS Building: Organization of American States, 17th Street at Constitution*
>   *Avenue, NW   with Albert Kelsey   1910*
> *Folger Shakespeare Library, East Capitol Street between 2nd and 3rd Streets, SE*
>   *with A. B. Trowbridge   1932*
> *Central Heating Plant, 13th Street between C and D Streets, SW   1933*
> *Federal Reserve Building, Constitution Avenue between 20th and 21st*
>   *Streets, NW   1937*
> *Calvert Street Bridge over Rock Creek Park   1935*
> *Connecticut Avenue Bridge over Klingle Valley, Connecticut Avenue between*
>   *Devonshire Place and Macomb Street, NW   1931*
> *National Naval Medical Center, Wisconsin Avenue, Bethesda, Maryland*
>   *with Frederick Southwick   1940*
> *Frederick Douglass Bridge over the Anacostia River   1949*

Cross, Eason
> *Watha T. Daniel Public Library, 7th Street and Rhode Island Avenue,*
>   *NW   1975*

Curtis and Davis
> *Forrestal Building: Department of Energy, Independence Avenue and 10th*
>   *Street, SW   1970*

Deigert and Yerkes
> *National Arboretum, 24th and R Streets, NE   1963*

Delano and Aldrich
> *Japanese Embassy, 2520 Massachusetts Avenue, NW   1931*
> *Post Office Department, Pennsylvania Avenue between 11th and 12th*
>   *Streets, NW   1934*

De Sibour, Jules Henri
> *Colombian Embassy, 1520 20th Street, NW   1905*
> *Canadian Embassy Chancery/Moore House, 1746 Massachusetts Avenue,*
>   *NW   1906*
> *Folger Building, 712–25 15th Street, NW   1906*
> *Peruvian Embassy Chancery/Wilkins House, 1700 Massachusetts Avenue   1909*
> *French Embassy/Lawrence House/later Hammond House/2221 Kalorama*
>   *Road, NW   1910*

National Trust for Historic Preservation/McCormick Apartments, 1785
Massachusetts Avenue, NW   1917
Foxtrappe Club/Mulligan House, 1601 R Street, NW   1911
Chevy Chase Club, Connecticut Avenue, Chevy Chase, Maryland
Investment Building (de Sibour's offices), 1511 K Street, NW
Luxembourg Embassy/Stewart House, 2200 Massachusetts Avenue
University Club, 1135 16th Street, NW
Yater Clinic/Ingalls Residence, 1780 Massachusetts Avenue, NW

Dessez, Leon E.
Vice-President's House, Observatory Circle, Massachusetts Avenue at 34th
Street, NW   1893

DeWitt, Roscoe
Library of Congress, James Madison Memorial Building, Independence Avenue
between 1st and 2nd Streets, SE   with Alfred Easton Poore (New York),
Homer Swanke (New York), A. P. Almond (Atlanta), and Jesse Shelton
(Atlanta)   1980

Dixon, Thomas (Baltimore, Maryland)
Church of the Ascension and St. Agnes, Massachusetts Avenue at 12th Street, NW
with Charles Carson   1875

Dominick, Theodore
Alexander Hawes House, 3210 Reservoir Road, NW   1937
André de Limur House, 3224 R Street, NW   1948

Dreyfuss, Edmund W.
Presidential Building, Pennsylvania Avenue and 12th Street, NW   1968
National Permanent Federal Savings and Loan, Georgetown Branch, 2901 M
Street, NW   1974

Dudley, Northrop
Church of St. Stephen and the Incarnation, 16th Street at Newton Street, NW
with Robert Tappan   1928

Edbrooke, W. J.
Old Post Office, 12th Street and Pennsylvania Avenue, NW   1899

Eggers and Higgins
Straus Memorial, 14th Street in Federal Triangle, NW   1947
Mellon Fountain, Constitution Avenue at 6th Street, NW   1952

Faulkner, Waldron
Venezuelan Embassy Residence/Strong House, 3712 32nd Street, NW   1929
Residence, 3419 36th Street, NW   1937
Waldron Faulkner House, 3415 36th Street, NW   1937

Faulkner, Winthrop. *See also* Wilkes and Faulkner
Winthrop Faulkner Houses, 36th and Ordway Streets, NW   1964, 1968, 1978

Faulkner-Faulkner (Chicago)
> *Sixth Church of Christ, Scientist, second stage, 4601 Massachusetts Avenue, NW 1978*

Faulkner, Fryer and Vanderpool
> *American Association for the Advancement of Science, 1515 Massachusetts Avenue, NW   1956*
> *Federal Office Building No. 6   1961*
> *American Chemical Society, 1155 16th Street, NW   1968*
> *American University, Ward Circle classroom building   1969*
> *George Washington University Hospital, Washington Circle and 23rd Street, NW   1970*
> *National Zoo master plan   1975*
> *George Washington University, classroom-office building   1970*
> *New Zealand Embassy, Observatory Circle, NW   with Warren Miles (New Zealand)   1979*

Faulkner, Kingsbury and Stenhouse
> *Armed Forces Institute of Pathology and Armed Forces Medical Museum, Walter Reed Army Medical Center, 6825 16th Street, NW   1953*
> *Brookings Institution, 1775 Massachusetts Avenue, NW   1960*

Faulkner, Stenhouse, Fryer & Faulkner
> *National Museum of American Art and National Portrait Gallery, Smithsonian Institution / Old Patent Office Building restoration and conversion, G Street between 7th and 9th Streets   1969*

Fischer, Milton
> *B'nai B'rith International, Rhode Island Avenue at 17th Street, NW   1957*
> *American Association of University Women, 2401 Virginia Avenue, NW   1960*

Fischer and Elmore
> *Embassy Row Hotel, 2015 Massachusetts Avenue, NW   1971*

Flagg, Ernest
> *Corcoran Gallery of Art, 17th Street at New York Avenue, NW   1897*

Florance, Colden
> *St. Alban's School academic center and gymnasium, National Cathedral Close, NW   1979*
> *Smithsonian Support Complex, Suitland, Maryland   1982*

Flournoy, Benjamin Courtney
> *Church of the Pilgrims, 2201 P Street, NW   1927*

Ford, Claude
> *Urban Village community housing project, Meridian Place, NW   1975*

Fraser, John
> *National Paint and Coatings Association/Brodhead House, 1500 Rhode Island Avenue, NW   1879*
> *James G. Blaine House, 2000 Massachusetts Avenue, NW   1882*

Frohman, Philip Hubert
> *Washington National Cathedral, Wisconsin Avenue at Massachusetts Avenue, NW 1919–73*
> *Church of the Annunciation, 39th Street at Massachusetts Avenue, NW*
> *St. Paul's Lutheran Church, Connecticut Avenue at Everett Street, NW*
> *Wesley Methodist Church, Connecticut Avenue at Jennifer Street, NW*

Fuller and Wheeler (Albany)
> *Denman-Hinckley House, 1623 16th Street, NW   1886*

Gilbert, Cass
> *Treasury Annex, Pennsylvania Avenue and Madison Place, NW   1919*
> *First Division Monument, State Place and 17th Street, NW   1924*
> *Chamber of Commerce Building, 1615 H Street, NW   1925*
> *Supreme Court, 1st Street at East Capitol Street, NE   1935*

Gitlin, Elliott
> *Georgetown Papermill apartment and housing complex, Grace and Potomac Streets, NW   1980*
> *Office building, 1140 19th Street, NW   1980*
> *Chancellor Condominium Apartments, 3 Washington Circle, NW   1981*

Goettelmann, Paul A.
> *Catholic University, Gilbert V. Hartke Theater, Harewood Road, NE   1970*

Goodhue, Bertram Grosvenor
> *National Academy of Sciences, Constitution Avenue at 21st Street, NW   1924*

Goodman, Charles M.
> *Hollin Hills housing development, Fairfax County, Virginia   1950*
> *River Park Apartments, Southwest renewal area   1962*
> *Hawthorne School, 6th and I Streets, SW   1964*

Graham, Anderson, Probst and White (Chicago)
> *State Department, C Street between 21st and 23rd Streets, NW   with Harley, Ellington and Day (Detroit)   1959*

Gruen Associates (successors to Victor Gruen)
> *Capitol Gallery office complex, Maryland Avenue and 6th Street, SW   1981*

Hadfield, George
> *Marine Barracks and Commandant's House, 8th and I Streets, SE   1805*
> *Arlington House: Custis-Lee Mansion, Arlington, Virginia   1820*

D.C. Courthouse, Old City Hall, 4th and D Streets, NW 1820–50
Van Ness Mausoleum, Oak Hill Cemetery, 30th and R Streets, NW 1833

Harbeson, Hough, Livingston and Larson
Rayburn House Office Building, Independence Avenue between 1st and South Capitol Streets, SW 1965

Hardenburgh, Henry
Willard Hotel, Pennsylvania Avenue and 14th Street, NW 1901

Harris, Albert L.
Army and Navy Club, Farragut Square, NW 1911

Harrison and Abramovitz
Central Intelligence Agency, Langley, Virginia with Frederick R. King 1959

Hartman-Cox
Mount Vernon College chapel and dormitory, Foxhall Road, NW 1970
St. Alban's Tennis Club, National Cathedral close, NW 1970
Euram Building, 21 Dupont Circle, NW 1971
Dodge Center, 3217 K Street, NW 1976
National Permanent Building, 1775 Pennsylvania Avenue, NW 1977
National Park Service Stable, Rock Creek Park, NW 1978
Folger Shakespeare Library addition, East Capitol Street between 2nd and 3rd Streets, SE 1981

Heaton, Arthur
Altamira Apartments, 1901 Wyoming Avenue, NW 1916

Heins and LaFarge
St. Matthew's Cathedral, 1725 Rhode Island Avenue 1899
Metropolitan Club, H Street at 17th Street, NW 1908

Hellmuth, Obata and Kassabaum
National Air and Space Museum, Smithsonian Institution, The Mall, IndependenceAvenue between 4th and 7th Streets, SW Gyo Obata, partner-in-charge 1976
Amalgamated Transit Union, 5025 Wisconsin Avenue at Garrison Street, NW 1981

Hill, James G.
Auditor's Building/Old Bureau of Engraving and Printing, 14th Street at Independence Avenue, SW 1879
Riggs Bank, 9th and F Streets, NW 1891

Hoban, James
The White House, 1600 Pennsylvania Avenue, NW 1792–1829

Holabird and Root and Burgee (Chicago)
Brotherhood of Teamsters, Constitution and Louisiana Avenues, NW 1956

International Union of Operating Engineers, 1125 17th Street, NW   1957
Federal Office Building No. 10, 800 Independence Avenue, SW   1963

Hornblower and Marshall

Indian Embassy Chancery annex/Edmunds House, 2111 Massachusetts
*   Avenue, NW   1885*
Fraser House, 1701 20th Street, NW   1890
Iraqi Embassy Chancery annex/Boardman House, 1801 P Street, NW   1893
Phillips Collection, 1600 21st Street, NW   1896
Hornblower House, 2030 Hillyer Place, NW   1897
Cross House, 2138 Bancroft Place, NW   1898
Morse studio-residence, 2133 R Street, NW   1902
National Geographic Society, Gardiner Greene Hubbard Memorial Library, 16th
*   and M Streets, NW   1902*
Johnston House, 1628 21st Street, NW   1905
Marine Corps Barracks rebuilding, 8th and I Streets, SE   1902–06
National Zoo, Monkey House, 3100 Connecticut Avenue, NW   1907
Lothrop House, 2001 Connecticut Avenue, NW   1908
National Museum of Natural History, Smithsonian Institution, Constitution
*   Avenue at 10th Street, NW   1904–11*

HTB Inc. (Oklahoma City and Washington)

National Press Building reconstruction, 14th and F Streets, NW   1983

Hunt, Richard M.

U.S. Capitol dome   with Thomas U. Walter   1851–65

Jacobsen, Hugh Newell

Lee House extension and remodeling, 2813 Q Street, NW   1968
Trentman House, 1350 27th Street, NW   1969
Renwick Gallery/Old Corcoran Gallery of Art interior restoration, Pennsylvania
*   Avenue at 17th Street, NW   1972*
Arts and Industries Building, Smithsonian Institution restoration, The Mall,
*   Jefferson Drive at 9th Street, SW   1976*
Robert Elliott House, 17 West Irving Street, Chevy Chase, Maryland   1977

Johnson, Philip

Dumbarton Oaks, Pre-Columbian Museum, 1703 32nd Street, NW   1963
Kreeger House, 2401 Foxhall Road, NW   1967
Kennedy Center, Terrace Theater, 2700 F Street, NW   with John
*   Burgee   1978*
Kennedy Center, Performing Arts Library interior design, 2700 F Street, NW
*   with IDA Associates   1979*

Johnson & Boutin (Donald S. Johnson and Harold L. Boutin)

Fort Myer Chapel
Our Lady of Victory, MacArthur Boulevard, NW

St. Stephen's Catholic Church, Pennsylvania Avenue at 24th Street, NW
St. Thomas Apostle Catholic Church, Woodley Road at 27th Street, NW

Justement, Louis

K Street Bridge over Rock Creek Park   1939
Massachusetts Avenue Bridge over Rock Creek Park   1940
U.S. District Court House, Constitution Avenue and 3rd Street, NW   1952
National Guard Association, 1 Massachusetts Avenue, NW   1959
Pan American Health Organization, 23rd Street and Virginia Avenue, NW
*   with Roman Fresnedo Siri   1964*

Keyes, Lethbridge and Condon

Forest Industries Building, 1619 Massachusetts Avenue, NW   1961
Columbia Plaza, 2400 Virginia Avenue, NW   1962
Tiber Island, 429 N Street, SW   1965
Carrollsburg Square, 4th and M Streets, SW   1965
Sunderland Building, 1320 19th Street, NW   1969
Washington Metropolitan Area Transit Authority, Operations Control Center, 5th
*   Street between F and G Streets, NW   1974*

King, Frederick Rhinelander

Phillips Collection annex, 1600 21st Street, NW   1960
Dumbarton Oaks Garden and Horticultural Library annex, 31st and R
*   Streets, NW   1963*

Kling, Vincent G., and partners (Philadelphia)

Government Employees Insurance Company, 5260 Western Avenue, NW
*   1959*
International Monetary Fund, 19th and G Streets, NW   with Clas, Riggs,
*   Owens and Ramos   1973*
National Housing Center, 15th and M Streets, NW   1974

Kohn Pedersen Fox

American Broadcasting Company, 1717 De Sales Street, NW   1980

Koubek, Vlastimil

Olmsted Building, 17th Street and Pennsylvania Avenue, NW   1962
American Psychological Association, 1200 17th Street, NW   1964
L'Enfant Plaza Hotel and Office Building   1970–73
Esplanade office complex, 20th and I Streets, NW   1979
Jefferson Building, 19th Street and Jefferson Place, NW

Lamb, Charles (New York)

Tivoli Theater, 3301 14th Street, NW

Lapidus, Morris

J. Finley House/Chalk House, 4th and O Streets, SW   1966

Latrobe, Benjamin H.
Washington Navy Yard Gate and Officers Quarters, M Street and 8th Street, SE 1804
Dumbarton House remodeling, 2715 Q Street, NW 1805
St. John's Church, Lafayette Square, 16th Street at H Street, NW 1816
The Capitol, Capitol Hill with others 1803–17
Decatur House, Lafayette Square, NW 1818
The White House, North Portico, 1600 Pennsylvania Avenue, NW 1829
The White House, East and West Terraces, 1600 Pennsylvania Avenue, NW
Van Ness House stables, 18th and C Streets, NW

Laws, Henry
Christ Church, 31st and O Streets, NW 1885

Lescaze, William
Longfellow Building, 1741 Rhode Island Avenue, NW 1941
Swiss Embassy, 2900 Cathedral Avenue, NW 1959

Little and Browne
Society of the Cincinnati/Anderson House, 2118 Massachusetts Avenue, NW 1905

Livingston, Goodhue. *See* **Trowbridge and Goodhue**

Lovering, William
Maples House, 619 D Street, SE 1796

Lundy, Victor A.
United States Tax Court, 2nd Street between D and E Streets, NW 1976

Lutyens, Sir Edwin
British Embassy, 3100 Massachusetts Avenue, NW 1931

Maginnis, Walsh, and Kennedy (Boston)
National Shrine of the Immaculate Conception, Michigan Avenue at 4th Street, NE 1918–59

Marsh and Peter
Old Evening Star Building, Pennsylvania Avenue and 11th Street, NW 1898

Marshall, James Rush
Embassy of Thailand, 2300 Kalorama Road, NW 1920

McKim, Mead and White
Page House, 1759 R Street, NW Stanford White, partner-in-charge 1897
Washington Club/Patterson House, 15 Dupont Circle, NW Stanford White, partner-in-charge 1903
Army War College, Fort Lesley J. McNair, SW 1908
Phillips Collection, Skylight Gallery, 1600 21st Street, NW 1917

Arlington Memorial Bridge over the Potomac River   1926–32
Memorial Gate to Arlington Cemetery   1926–32
John Philip Sousa Bridge over Anacostia River   1940
The White House, East Gallery and Executive Office Wing   1902, 1948–52

Meigs, Gen. Montgomery C.

The Capitol, Capitol Hill   with others   1851–65
Cabin John Aqueduct Bridge over Cabin John, Maryland   1859
*Arts and Industries Building, Smithsonian Institution, The Mall, Jefferson Drive
   at 9th Street, SW   1881   with Cluss and Schulze*
Old Pension Building, F Street between 4th and 5th Streets, NW   1883

Mesrobian, Mihran

Wardman Park annex, Connecticut Avenue at Woodley Road, NW   1918
Carlton Hotel, 16th Street at K Street, NW   1926

Meyers, John G.

*Columbia Historical Society/Heurich House, 1307 New Hampshire Avenue,NW
   1880*

Mies van der Rohe, Ludwig (Chicago)

Martin Luther King Memorial Library, G Street at 9th Street, NW   1972

Mills, Robert

The Capitol, Capitol Hill   with others   1836–51
*National Museum of American Art and National Portrait Gallery, Smithsonian
   Institution/Old Patent Office Building, G Street between 7th and 9th
   Streets, NW   with William Elliot, Edward Clark, and others   1836–67*
*Tariff Commission/Old Post Office, 7th and 8th between E and F Streets, NW
   1839–69*
*Treasury Building, 1500 Pennsylvania Avenue, NW   with Thomas U.Walter
   1836–69*
Washington Monument, The Mall at 15th Street, NW   1884

Mills, Petticord and Mills

Peoples Life Insurance Company, 601 New Hampshire Avenue, NW   1958
*National Museum of Natural History wings, Constitution Avenue between 9th
   and 12th Streets, NW   1965*
*American Home Economics Association, 2010 Massachusetts Avenue, NW
   1969*
George Washington University Law Library, 718 20th Street, NW   1968
*Eastern Liberty Federal Savings and Loan Building, 600 Pennsylvania
   Avenue, SE   1976*

Moore, Arthur Cotton

Canal Square, 1054 31st Street, NW   1971
*Old Post Office Building renovation, Pennsylvania Avenue at 12th Street, NW
   1978–81*

Architects and Their Buildings

Moretti, Luigi
> *The Watergate Apartments and office buildings, Virginia and New Hampshire Avenues, NW   with Corning, Moore, Elmore and Fisher   1964–72*

Morsell, Samuel T.
> *Metropolitan AME Church, 1518 M Street, NW   1881*

Mullett, Alfred B.
> *Executive Office Building/Old State, War and Navy Building, 17th Street and Pennsylvania Avenue, NW   1871–88*
> *Apex Liquor Building, 633 Pennsylvania Avenue, NW   1888*
> *District of Columbia Jail, 17th and B Streets, SE*
> *Tariff Commission/Old Post Office alterations, 7th and 8th between E and F Streets, NW*

Murphy, C.F., Associates (Chicago)
> *J. Edgar Hoover Building: Federal Bureau of Investigation, Pennsylvania Avenue between 9th and 10th Streets, NW   1975*

Murphy, Frederick Vernon
> *Apostolic Delegation, 3339 Massachusetts Avenue, NW   1938*
> *National Conference of Catholic Bishops, facade,1312 Massachusetts Avenue,NW 1949*

Neratov, Alexander
> *St. Nicholas Cathedral, 3500 Massachusetts Avenue, NW   1963*

O'Connor, Jerome
> *National Grange, 1616 H Street, NW   1959*

O'Connor and Killham (New York)
> *National Library of Medicine, 8600 Wisconsin Avenue, Bethesda, Maryland   1962*

Olmsted, Frederick Law
> *Trolley waiting station, U.S. Capitol Plaza   1876*
> *Capitol Grotto, U.S. Capitol grounds   1879*

Orr, Douglas W.
> *Robert A. Taft Memorial, U.S. Capitol grounds near Louisiana Avenue, NW 1959*

Owings, Nathaniel
> *Granite Fountains, Constitution Avenue at the Ellipse, NW   with David Childs   1967*

Page, Harvey
> *Women's National Democratic Club/Weeks House, 1526 New Hampshire Avenue, NW   1892*

Peaslee, Horace P.
Meridian Hill Park, 16th Street between Florida Avenue and Euclid Street, NW
1920
Peruvian Embassy, 3001 Garrison Street, NW   1924
St. John's Church Parish House remodeling, 1525 H Street, NW   1955
Episcopal Home addition, 3124 Q Street, NW   1957
Cosmos Club/Townsend House addition, 2121 Massachusetts Avenue, NW
1958

Pei, I. M.
Town Center Plaza, M Street between 3rd and 6th Streets, SW   1961
Slayton House, 3411 Ordway Street, NW   1962
L'Enfant Plaza, north and south buildings and plaza, SW   1965
Third Church of Christ, Scientist, 16th and I Streets, NW   1972
National Gallery of Art, East Building, The Mall, Constitution Avenue between
3rd and 4th Streets, NW   1978

Pelz, Paul. *See also* **Smithmeyer and Pelz**
Argyle Guest House, 2201 Massachusetts Avenue, NW   1901
Playhouse Theater, 725 15th Street, NW   1906

Perkins & Will (Chicago)
Federal Deposit Insurance Corporation, 550 17th Street, NW   with Chatelain,
Gauger and Nolan   1963
University Medical Building, 2143 K Street, NW   1965

Pierson and Wilson
Library of Congress John Adams Building, 2nd Street at Independence Avenue, SE
1938

Platt, Charles A.
Freer Gallery of Art, Smithsonian Institution, The Mall, Jefferson Drive at 12th
Street, SW   1923
Corcoran Gallery of Art addition, 17th Street at New York Avenue, NW
1927

Poore, Alfred Easton. *See* **DeWitt, Roscoe**

Pope, John Russell
Brazilian Embassy, 3000 Massachusetts Avenue, NW   1909
House of the Temple, Scottish Rite, 1733 16th Street at S Street, NW   1910
White-Meyer House, 1624 Crescent Place, NW   1911
Myers House, 2320 S Street, NW   1912
Meridian House: Washington International Center, 1630 Crescent Place, NW
1920
Daughters of the American Revolution, Constitution Hall, 18th and D Streets, NW
1929

National City Christian Church, Thomas Circle, 14th Street at Massachusetts Avenue, NW   1930
American Pharmaceutical Association, Constitution Avenue between 22nd and 23rd Streets, NW   1934
National Archives, Constitution Avenue at 7th Street, NW   1935
Second Division Memorial, Constitution Avenue near 17th Street, NW   1936
National Gallery of Art, West Building, The Mall, Constitution Avenue between 4th and 7th Streets, NW   1941
Jefferson Memorial, Tidal Basin, SW   1943

Porter, Lockie and Chatelain
Scottish Rite Temple, 2800 16th Street, NW   1940

Prassas, Milton J.
Sts. Constantine and Helen Greek Orthodox Church, 4115 16th Street, NW 1953
Christ Church of Washington, Massachusetts Avenue at Idaho Avenue, NW 1967

Protopapas, Archie
Saint Sophia: Greek Orthodox Cathedral, Massachusetts Avenue at 36th Street, NW   1956

Rankin, Kellogg and Crane
Department of Agriculture, 14th and Independence Avenue, SW   1905-30

Renwick, James
Smithsonian Castle building, The Mall, Jefferson Drive, SW   1849
Oak Hill Cemetery Chapel, 29th and R Streets, NW   1850
Renwick Gallery/Old Corcoran Gallery of Art, Pennsylvania Avenue at 17th Street, NW   1859
St. John's Church remodeling, Lafayette Square, 16th Street at H Street   1883
St. Mary's Episcopal Church, 730 23rd Street, between H and G Streets, NW with Aspinwall and Russell   1886

Richardson, H. H.
Lutheran Church Center, 2633 16th Street, NW   removed to present address in 1902   1885

Robinson, Hilyard R.
Langston Dwellings, off Benning Road between 21st and 24th Street, NE 1935

Rossi, Mario
Islamic Center, 2551 Massachusetts Avenue, NW   with Irwin Porter and Sons 1957

Saarinen, Eero
Dulles International Airport Terminal, Chantilly, Virginia   1962

Samperton, John S.
> *C & P Telephone Company Building, 1200 H Street, NW 1970*

Sanson, Ernest (Paris)
> *Eastern Star Temple/Belmont House, 1618 New Hampshire Avenue, NW*
> *with Horace Trumbauer 1909*

Satterlee, Nicholas
> *Capitol Park Apartments, 4th and I Streets, SW with Chloethiel Woodward*
> *Smith 1963*
> *Chevy Chase Branch Library, Connecticut Avenue at McKinley Street, NW*
> *1967*
> *Logan Circle restoration plans 1969*

Sauginet and Staats (Fort Worth, Texas)
> *Mt. Vernon Place United Methodist Church, Massachusetts Avenue at 9th*
> *Street, NW 1917*

Schneider, Thomas Franklin
> *National Park Seminary, Forest Glen, Maryland 1887*
> *Cairo Apartments, 1615 Q Street, NW 1894*

Scholz, Robert O.
> *General Scott Apartments, 1 Scott Circle, NW 1942*
> *Bay State Apartments, 1701 Massachusetts Avenue, NW*
> *Boston House, 1711 Massachusetts Avenue, NW*
> *World Center Building, 16th and K Streets, NW*

Simmons, Stanley
> *Barr Building, 910 17th Street, NW 1930*

Simon, Louis A.
> *Internal Revenue Service, Constitution Avenue and 10th Street, NW 1935*
> *Government Printing Office Building No. 3, North Capitol Street at H Street, NW*
> *1938*

Siri, Roman Fresnedo (Uruguay)
> *Pan American Health Organization, 23rd Street and Virginia Avenue, NW*
> *1964*

Skidmore, Owings & Merrill
> *International Bank, 18th and G Streets, NW 1970*
> *Gonzaga High School Gymnasium 1974*
> *Hirshhorn Museum and Sculpture Garden, Smithsonian Institution, The Mall*
> *Independence Avenue at 8th Street, SW Gordon Bunshaft,*
> *partner-in-charge 1974*
> *Pool and Ice Skating Rink, The Mall between 7th and 9th Streets, NW 1974*

Capitol Reflecting Pool, Grant Memorial, East end of the Mall, at 1st Street, NW 1976

Constitution Gardens, The Mall along Constitution Avenue between 17th Street and Bacon Drive, NW 1976

Mall Master Plan 1965 and 1976

Office Building, 1101 Connecticut Avenue, NW 1978

Four Seasons Hotel and Georgetown Plaza 1979

Office building, 1100 15th Street, NW 1981

Office building, 1201 Pennsylvania Avenue, NW 1981

Shoreham Hotel renovation, 2500 Calvert Street, NW 1983

Smith, Chloethiel Woodward

Capitol Park Apartments, 4th and I Streets, SW with Nicholas Satterlee 1963

Wheat Row, Harbor Square, 4th Street, SW 1966

Waterside Towers, 905–947 6th Street, SW 1970

Town Center Plaza, SW 1972

Waterside Mall, 400 M Street, SW 1972

Young Women's Christian Association, 9th and G Streets, NW 1981

Washington Square, Connecticut Avenue at L Street, NW 1982

Smithmeyer and Pelz

Healy Building, Georgetown University 1879

Library of Congress, Thomas Jefferson Building, 1st Street between East Capitol Street and Independence Avenue, SE 1886–97

Smith Segreti and Tepper

Office building, 1776 G Street, NW 1979

Office building, 2833 M Street, NW 1981

Steinmann, Cain and White

National Museum of American History, Smithsonian Institution, The Mall, Constitution Avenue at 14th Street, NW Walker O. Cain, partner-in-charge 1964

Stone, Edward Durell

National Geographic Society, 17th Street at M Street, NW 1964

Nassif Building: Department of Transportation, 7th Street between D and E Streets, SW 1969

Georgetown University Law Center, 600 New Jersey Avenue, NW 1971

John F. Kennedy Center for the Performing Arts, 2700 F Street, NW, between Rock Creek Parkway and New Hampshire Avenue, NW 1959–71

Stone, Maricini and Patterson

Walter Reed Hospital, Walter Reed Army Medical Center, 16th Street and Alaska Avenue, NW 1979

Swartwout, Egerton (New York)

National Baptist Memorial Church, 1501 Columbia Road, NW 1933

Tappan, Robert
> *Church of St. Stephen and the Incarnation, 16th Street at Newton Street, NW*
> *with Northrop Dudley   1928*

Tauber, Pieter H.
> *Netherlands Embassy Chancery, 4200 Linnean Avenue, NW*

Thornton, Dr. William
> *The Octagon: American Institute of Architects Foundation/Tayloe House, New*
> *York Avenue at 18th Street, NW   1799–1800*
> *The Capitol, Capitol Hill   with others   1793–1802*
> *Woodlawn Plantation, Fairfax County, Virginia   1800–05*
> *St. John's Church, Georgetown, Potomac and O Streets, NW   1804–09*
> *Tudor Place: Peters House, 31st and Q Streets, NW   1815*

Totten, George Oakley, Jr.
> *Warder-Totten House, Reconstruction of H. H. Richardson House, 2633 16th*
> *Street, NW   1902*
> *Inter-American Defense Board, 2600 16th Street, NW   1906*
> *Pakistan Embassy, 2315 Massachusetts Avenue, NW   1908*
> *Turkish Embassy/Everett House, 1606 23rd Street, NW   1914*
> *Ecuadorian Embassy, 2535 15th Street, NW   1922*
> *Spanish Embassy, 2801 16th Street, NW   1923*

Trowbridge and Livingston
> *American Red Cross, 17th Street between D and E Streets, NW   1917*

Trumbauer, Horace
> *Eastern Star Temple/Belmont House, 1618 New Hampshire Avenue, NW*
> *with Ernest Sanson (Paris)   1909*

Urbahn, Max O. Associates
> *Federal Home Loan Bank Board Building, G Street at 17th Street, NW   1978*

Vaughan, Henry (Boston)
> *Washington National Cathedral, Wisconsin Avenue at Massachusetts Avenue, NW*
> *with George F. Bodley   1907–16*

Vaux, Calvert
> *Gallaudet College, President's House, 7th Street and Florida Avenue, NE   with*
> *Withers   1867*
> *Francis Dodge House, Q Street at 30th Street, NW   1854*

Vercelli, Peter (ICON)
> *Eleven Dupont Circle office building, 11 Dupont Circle, NW   1977*
> *The Flour Mill apartments and stores, Grace and Potomac Streets, NW   1980*

Voorhees, Gmelin and Walker
> *C & P Telephone Company Building, 730 12th Street, NW   1930*

Voorhees, Walker, Smith & Smith
> *AFL/CIO Building, 16th Street at I Street, NW   1956*

Wagoner, Harold E. (Philadelphia)
> *First Baptist Church, 16th and O Streets, NW   1955*
> *National Presbyterian Church and Center, 4125 Nebraska Avenue, NW   1968*

Walter, Thomas U.
> *Treasury Building, 1500 Pennsylvania Avenue, NW   with Robert Mills*
> *1836–69*
> *The Capitol, Capitol Hill   with others   1851–65*

Warnecke, John Carl
> *John F. Kennedy Grave, Arlington Cemetery, Arlington, Virginia   1966*
> *Federal Office Building No. 7: New Executive Office Building, 17th and H*
> *   Streets, NW   1968*
> *U.S. Court of Claims, 717 Madison Place, NW   1968*
> *Lauinger Library, Georgetown University   1970*
> *Mazza Gallerie shopping mall, Wisconsin and Western Avenues, NW   1978*
> *Hart Senate Office Building, Capitol Hill   1981*
> *Office building, 2000 Pennsylvania Avenue, NW   1981*

Warren, H. Langford (Boston)
> *Church of the Holy City, Swedenborgian, 1611 16th Street, NW   1895*

Warren, Miles (New Zealand)
> *New Zealand Embassy, Observatory Circle, NW   with Faulkner, Fryer and*
> *   Vanderpool   1979*

Warren and Wetmore
> *Mayflower Hotel, Connecticut Avenue at De Sales Street, NW   1924*
> *Italian Embassy, 2700 16th Street, NW*

Weese, Harry (Chicago)
> *Arena Stage, 6th Street at M Street, SW   1961*
> *Channel Square, 325 P Street, SW   1968*
> *Arena Stage, Kreeger Theater addition, 6th Street at M Street, SW   1971*
> *Metro subway system   consulting architect   1975–85*

Weihe Black Jeffries Strassman and Dove
> *Mills Building, 1700 Pennsylvania Avenue, NW   1966*
> *Office building, 1730 Pennsylvania Avenue, NW   1972*
> *National Rural Electric Cooperative Association, 1800 Massachusetts Avenue, NW*
> *   1978*
> *Westbridge condominium and office building, 2555 Pennsylvania Avenue, NW*
> *   1978*
> *ASAE Building, 1575 Street, NW   1979*

Bibliography

Architecture

Commission of Fine Arts. *Massachusetts Avenue Architecture*, vol. 1, 1973; *Massachusetts Avenue Architecture*, vol. 2, 1975; *Sixteenth Street Architecture*, vol. 1, 1978. Washington, D.C.: Government Printing Office. A series of reasonably priced official studies prepared by J. L. Sibley Jennings and Sue A. Kohler; exhaustive in its description of the history and architectural details of the principal residences of these avenues; contains photographs, elevations, and floor plans.

Cowdrey, Albert E., for the Chief of Engineers. *A City for the Nation: The Army Engineers and the Building of Washington, D.C., 1790–1967*. Washington, D.C.: Government Printing Office, 1978. A narrative of the unique role of the talented and resourceful Army Corps of Engineers in creating the city of Washington.

Cox, Warren J., Jacobsen, Hugh Newell, *et al.*, for the Washington Metropolitan Chapter of the American Institute of Architects. *A Guide to the Architecture of Washington, D.C.* 2nd ed. New York: McGraw-Hill, 1974. An authoritative guide with excellent small photographs; organized in the form of walking tours of the city.

Craig, Lois A., and the staff of the Federal Architecture Project. *The Federal Presence: Architecture, Politics and Symbols in U.S. Government Building*. Cambridge, Mass.: MIT Press, 1977. A pictorial and critical survey of government buildings in the capital and throughout the country.

Myer, Donald B., for the Commission of Fine Arts. *Bridges and the City of Washington*. Washington, D.C.: Government Printing Office, 1974. Plans, photographs and drawings of bridges over the Anacostia and Potomac Rivers, and over Rock Creek— old, proposed and never built, and still surviving.

Withington, Charles F., for the U.S. Geological Survey. *Building Stones of Our Nation's Capital*. Washington, D.C.: Government Printing Office, 1975. Geological descriptions of the building stones used in the city's major public buildings.

Art

Getlein, Frank, and Lewis, Jo Ann. *The Washington D.C. Art Review*. New York: Van-

Bibliography

guard, 1980. Brief descriptions of the collections in the public museums, as well as a
listing of the special interests of Washington's private commercial galleries.

Guides

Cameron, Robert. *Above Washington*. San Francisco: Cameron & Co., 1980. Washington photographed from the air in pictures of remarkable clarity; aspects of the city
that can be seen in no other way.

Hodges, Allan A. and Carol A. *Washington on Foot*. Washington, D.C.: Smithsonian
Institution Press, 1977. A pocket-size compendium of 25 walking tours; includes a
conscientious restaurant guide.

Historic Georgetown, Inc. *A Walking Guide to Historic Georgetown*. Reprint. 1980. A
50-page guide with maps and photographs.

Thomas, Bill and Phyllis. *Natural Washington*. New York: Holt, Rinehart & Winston,
1980. A nature lover's guide to the area's parks, trails, and gardens.

History

Goode, James M. *Capitol Losses: A Cultural History of Washington's Destroyed Buildings*.
Washington, D.C.: Smithsonian Institution Press, 1979. Pictures and lively descriptions of lost buildings.

Green, Constance McLaughlin. *Washington: A History of the Capital, 1800–1950*.
Princeton: Princeton University Press, 1962. A comprehensive social history.

Junior League of Washington. *The City of Washington: An Illustrated History*. New
York: Alfred A. Knopf, 1977. A pictorial evocation of the city's social and cultural
history in the style of a family album.

Plan of the City

Gutheim, Frederick, and Washburn, Wilcomb E. *The Federal City: Plans and Realities*.
Washington, D.C.: Smithsonian Institution Press, 1976. A useful summary of the
city's development from the L'Enfant Plan to the present.

Reps, John W. *Monumental Washington: The Planning and Development of the Capital
Center*. Princeton: Princeton University Press, 1967. Describes attempts to create
"Civic Beauty" in the capital.

Spreiregen, Paul D., editor. *On the Art of Designing Cities: Selected Essays of Elbert Peets*.
Cambridge, Mass.: MIT Press, 1968. Discusses the planning of Washington in the
context of other capitals and cities; the most original work in the field.

Restaurants

Richman, Phyllis C. *The Best Restaurants (& others): Washington, D.C. (and Environs)*.
Washington, D.C.: *Washington Post* and 101 Productions, 1980. A candid and critical
guide enhanced by facsimiles of restaurant menus.

Statues and Monuments

Goode, James M. *The Outdoor Sculpture of Washington, D.C.* Washington, D.C.:
Smithsonian Institution Press, 1974. A comprehensive (512-page) guide; authoritative
and entertaining.

Index

Grateful acknowledgment is made to the following
for permission to reprint from previously published material:

Houghton Mifflin Company: Excerpt from *The Spaces in Between: An Architect's Journey* by Nathaniel Alexander Owings. Copyright © 1973 by Nathaniel Alexander Owings. Reprinted by permission of Houghton Mifflin Company.

The New York Times Company: Excerpts from obituary of Duncan Phillips, 1966; article by Hilton Kramer, 9 June 1974; review of opening of Kennedy Center by Ada Louise Huxtable, 6 June 1978. Copyright © 1966, 1974, 1978 by The New York Times Company. Reprinted by permission.

The New Yorker Magazine, Inc.: Excerpt from "The Hirshhorn" by Harold Rosenberg, 4 November 1974 issue. Reprinted by permission. Copyright © 1974 by The New Yorker Magazine, Inc.

Smithsonian Institution Press: Excerpt from *The Outdoor Sculpture of Washington, D.C.* by James M. Goode, page 246. Copyright © Smithsonian Institution Press, Washington, D.C., 1974. Reprinted by permission of the Smithsonian Institution Press.

The Washington *Post:* Excerpts from articles dated 9/25/71; 1/19/77; 10/25/79; 9/28/80. Copyright © 1971, 1977, 1979, 1980 by The Washington *Post.* Reprinted by permission.